Britain Confronts the Stalin Revolution: Anglo-Soviet Relations and the Metro-Vickers Crisis

Britain Confronts the Stalin Revolution: Anglo-Soviet Relations and the Metro-Vickers Crisis

Gordon W. Morrell

Wilfrid Laurier University Press

[WLU]

Canadian Cataloguing in Publication Data

Morrell, Gordon W., 1958-
 Britain confronts the Stalin revolution : Anglo-
Soviet relations and the Metro-Vickers crisis

Includes bibliographical references and index.
ISBN 0-88920-250-8

1. Electric power-plants – Soviet Union.
2. Metropolitan Vickers Electrical Co.   3. Trials
(Sabotage) – Soviet Union.   4. Great Britain –
Relations – Soviet Union.   5. Soviet Union –
Relations – Great Britain.   I. Title.

DK266.3.M67 1995   947.084   C94-932344-6

Cover design: Jose Martucci, Design Communications

Cover illustrations, clockwise: Anna Kutuzova; Soviet and British accused in
the dock; Andrei Vyshinskii, the Public Prosecutor. Photos supplied by the
owners of the Strang Papers, the Master and Fellows of Churchill College
Cambridge, and reproduced courtesy of SOVFOTO/EASTFOTO.

Printed in Canada

*Britain Confronts the Stalin Revolution: Anglo-Soviet Relations and the Metro-
Vickers Crisis* has been produced from a manuscript supplied in electronic
form by the author.

Contents

Illustrations

Acknowledgements

I have incurred a host of professional and personal debts in the research and writing of this study and would like to acknowledge them here. My mentors at Michigan State University, especially Donald Lammers and Lewis Siegelbaum, have continued to offer advice and support over the course of my project and I count myself fortunate to have had their guidance to draw upon. I would also like to thank my other friends and colleagues at Michigan State University, Denison University, the University of Waterloo, and the University of British Columbia for their support and friendship over the past few years as I made my way from one teaching assignment to another.

The archivists and staff at the Public Record Office in Kew, Cambridge University Library, Birmingham University Library, Churchill College Archives, the Arts Faculty Library at the University of Waterloo, and the Michigan State University Library have all facilitated my research in many varied and important respects.

This book has been published with the help of a grant from the Social Science Federation of Canada, using funds provided by the Social Sciences and Humanities Research Council of Canada.

My editor at Wilfrid Laurier University Press, Maura Brown, and the Press's Director, Sandra Woolfrey, have been encouraging throughout the process which has been a most enjoyable experience for me.

Finally, I would like to thank publicly my family and, most importantly, my wife, Kathy, who has provided me with the love and friendship necessary to see this project and our many other challenges through. This book is dedicated to her.

Introduction:
Perspectives and Sources

> Russian politics like opium, seems infallibly to provoke
> the most fantastic dreams and imaginings on the part of
> the people who study them.
> — E.A. Walker, British Embassy, Moscow 1931

When, in early March 1933, the Economic Administration (EKU) section of the Soviet secret police (OGPU) arrested six British engineers employed by the Metropolitan-Vickers Electrical Export Company (MVEEC) on technical assistance contracts in the USSR, it provoked a confrontation that brought Anglo-Soviet relations to the brink of disaster and resurrected the spectre of the show trials and purges of the technical intelligentsia that had shaken Soviet society from 1928 to 1931. The affair erupted just as the First Five-Year Plan was giving way to the Second *Piatiletka* and as the murderous famine of 1932-33, which took the lives of millions of Soviet peasants in the Ukraine and elsewhere, reached its height. The "Revolution from above," as these early years of Stalin's leadership are sometimes called, utilized massive and often violent campaigns to collectivize agriculture and emphasized a rapid tempo of development for heavy industry. While the Soviet "experiment" could boast of some triumphs, in the winter of 1933 there was still more than enough tragedy.

On the face of it, a quarrel with Great Britain, a power which had already shown itself quite capable of severing relations with the Soviet Union in 1927, only aggravated the position of the Soviet government in the international arena. The arrests occurred on the heels of the British decision to act upon provisions in the Ottawa Agreements of 1932 and abandon the 1930 Anglo-Soviet trade agreement in favour of a

1

new, more "equitable" trade arrangement with the Soviet Union.[1]
Over the course of this confrontation, the French and American governments, as well as British and American businessmen, made their
concerns about the Soviet action known to both sides in the conflict.

The difficulties with Britain that the arrests intensified were compounded by events in Germany which saw Hitler's Nazi Party rapidly
and ruthlessly consolidate its hold on power. The USSR, already virtually isolated in an international system of "capitalist" powers, now
found that Germany, the only major power with which the USSR had
managed any genuine accord, was moving away from a relationship
that had developed from the Rapallo Agreements of 1922.[2] Soviet diplomatic efforts over the subsequent months of the Metro-Vickers crisis
were devoted to minimizing the effects of these unsettling events.

The central thesis that emerges from this study is that the Metro-
Vickers crisis must be understood in both its international and domestic contexts, and more than this, I maintain that the relationship between the international and domestic forces must be appreciated as
they operated in the economic, cultural, ideological, legal, diplomatic,
technological, strategic, and personal spheres. In my effort to recast the
Metro-Vickers crisis within this broad thematic framework, I have
drawn on the work of many other historians and some political scien-
tists and in the process have found that, all too often, scholars who
have much to offer each other have, because of methodological or disciplinary fracturing, talked past one another, or worse, not attempted a
dialogue at all. To some extent, then, this treatment involves creating a
synthesis as well as offering my own original research and analysis;
hence, a brief sketch of some of the more important contributions to
the understanding of the Metro-Vickers crisis is in order.

In one of the earliest studies of the crisis, Donald Lammers placed it
within the context of Anglo-Soviet interstate relations and raised many
of the key questions which have occupied scholars since.[3] Lammers al-
luded to the importance of the Soviet domestic scene, but with few Soviet documents available and with his main interest being interna-

---

1 I. Drummond, "Empire Trade and Russian Trade: Economic Diplomacy in the Nineteen-Thirties," *Canadian Journal of Economics/Revue canadienne d'économique*, 5, 1
(1972): 35-47.

2 J. Haslam, *Soviet Foreign Policy, 1930-1933: The Impact of the Depression* (London: Macmillan, 1983), p. 6.

3 D. Lammers, "The Engineers' Trial (Moscow 1933) and Anglo-Soviet Relations,"
South Atlantic Quarterly, 62 (1963): 256-67. See also the related article by D. Lammers,
"The Second Labour Government and the Restoration of Relations with Soviet Rus-
sia (1929)," *Bulletin of the Institute of Historical Research*, 37 (May 1964): 60-72.

tional relations, he pursued an analysis that revolved around the conflict between the two governments in the aftermath of the Ottawa Agreements of 1932. He examined the economic and diplomatic levers exercised in the resulting test of strength, which was, in Lammers' view a small, but significant victory for the British. The engineers were guilty, if such a term is applicable at all, of small "indiscretions" that were trumped up, in the paranoia of Stalin's Russia, as criminal acts.

The most serious challenge to such a portrait of the international dimensions of the Metro-Vickers affair was offered by Gail Owen more than a decade later.[4] Her analysis was more avowedly economic in nature and placed the arrest and trial of the British engineers in the context of Anglo-Soviet trade relations. By establishing that the Soviets in practice came out ahead in bilateral trade relations after the Metro-Vickers crisis, she argued that the test of strength in the early months of 1933 was a carefully plotted Soviet strategy for wearing the British down on all fronts. Stalin held "all the cards" in such a contest, since he knew the USSR would need the British proportionately less in the coming months than the British needed the Soviets. For Owen, what eventually occurred was deviously planned in advance. Moreover, the case against the engineers was not a simple frame-up in Owen's view. The confessions of two of the men, coupled with their general conduct during the trial, created the impression that, "even under Western law" their innocence was not nearly so apparent as the British would have liked.[5]

Owen also included an important Soviet domestic issue in her presentation — that of the OGPU's relationship with Stalin. In the aftermath of the case the OGPU was purged and Stalin's "creature," Akulov, was promoted to become the Prosecutor of the USSR — allegedly the better to control the head of the secret police, Menzhinskii. This suggested to Owen that Stalin had initiated the investigation in order to provoke Menzhinskii's OGPU apparatus into committing errors which would justify Stalin's subsequent disciplinary action against the OGPU. This view conflicts with the explanation offered below, primarily because of the absolute primacy given to Stalin's place from beginning to end. Undoubtedly it was the case that when Stalin wished to direct such affairs, he could, but it seems more consistent with the available evidence to argue that the OGPU initiated the arrests without consulting Maxim Litvinov, the Commissar of Foreign Affairs, and this

---

4 G. Owen, "The Metro-Vickers Crisis: Anglo-Soviet Relations between Trade Agreements, 1932-1934," *Slavonic and East European Review*, 44, 114 (1971): 92-112.
5 Ibid., p. 100 n. 50.

lapse unexpectedly produced an international incident which prompted Stalin to discipline the OGPU at home. This also appears to be a rare instance where Litvinov's Commissariat of Foreign Affairs (Narkomindel) managed to convince Stalin that international, rather than domestic, issues deserved primary consideration.

The most recent examination of these issues that concentrated mainly on their international dimension was developed by Jonathan Haslam.[6] By utilizing recent Western and Soviet scholarship, Haslam's portrait suggested that the engineers were guilty of industrial espionage broadly defined, but that the British trade embargo and political leverage were successful in convincing the Soviets that the six British subjects should be expelled rather than imprisoned. Soviet isolation "was too high a price to pay" in the international setting of 1933.[7]

The second branch of scholarship that has dealt with the Metro-Vickers trial has considered it primarily as a part of the domestic political scene in the early Stalin years which saw political show trials and purges wrack the upper echelons of most sectors of Soviet society. This was particularly clear in Robert Conquest's *The Great Terror: Stalin's Purge of the Thirties* (1973), which characterized the trial of 1933 as preparation for Stalin's development of the grim machine which gripped Soviet society from 1936 to 1938 and operated with the terroristic apparatus of night arrest, OGPU interrogation, dubious terror-inspired "confessions" and the public show trial. That the key defendants among the engineers were British subjects whose cause was taken up by the British government was a point to be noted in passing. Little about the trial, in Conquest's view, suggested that it was in any fundamental way unique. It was simply a pallid foreshadowing of the mass political violence that was to come later.

With the increasing interest in the relationship between state and society in the Soviet Union during the interwar years has come a better understanding of the forces that were at work at various levels of Soviet society.[8] In this context the work by Kendall Bailes and Hiroaki

---

6 J. Haslam, *The Soviet Union and the Struggle for Collective Security, 1933-1939* (London: Macmillan, 1984).

7 Ibid., p. 19.

8 The sometimes painful debates over the merits and typologies of recent work on the history of the Soviet Union in the 1930s are replete with straw men (and women), but appear to demonstrate some willingness to rethink methods, evidence, and paradigms. See *The Russian Review*, 45, 4 (1986) and the second "round" of responses in *The Russian Review*, 46, 4 (1987). I have found it necessary to rely on contributors from all sides of the debate concerning the over-dichotomized formulations: Stalinism as "revolution from above or below," "social" versus "political" history, or the "totalitarian" model versus the "institutionalized-pluralism" model.

Kuromiya is important for the Metro-Vickers case, since they place the trial not, as Conquest does, at the beginning of the Great Purges, but rather at the end of the assault on technical specialists which occurred primarily from 1928 to 1931.[9] The Metro-Vickers trial fits somewhat awkwardly into such an analysis, since it is generally argued that by June 1931 such assaults had been largely curtailed by the Soviet leadership. The return to the arrests of engineers in the electrical industry in March 1933 was, for Bailes and Kuromiya, more a reminder of politics past than a grim foreshadowing of things to come.[10] Here, too, little is made of the international implications of the case, but the relationship of the arrested "bourgeois" electrical engineers to the politics of Soviet industrial development is emphasized.

The presentation outlined below draws on the contributions of all of these scholars and many others, too,[11] and tries to bring them into an effective synthesis. Beyond exploring both the international and domestic factors and the relationship between them, however, this work also recasts the Metro-Vickers crisis in a chronological framework that underscores the importance which the political, economic, social, and cultural changes in Soviet domestic life during the period of the New Economic Policy (NEP, 1921-28) and the First Five-Year Plan (1929-32) had on those foreign firms, such as the MVEEC, which were involved in technology transfer.

The crisis also conveys much about the changes occurring in Britain in response to the challenges posed by "totalitarian" societies in the century of total war. To take an example, one of the chief charges against the British accused during the trial was that of economic espionage, and it now appears that the MVEEC was connected to Britain's Industrial Intelligence Centre (IIC), created in 1931 precisely to develop an industrial intelligence network which could provide information on

---

9 K. Bailes, *Technology and Society under Lenin and Stalin: Origins of the Technical Intelligentsia* (Princeton, NJ: Princeton University Press, 1978). A complete discussion of Bailes' position can be found in his dissertation; H. Kuromiya, *Stalin's Industrial Revolution: Politics and Workers, 1928-1932* (Cambridge: Cambridge University Press, 1988).

10 On this point Bailes and Kuromiya appear consistent with the approach of J. Arch Getty, *Origins of the Great Purges: The Soviet Communist Party Reconsidered, 1933-1938* (Cambridge: Cambridge University Press, 1985). Getty insists that there were many types of "purges" of which the Great Terror of 1936-38 was a distinct and particularly grim type.

11 Here I would like to thank in particular Donald Lammers and Lewis Siegelbaum at Michigan State University, and R.W. Davies at the University of Birmingham for their generous efforts to improve my understanding of the many facets of this subject.

all military-industrial assets available to states in peace-time which might be considered as potential war-time assets as well. By developing an institution which would provide data on societies such as Stalin's USSR, with its one-party state, command economy, and foreign trade monopoly, the British effectively changed the definition of what "intelligence" and "intelligence gathering" would mean in the twentieth century, and the Metro-Vickers crisis was, in part, the result.

The organizational structure of this study is built around an examination of the root causes, the course, and the consequences of the Metro-Vickers crisis at three levels, which can be characterized as the local, national, and international dimensions of the case. At the local level, the relationship between the MVEEC and the Soviet authorities is considered in chapters 1 and 2. The first focusses on the close and easy collaboration evidenced during the period of the New Economic Policy (1921-28) and saw the British firm make major contributions to the electrification of the USSR. The second chapter examines the impact that the national strategy embodied in the First Five-Year Plan (1929-32) and the concurrent "Stalin Revolution" had on the local relationship between the MVEEC and its Soviet employees and associates in the electrical industry. Many of the Russian engineers who had enjoyed favour during the NEP period and who had worked alongside the MVEEC engineers were now swept up in this Stalinist movement. As this examination makes clear, prior to the arrests of March 1933, there was growing evidence that the Stalinist commitment to the promotion of "red," as against "bourgeois," experts in industry would have grim consequences for foreign firms as well as the Soviet technical intelligentsia.

Chapter 3 takes up the state-vs.-state confrontation that erupted immediately after the arrests, when the British government, strongly encouraged by the uncharacteristically shrill recommendations of its Ambassador in Moscow, Sir Esmond Ovey, waded into the affair. While there is evidence suggesting that the MVEEC had already been cooperating with a branch of the British intelligence service, the Industrial Intelligence Centre, in the public drama that emerged the MVEEC, the Foreign Office, and Ramsay MacDonald's Tory-dominated National Government all sought to portray the case as a trumped-up and frivolous consequence of Soviet paranoia. Though the efforts of the British authorities could not prevent the trial which would follow in mid-April, it does appear that the Soviet Commissar for Foreign Affairs, Maxim Litvinov, was prompted to intercede on behalf of the British engineers in the first of his attempts to avoid an all-out breach with Britain.

Chapter 4 examines the experience of arrest and interrogation that the MVEEC engineers endured prior to the trial. This provides a rare opportunity to document the process used by the Stalinist legal/penal system to wring the necessary "confessions" from its prisoners. The techniques employed with the British prisoners, while never "third-degree," were very effective with two of the engineers and reveal much about the tapestry of the case that the Public Prosecutor, Andrei Vyshinskii, would weave once the trial began. By penetrating deeply into the personal quandaries of the accused, important evidence surfaces about the difficulty these men and women faced when trying to comprehend the changing nature of Soviet legal culture. While at some levels the British and Russian accused shared the same confusion about Soviet law and criminal procedures, there was an additional level at which the British were unable to see clearly that practices which were common in the business world of the West and were tolerated during the NEP were decidedly unacceptable in the climate of the Stalin revolution.

The trial itself is the subject of chapter 5 and is examined in large part as a case study of what was Vyshinskii's first show trial as Stalin's Public Prosecutor. In scale, the use of "evidence," and orchestration, the Metro-Vickers trial was a model of what was to come later in the Great Purge trials of 1936-38, although the international dimension did influence the efforts of the defence counsel and undoubtedly was responsible for the relatively generous verdicts meted out to the British defendants. This is also one of the few instances where students of the Soviet legal system have access to extensive written depositions and testimony of the defendants who survived the ordeal, and who were, in the case of the six British MVEEC engineers, ultimately expelled from the USSR and debriefed by the Foreign Office.

In my discussion of the trial I have paid particular attention to the role the trial played in shaping the debate in the Soviet legal community at the time. Though there is no other study of the Metro-Vickers trial that pursues this theme, I have drawn extensively from the work of Robert Sharlet, Peter Solomon, Piers Beirne, and especially Eugene Huskey to locate the Metro-Vickers trial within the context of Stalinist judicial politics in the early 1930s.[12] The position taken here is that legal

---

12 See E. Huskey, *Russian Lawyers and the Soviet State: The Origins and Development of the Soviet Bar, 1917-1939* (Princeton, NJ: Princeton University Press, 1986); E. Huskey, "Vyshinskii, Krylenko, and the Shaping of the Soviet Legal Order," *Slavic Review*, 46, 3/4 (1987): 414-28; P. Solomon, "Local Political Power and Soviet Criminal Justice, 1922-1941," *Soviet Studies*, 37, 3 (1983): 305-329; R. Sharlet and P. Beirne, "In Search of

"moderates" such as Andrei Vyshinskii, used the trial to promote their vision of a more professional and centralized legal structure against the aspirations of the legal "nihilists," such as E.B. Pashukanis and N.V. Krylenko, who were their rivals.

Chapter 6 examines the consequences of the Metro-Vickers affair for Anglo-Soviet relations and the MVEEC. In the first instance, the impact of the mutual trade embargoes put into effect after the trial is considered alongside the difficulties the Soviets were having with Japan, Germany, and the United States. For students of Maxim Litvinov's career the Metro-Vickers crisis may well have been the first major moment where the Foreign Commissar's Anglophile approach to Soviet security made itself felt. Here, the Soviet conflict with Britain is considered in light of the difficulties which the OGPU action created for Soviet diplomacy, and an effort is made to assess the relative importance that economic and political considerations had on the containment and resolution of the crisis. The crisis also revealed much about the way in which international law would be used by both the National Government and the Labour Party to shape the debate about Anglo-Soviet relations during the period.

The consequences of the trial for the MVEEC, its Soviet employees, and the Soviet domestic context in the years following the apparent resolution of the 1933 affair are also examined in the final chapter. Though the issue quickly disappeared from the front pages of the Western press, the consequences for those tainted by association with the MVEEC continued to have dangerous implications and, as a result, the Company substantially altered the way it did business in the USSR for the remainder of the 1930s. The dogged efforts of the MVEEC to remain in the USSR, despite Foreign Office recommendations to abandon their operations, raises questions about the MVEEC's policy itself and about the Soviet view of the "foreign threat" following the trial. As the experience of the MVEEC would prove throughout the remainder of the 1930s, their presence would be tolerated and closely scrutinized by the Soviet authorities, but rarely would they be rewarded with any major contracts.

Historians are almost never satisfied with the nature and extent of their documentation, and in studies where the intelligence services from at least two countries are involved, the potential problems are

---

Vyshinsky: The Paradox of Law and Terror," *International Journal of the Sociology of Law*, 12 (1984): 153-77; and R. Sharlet, "Stalinism and Soviet Legal Culture," in R. Tucker, ed., *Stalinism: Essays in Historical Interpretation* (New York: W.W. Norton, 1977), p. 155-79.

even more complex. This is particularly true on the Soviet side, where the records of the secret police, in general, remain closed and are under the control of Boris Yeltsin's presidential archive. I have made use of the published diplomatic correspondence, the various branches of the Soviet press, recent monographs by Soviet scholars on related themes of industrialization, memoir material, and the verbatim report of the Metro-Vickers trial, which all help to provide the basis of the arguments made regarding Soviet behaviour. I have tried to be very clear about lines of reasoning which are clearly circumstantial. The role of Stalin in the affair remains something of a mystery though here, too, I have attempted to outline the range of possibilities that coincide with what Western scholars think they know about the nature of the Stalinist regime.

On the British side, the available material is much more abundant, although gaps remain in the documentation of the MVEEC itself and the records of the British Intelligence community that directed its attention to this case. The former defect will almost certainly never be overcome since, according to the archivist of the General Electric Switchgear Company, the firm's archive for the MVEEC no longer exists.[13] I have made use of the papers of Vickers Director, Sir Vincent Caillard, which deal with MVEEC affairs in the 1920s when Vickers was a major shareholder. Some important records of the Company are also to be found in the 371 Foreign Office files that pertain to the trial as a considerable body of MVEEC contracts with the Soviet Union was sent to Anthony Eden just prior to his visit to the USSR in February 1935. It is likely that these may be the only copies outside of the former Soviet Union still extant.

Since the case caused a substantial stir in Britain and other Western countries, the press coverage of the arrests and trial is also a revealing source of information. Several prominent reporters who attended the trial in Moscow, including Eugene Lyons, Will Duranty, and the young Ian Fleming, provided accounts of the proceedings in their press reports and in later books.[14] In Britain, the press was divided about the economic and political dimensions of the Anglo-Soviet clash, and one *News Chronicle* reporter, A. Cummings, published an entire book on

---

13 I would like to thank Mr. N.D. Davies, Finance Director of GEC Switchgear Limited in Manchester, for his efforts to locate any remnants of the MVEEC archive.

14 E. Lyons, *Assignment in Utopia* (New York: Harcourt, Brace, 1937); W. Duranty, *I Write as I Please* (New York: Simon and Schuster, 1935); J. Pearson, *The Life of Ian Fleming* (New York: McGraw-Hill, 1966); and H. Zeiger, *Ian Fleming: The Spy Who Came in with the Gold* (New York: Duell, Sloan and Pearce, 1965).

what he considered the poor conduct of the British government.[15] In general those papers on the liberal left, such as the *Manchester Guardian*, were critical of the British government's high-handed behaviour, while, equally predictably, *The Times* was supportive of the efforts of Whitehall. The whole affair revealed and reinforced the profound and often antagonistic feelings which only the Soviet Union could elicit in Britain.

As mentioned earlier, the issue of British intelligence gathering played an important role in the arrest of the engineers, and there is oblique evidence in the correspondence of the Foreign Office that MI5 took a direct interest in the case. The records of the IIC can be found in the CAB 48 series, and although these too are incomplete, they do reflect the type of interest that the IIC had in MVEEC.

There remains the voluminous collection of relevant documentation from the other branches of the British government. A combination of the private papers of key players in the crisis, the Cabinet papers, the records from the Board of Trade and its related branch, the Department of Overseas Trade, and the Hansard debates from Parliament have been helpful in developing a sense of the overall response of the government. Clearly the most important source of this type is the correspondence and minutes of the Foreign Office. As the crisis developed, the normal flow of information and commentary between the Foreign Office and its Moscow embassy increased substantially, and the attention of the Northern Department officials was brought to bear on the Metro-Vickers case.

Forming an especially important segment of this material were the depositions that the arrested engineers[16] made to the Foreign Office of-

---

15 A. Cummings, *The Moscow Trial* (London: Victor Gollancz, 1933).

16 The arrested engineers were Allan Monkhouse, Leslie Thornton, Charles Nordwall, Albert Gregory, John Cushny, and William MacDonald. Their depositions are found in a series of Foreign Office and Company files. See the memorandum by William Strang (British Chargé d' Affaires in Moscow), which includes a deposition by William MacDonald in FO 371/17263 N5059/1610/38, 3 July 1933. William MacDonald provided a second, more detailed account in C.S. Richards (MVEEC) to Foreign Office, 20 July 1933, FO 371/17264 N5681/1610/38. Leslie Thornton's deposition is included in C.S. Richards to Foreign Office, 20 July 1933, FO 371/17264 N5682/1610/38 [hereinafter cited as MacDonald, Foreign Office Deposition, 3 July 1933, MacDonald, Foreign Office Deposition, 20 July 1933, and Thornton, Foreign Office Deposition, 20 July 1933]. The depositions of the other arrested engineers can be found in the memo by Wylie (Foreign Office), Interviews of Monkhouse, Cushny, Gregory, and Nordwall conducted at Bush House (MVEEC headquarters) and the Foreign Office, 9 May 1933, FO 371/17272 N3487/1610/38 [hereinafter cited as the Bush House Interviews, 9 May 1933]. Nordwall provided a separate installment later in May. See

ficials following their release and expulsion from the Soviet Union. This material is supplemented and largely substantiated by the memoir account of the manager of MVEEC operations in Moscow, Allan Monkhouse, *Moscow, 1911-1933*, which was published in 1933. Previous studies of the case have not availed themselves of the material presented in these depositions and have thereby been deprived of important material related to the interaction between the MVEEC engineers and the changing Soviet context that enveloped them.

Typically the Metro-Vickers crisis has been treated as either a Soviet domestic concern or a critical moment in Anglo-Soviet relations. This study argues that it was both these things simultaneously and that this was a case where foreign and domestic policy created a troubling synergy.

Richards (MVEEC) to Collier (Foreign Office), 23 May 1933, FO 371/17272 N3904/160/38. One other MVEEC engineer, Tearle, who was named in the trial, but not arrested, provided a statement to the Foreign Office after the trial. See Richards to Collier, 26 May 1933, FO 371/17272 N3993/1610/38.

1

Building Lenin's Dream: The MVEEC and Soviet Electrification, 1922-27

> Communism equals Soviet Power plus the Electrification of the entire country. — V.I. Lenin, 1920

From 1922 to 1927, the participation of the MVEEC in the electrification of the USSR was an undoubted success both for the Company and for the Soviet authorities. In part this was due to the willingness of Lenin's regime to draw on the talents of "class" enemies, both at home and abroad, during the period of the New Economic Policy; and, in part, the success was due to the background and experience of the British firm itself. The Soviet electrification plan, endorsed by Lenin and orchestrated by the State Commission for the Electrification of Russia (GOELRO),[1] stressed massive projects based in substantial measure on the latest and best Western technology. The MVEEC proved itself to be one of the most technically ambitious foreign firms during these years and was, due to the Russian experience of many its engineers, well placed to help fulfill Lenin's dream. Since one of the central issues of the Metro-Vickers crisis revolves around the politics of this technology transfer and the implementation of the Soviet plan, it is necessary to

---

1 The best examination of Russian electrification is Jonathan Coopersmith's, *The Electrification of Russia, 1880-1926* (Ithaca: Cornell University Press, 1992). See also Allan Monkhouse's report, "Electrical Developments in the U.S.S.R.," *Proceedings of the Institute of Electrical Engineers* (London), 76 (June 1935): 601-46.

explore the background of the policies and personnel that shaped the character of the early years of Soviet electrification.

In large part, the GOELRO strategy adopted by the Communist Party in December 1920 was the product of the technological vision and political activity of a group of electrical engineers, led by the Bolshevik, Gleb Krzhizhanovskii, who pressed Lenin and his infant regime to pursue electrification as the cornerstone of the state industrialization program. In devising propaganda to support the plan, Lenin's coinage, "communism equals Soviet power plus the electrification of the entire country," not only reflected the central role electrification was thought to play in the success of the Soviet experiment at the time, but also captured the power of the almost utopian vision[2] that the electrical engineering cadre, both the Bolsheviks and non-Bolsheviks, sought to promote. Jonathan Coopersmith has compared Krzhizhanovskii's role in this context to the influence that Edward Teller had with Ronald Reagan and the USA's Strategic Defence Initiative of 1983. Acting both as confidants and technical experts, these men pushed utopian plans in which the leader already had an interest and where the necessary ideas and institutions already existed. In both instances the leaders invested much political capital, and neither plan survived criticism intact.[3] In the Soviet context, the Leninist program for electrification promised to eliminate the urban-rural divide, centralize and rationalize the economy, and transform its social and economic foundations on the basis of a network of regional power stations.

The Soviet electrical experts who sponsored the scheme, and who would work so successfully alongside the MVEEC engineers during the NEP, were drawn largely from what Kendall Bailes has termed the "old specialists."[4] They had received their technical training prior to the Revolution and, while many were politically active Bolsheviks, they were professionally and socially at ease with the British contingent. Most had been involved in the electrical industry well before the 1917 Revolution through the Bolshevik-dominated Moscow section of the 1886 Company, Russia's largest utility, and the St. Petersburg Technological Institute. During the last two decades of Tsarist rule the basis of the "old-boy network" which operated during the period of the

---

2 For an excellent treatment of the role of "utopian vision" in the Bolshevik experiment, see Richard Stites, *Revolutionary Dreams: Utopian Vision and Experimental Life in the Russian Revolution* (Oxford: Oxford University Press, 1989).

3 Coopersmith, *The Electrification of Russia*, p. 152.

4 Bailes, *Technology and Society*, Part 2: "The Old Specialist and the Power Structure, 1928-1931."

NEP was formed. The 1886 Company employed future director of the GOELRO, Krzhizhanovskii, the engineer-manager of the Shatura project, Aleksandr Vinter, and many others who were, according to Billington, a kind of "electrician's mafia" during the late Tsarist period when the desperate need to proceed with electrification caused the regime to overlook these engineers' political views.[5]

This GOELRO cadre, trained during the Tsarist period, understood that Russian backwardness could only be overcome by learning from the more advanced capitalist economies, and they were at home in the international community of electrical experts. The plan for Soviet electrification was therefore predicated on the resumption of normal economic and diplomatic relations, and it was assumed that foreign goods and foreign technical expertise would be necessary to launch and complete the 10-year project. For these men, then, the key qualification for participation in the Soviet experiment was "expertism" not Bolshevism, and it was for this reason that as long as this group dominated Soviet electrification, non-communists and foreigners were welcome as long as they were able.[6]

The GOELRO program and its proponents were not without their detractors, however, and some of these had strong institutional backing indeed. Two of the most important groups were the Commissariat of Agriculture and the Peoples Commissariat of Internal Affairs (NKVD)[7] who opposed the GOELRO plan on the grounds that it was too urban-based and that its centralized structure removed control and initiative from the local authorities, which the NKVD, in particular, sought to defend. These were reasonable criticisms, raised by powerful

---

5 James Billington, *Fire in the Minds of Men: Origins of the Revolutionary Faith* (New York: Basic Books, 1980), p. 448, 453-55; and Coopersmith, *The Electrification of Russia*, p. 26.

6 The term "expertism" is Coopersmith's (see ibid., p. 140). For an important examination of the evolution of this uneasy relationship between "bourgeois experts" and the Soviet state, see Loren Graham's, *The Ghost of the Executed Engineer* (Cambridge, MA: Harvard University Press, 1993).

7 During the 1920s the structure of the Russian and Soviet policing structures changed many times. For a brief period at the outset of the New Economic Policy the political police — State Political Administration (GPU) — was part of the Russian Federation's NKVD. When the USSR was formed in 1923 the GPU was raised to federal status as the OGPU (Unified State Political Administration) and was not integrated into the NKVD until the 1934 reorganization created the USSR's NKVD. Unlike the GPU/ OGPU which was charged with the task of "unmasking" counter-revolutionaries, spies, and terrorists, the NKVD's interest in electrification during the 1920s may well have stemmed from its responsibilities over the provision of utilities through the *kommunalnoe khoziaistvo* agency. For a recent discussion of these developments, see A. Knight's, *The KGB: Police and Politics in the Soviet Union* (London: Unwin & Hyman, 1990), p. 13-17.

foes, and were echoed by peasant organizations and other electrical engineering specialists who sought to challenge the current hegemony of the GOELRO planners.[8] All of these challenges foreshadowed the more violent trauma that the electrical specialists associated with the GOELRO would suffer once they lost control of the process, as they did when the Stalin Revolution enveloped them.

To a significant degree, the characteristics of the Metropolitan-Vickers Electrical Export Company and its personnel were shaped by experiences that paralleled those of the GOELRO and its leading cadre. Like the GOELRO, the MVEEC was a very new venture, having been formed in 1919 in a manner that allowed it to draw on the knowledge and experience that its newly acquired personnel had gained while working on Tsarist projects for British Westinghouse prior to the Bolshevik Revolution.

The driving force behind the creation of the MVEEC was Douglas Vickers, who, as head of the great Vickers Company, believed that the shape of the post-war economy required that Vickers acquire an electrical interest to compete with Germany's AEG and Siemens and the American concern of General Electric. In 1919, Vickers decided to purchase the Metropolitan Carriage, Wagon and Finance Company, which was headed by the industrialist Dudley Docker, who himself had been so impressed by the German achievement at cartelization that he had acquired British Westinghouse in 1917. In the end, Vickers paid almost 13 million pounds for the various Metropolitan interests — a high price according to the financial experts in the City. Douglas Vickers was willing to pay the price both because he foresaw a great industrial expansion and rationalization in the works and because he believed that Docker's own global vision and reputation added value to the new Vickers enterprise.[9]

Following the aquisition, in September 1919 the new MVEEC was formed to handle electrical exports, and it moved quickly by opening offices in Brussels, Bombay, Calcutta, Johannesburg, Melbourne, and Sydney. With the global backing of its parent company, Vickers, and its mandate to participate in the development of international electrifica-

---

8 See Coopersmith's analysis in *The Electrification of Russia*, p. 127, 162-63.
9 For a full discussion of these transactions, see J. Scott, *Vickers: A History* (London: Weidenfeld & Nicholson, 1962), p. 140-42. See also J. Dummelow, *1899-1949* (Metropolitan-Vickers Electrical Company, 1949), p. 74; A. Monkhouse, *Moscow, 1911-1933* (Boston: Little, Brown, 1934), p. 27-29; and A. Sutton, *Western Technology and Soviet Economic Development, 1917-1930* (Stanford: Hoover Institution Press, 1971), p. 199.

tion, the MVEEC looked well placed to take advantage of new opportunities for growth.[10]

MVEEC interest in the possibilities for trade with Soviet Russia developed naturally out of the experience which its British Westinghouse staff had gained before the Bolshevik Revolution. The Company's official account of its first approaches to the Bolshevik regime in 1922 stresses the role of future director C.S. Richards and manager of European operations A. Simon. These men had a "wide and personal knowledge of the country and were confident of the stability of the new republic."[11] They initiated a long series of contracts with the GOELRO for electrical machinery, technical training for Soviet engineers in Manchester, technical assistance, and the sale of patents that would total some 5 million pounds between the wars.[12] Since the British government throughout the 1920s was reluctant to extend long-term credits to the Soviet government, the MVEEC had to arrange the financing for such contracts itself.[13]

The MVEEC's willingness to take risks with the Soviet Union was combined with the Soviets' interest in adopting the latest and, in certain instances, untried designs the British company could produce. Dividends were gained on both sides in 1926 when a new MVEEC generator in a Soviet plant set a world record for kilowatt output. Undoubtedly such success was a key reason for the firm being the only British enterprise to have an office at Electro-Import in Moscow at this time.[14] As will be seen later, close proximity to Soviet authorities and the development and application of innovative technology in the Soviet context could create problems, too.

Though the First Five-Year Plan would feature the rapid development of mining, metallurgy, and machine building — often called the "American" industrial strategy — rather than the chemical and electrical scheme preferred by Germany, between 1923 and 1933 the country's electrical capacity dramatically increased. During that 10-year period, 56 large electric power stations were constructed, 10 of which had capacities in excess of 100 000 kW. By 1930, about 90 percent of these new Soviet electrification projects were fitted with imported boilers,

---

10 See Dummelow, *1899-1949*, p. 81-82.

11 Ibid., p. 82.

12 Ibid.

13 The Second Labour Government did eventually extend long-term credit guarantees to the Soviet Union in 1931, but the MVEEC contracts were never underwritten by such governmental guarantees.

14 Sutton, *Western Technology*, p. 199.

turbines, and generators.[15] Soviet reliance on imported machinery and
equipment would ease substantially by 1934,[16] but in these early years
the MVEEC's role, particularly in the larger stations, placed it among
the most important of the foreign firms participating in these projects.[17]
It was the sole foreign contributor to the MOGES (Moscow), Zuevka,
and Chelyabinsk stations and collaborated on the Shatura, Krasnyi
Oktiabr', Gorki, Shterovka, and Baku stations with Brown-Boveri, Sie-
mens-Schukert, and AEG.[18]

The collaboration between the MVEEC and the Soviet electrical authorities was much more than just a cash transaction, of course. To
some extent the MVEEC personnel involved were drawn to Russia and
its technologically ambitious project for reasons similar to those which
excited engineers in Russia. Like Krzhizhanovksii and his cadre of
GOELRO engineers, several of the MVEEC engineers participated in
the international community of electrical specialists and had worked in
Tsarist Russia on major schemes such as the Moscow tramway, the Ko-
lomna industrial works south of Moscow, and the Dynamo Works of
Russian General Electric. These men travelled widely in the country
and consulted on projects in a variety of regions, including Central
Asia, Siberia, and Ukraine. Over the course of the 1920s there was
probably not a major industrial region of the country that at least one
of them had not visited. It would eventually transpire that such intimate knowledge of the Soviet industrial sector was not necessarily a
good thing, but for a relatively new company embarking on a technologically and politically risky relationship with the infant Bolshevik regime, such men were undoubtedly assets.

Beyond the professional rewards that the Soviet experiment held
out for the MVEEC and its leading engineers were the personal connections some of the MVEEC staff had with Russia. Since some of these
connections and experiences were to prove fateful during the tribulations of 1933, it is necessary to trace the background of these men in
some detail.

The outbreak of the Great War in 1914 found Leslie Thornton, fellow engineer Allan Monkhouse, and Richards all in Russia. Given their
familiarity with Russia and their technical expertise, they were in-

---

15 B. Weitz, ed., *Electrical Power Development in the U.S.S.R.* (Moscow: INRA Publishing
    Society, 1936), p. 100-101. See Appendix A, "Electrical Capacity and Production in
    the USSR."
16 Ibid.
17 Monkhouse, "Electrical Developments in the U.S.S.R.," p. 601.
18 Sutton, *Western Technology . . . 1930-1945*, p. 169.

structed by the British Embassy to remain in Russia and assist with work in the munitions industry. When the Tsarist government fell, Richards and Thornton made their way to Murmansk, where their general knowledge of the country was used by the British intelligence staff.

Monkhouse was later to find that his technical tasks in the munitions industry were to have unexpectedly profound political ramifications as well. In the spring of 1917 he was, "like most other foreigners in Moscow," commissioned by the Provisional Government to be a special constable in the militia. Apparently the Kerensky regime felt that foreigners who had a stake in the continuance of the Provisional Government's war policy were reliable allies. For a short time after the October Revolution Monkhouse remained connected with the munitions industry, but in December 1917 he was arrested by a Revolutionary Court on charges of wrecking. The wrecking of various munitions factories had indeed occurred, though, as Monkhouse's memoirs later argued, such destruction was prompted by the fear of Germany's advancing army and not by a desire to destroy assets claimed by the revolutionary government. Characteristically the British technician also claimed that "wrecking activities of this nature are heart-rending to an engineer" and that he was not personally involved in the operation. Fortunately for Monkhouse when faced with these dire circumstances, his proficiency in Russian served him well and he escaped execution by directing the Court to the records of munitions production in the safe of the Union of Zemstvos. The papers there apparently made clear the motives and circumstances behind the "wrecking."[19]

After the Bolsheviks signed the Brest-Litovsk Treaty which ended the Russian war effort against the Central Powers, the British engineers were advised at a meeting of the British Club in Moscow that their continued presence in Russia no longer served British policy. In March 1918, Monkhouse secretly made his way with about 60 other British engineers to Vladivostok, and from there to Canada where he helped train Zionist battalions[20] in Nova Scotia. When he returned to London with these battalions in July 1918, he was debriefed by the War Office on the situation in Russia. It was at this point that Monkhouse was formally brought into the British army and, while stationed at Berkenstead Camp in the Officers Training Corps, he prepared a political

---

19 Monkhouse, *Moscow*, p. 55-66.
20 These battalions were recruited from the Russian Jewish community in New York and were trained primarily to fight in Palestine against the Turks.

summary for various "political authorities"[21] on the fall of the Tsarist government and the competing political parties that were active in Russia at that time.

Monkhouse's absence from Soviet Russia was short-lived. In 1919 he was posted to Archangel to act as an interpreter for British Military Intelligence and to assist a unit of the Royal Engineers Railway Operating Division. There he renewed his acquaintance not only with the war-torn country, but with Richards and some 30 of those same British engineers with whom Monkhouse had fled to Vladivostok. In addition to serving as an interpreter, Monkhouse was charged with rationing food to the civilian population of about 2 700 and maintaining the readiness of the armoured train. His investigations into the needs of the local population brought him into contact with the local Menshevik leader, Lomonosov, a worker who greatly impressed Monkhouse with his willingness to lead by example. This close contact with Russians in the area earned him the reputation of being a Russophile.

> Under the circumstances I [Monkhouse] felt it my duty to allow this impression to remain, because unfortunately many of our Allied officers in the district had evidently been accustomed to dealing with Asiatic and dark races, and were inclined to treat our Russian Allies in the manner which they had previously adopted towards less enlightened peoples.[22]

When it became clear in July 1919, that the British forces would be withdrawing from Archangel, Monkhouse was asked to help communicate the bad news to the "White" defenders of the region. From his evaluation of the leadership of the White forces in the Archangel area and his knowledge of the attitudes of the peasants and workers in the region, Monkhouse concluded that Kolchak's forces had little hope of retaining local control once the British left.[23]

C.S. Richards' activities in Russia during the Great War also had difficult moments which would later haunt the MVEEC. In 1916 he was under orders from David Lloyd George (Minister of Munitions) to help out in the Russian munitions industry; in particular, he was to facilitate the transfer of munitions that were to come to Russia with Lord Kitchener on the ill-fated *Hampshire*. Early in 1918, with the Civil War

---

21 Monkhouse does not disclose who these groups were, although the term "authorities" suggests that they were in some sense "governmental" groups, possibly in the intelligence services. See Monkhouse, *Moscow*, p. 85-90.

22 Ibid., p. 95.

23 Admiral Aleksandr Kolchak was leader of the White forces in Siberia. Ibid., p. 67, 82-107; and Dummelow, *1899-1949*, p. 82.

now erupting in Russia, Richards was instructed by Lord Robert Cecil (Parliamentary Under-Secretary of State for Foreign Affairs) to obtain a sum of about one million roubles from the British Embassy in Petrograd and deliver it to General Iudenitch, commander of the White Russian forces in the Baltic. He travelled by sleigh and crossed through a "Red" frontier north of Sortavalla on the strength of his British passport. Arriving in Petrograd just after all the Embassy staff had left, he found the Consular staff in charge of the Embassy. They refused to give Richards the money, since they had not received the appropriate instructions. He met with Iudenitch, but was told that it was too late for such measures in any case. After this unsuccessful mission, Richards was posted to Colonel Thornhill, head of Army Intelligence at Murmansk, and from May 1918 to November 1919 he worked as an Army Intelligence Officer in both Murmansk and Archangel.[24] When these episodes in the careers of Richards and Monkhouse surfaced in 1933, the Foreign Office made much of the distinction between "Army Intelligence," in which both Richards and Monkhouse served, and the "Secret Service," which had never employed either man. The Soviet authorities were decidedly less convinced of the importance of such distinctions.

This professional involvement and expertise was reinforced by the Russian family connections of the MVEEC's European manager, A. Simon, and one of the senior engineers, Leslie Thornton. Thornton had been born in St. Petersburg, and his father had owned a woolen mill in Moscow prior to the Revolution. As for Simon, a portion of his family continued to live in the Soviet Union and throughout the 1920s Simon had his employees deliver various goods to his sister-in-law in Moscow.[25]

It is apparent from the accounts of Thornton and Monkhouse that their experience as foreign experts was profoundly shaped by the changing relationship they had with the Soviet electrical engineering community. For most of the period of the NEP they worked shoulder to shoulder with both communist and non-communist Russian experts, but after 1928 many of these experts and their associates became increasingly suspect in the eyes of the Stalinist authorities who were implementing the First Five-Year Plan.

---

24 Memorandum by Sir L. Oliphant, *Documents on British Foreign Policy*, 2nd series, VII, 1929-1934, eds. Woodward and Butler (London: Her Majesty's Stationary Office, 1957) (hereinafter cited as *DBFP*), #409, 15 April 1933.

25 See Thornton's account in his debriefing statement: C.S. Richards to Foreign Office, 20 July 1933, FO 371/17274 N5681/1610/38 (hereinafter cited as Thornton, Foreign Office Deposition, 20 July 1933).

Perhaps the most important of the men directly involved in the temporary alliance between party and non-party electrical engineers in the experience of the MVEEC were two engineer-managers, the non-communist, Genrikh Graftio and the Bolshevik, Aleksandr Vinter. Both men had had direct access to Lenin during the debates that would shape GOELRO priorities, and the former, an electrical engineer, was made head of the construction of the Volchov hydroelectric station outside of Leningrad to which Monkhouse was assigned in 1926. He had been put in charge at Lenin's insistence, despite being a former Tsarist official and despite having been arrested after the Revolution.[26] As has been demonstrated elsewhere,[27] such an accommodation with bourgeois specialists was a general feature of Soviet development until 1928. Monkhouse found the esprit de corps and enthusiasm of the staff at the Volchov station outstanding and, despite the cost overrun involved with the project, it "constituted a fine example of what could be accomplished in the U.S.S.R. under proper leadership and control."[28] Graftio organized regular social evenings between the foreign specialists and their Soviet counterparts and established a professional collegiality between the two groups. However, Graftio's status suffered an eclipse because of the excessive cost of the Volchov project, and Vinter rose to the top ranks of the hydroelectric engineering management in the USSR, culminating in his directorship of the gigantic Dneprostroi hydroelectric project.[29]

Vinter was in some respects atypical of the "bourgeois" specialists. As noted above, he was, along with his sponsor, Krzhizhanovskii, part of the Bolshevik cadre that learned their trade with the 1886 Company. Vinter was the son of a tradesman and had been expelled from Kiev University in 1901 for revolutionary activity. Prior to the Great War he had become a Social Democrat. He later studied engineering at Petrograd University under the future Bolshevik diplomat, Leonid Krasin, and had subsequently married the Bolshevik's sister. It seems likely that Krasin's early membership in the Presidium of the Supreme Economic Council and his promotion of the newly formed Electrotechnical Council could only have strengthened Vinter's position in the industry. Alongside these formidable political connections he had a reputation

26 Coopersmith, *The Electrification of Russia*, p. 148.

27 Bailes, *Technology and Society*, p. 51.

28 Monkhouse, *Moscow*, p. 142.

29 A. Rassweiler, *The Generation of Power: A History of Dneprostroi* (New York: Oxford University Press, 1988), p. 64-65.

as a problem solver and did not shy away from being held accountable for his decisions. At the time of his appointment to the Dneprostroi he was also rumoured to be a friend of the Chair of the Supreme Council for the National Economy (VSNKh), Aleksei Rykov.[30]

Monkhouse's involvement with Vinter came earlier, in 1924, at the Shatura power station east of Moscow. His account exudes an excitement and pride that came from working on what Monkhouse called "the first fruits of Lenin's electrification scheme." Vinter's administrative methods were generally well respected by those who worked under him. Richards reported on a revealing aspect of Vinter's approach in 1925 when, towards the end of the Shatura project, Vinter provoked a protest from the local Party officials, who complained that party members were the first to be laid off as the workforce to construct the station was reduced to the level necessary to operate it. The local officials complained that under the communist system the workers, and not Vinter, were the owners and that their wishes should be given priority. According to Richards, Vinter retorted, "I have been appointed by the people's Government to build this Power Station for the people. Anyone interfering with me is acting against the will of the people; he will be dealt with accordingly."[31] It was widely held around Shatura that Vinter's decision was supported by Trotsky, and the matter was left in Vinter's hands.[32] A further indication of Vinter's status with the authorities came during Thornton's interrogation. The British engineer had mentioned that Vinter had personally ordered switchgear equipment which had turned out to be faulty and was told by the interrogator, Zhelesnikov, not to mention Vinter's name again.[33] Even at the height of the most important investigation of the electrification industry in the USSR, Vinter was untouchable. While there will be much more to say about this later, it was insights such as those noted above that made the MVEEC engineers valuable sources for political as well as industrial intelligence, once Britain's Industrial Intelligence Centre was established.

On several other occasions Monkhouse was deputed to escort around the MVEEC's sites important figures such as Trotsky, who headed the Main Concessions Committee at the time and was in

30 Ibid., p. 19, 66.
31 Sir Philip Nash (MVEEC Director) to Caillard, 7 April 1925 (Sir Vincent Caillard [Vickers Director] MSS), contains Richards' report.
32 Rassweiler, *The Generation of Power*, p. 113.
33 Thornton, Foreign Office Deposition, 20 July 1933.

charge of Glavelektro.[34] The British engineer was surprised by the revolutionary's interest in technical detail, but was reminded by Trotsky that he had studied engineering as a young man.[35] Monkhouse also conducted the tours of the site for Krasin when he visited Shatura, and this contact with the leading figures undoubtedly reflected the MVEEC's reputation and Monkhouse's own personal standing as a foreign expert in the electrification industry.

Monkhouse maintained close contact with a number of the over 150 research institutes in Leningrad during this period. He met such famous figures as I. Pavlov and was part of a British delegation which presented the President of the Soviet Academy of Science, V. Karpinskii, with souvenirs of the Faraday Centenary. Overall he found the researchers and senior students to be very similar in education and calibre to those in Britain, but observed that the younger students were rather poorly prepared. This latter group tended to stress social and political work, and it is from this group that the upcoming generation of "red specialists" would undoubtedly be drawn.[36]

It is clear from Monkhouse's account of the MVEEC's involvement with the technical intelligentsia in the electrical industry that the British engineers much preferred to work and socialize with Russian engineers and managers who were trained prior to the Soviet period. Whether old-Bolshevik or non-communist, the key for Monkhouse, as it was for the Russians who promoted the GOELRO plan, was expert knowledge, not political "redness." To some extent it might even be argued that the tone of Monkhouse's memoir, which is that of a lament for a lost opportunity, rather than an indictment of the USSR, comes out of his conviction that many of the Russian engineers with whom he worked, in particular those who came from the "old-school," were men who were cast aside, as he was, after devoting themselves to a monumental and valuable component of the Soviet experiment. Alongside Monkhouses's high-powered encounters with prominent Soviet politicians and engineers, the daily difficulties associated with the somewhat primitive living conditions of his family and colleagues paled in significance. Monkhouse claimed that the long days and collegial circumstances made this an experience which helped form "the optimistic view which [he] always maintained as to the ultimate out-

---

34 Glavelektro was formed in 1921 as the successor to the Extraordinary Commission for Electricity Supply in Moscow.

35 Monkhouse, *Moscow*, p. 111.

36 Ibid., p. 142-43.

come of events in the U.S.S.R."[37] Only the experience of his arrest and trial served to give him pause in this regard.[38]

The profile of the MVEEC's personnel and their immediate community reveals important aspects of their involvement with Soviet society as well. One of the striking features of the six men arrested in 1933 is that while all were British subjects, only two, MacDonald and Gregory, were born in England. The others were born in Russia (Thornton), New Zealand (Monkhouse), Germany (Nordwall), and South Africa (Cushny). It is thus reasonable to suggest that living and working in foreign environs was nothing new to these engineers. Indeed, all those born outside of the UK had a passable command of Russian. According to Thornton, he and Monkhouse could be mistaken for natives when outside of Moscow and Leningrad.[39]

There was a generation gap in the MVEEC's cadre as well. In 1933, the most senior of the men, acting-manager Monkhouse, chief engineer Thornton, and electrical engineer Gregory were aged 46, 45, and 47 respectively.[40] All were married, and it is known that their families resided with them in the Soviet Union for short stints throughout this period.[41] This may have added a sense of normalcy to their lives, but it was clearly difficult for some. For example, by 1933 Thornton's wife had returned the UK, and it was universally reported by the other engineers that he had been in a state of nervousness and periodic depression for much of her absence.[42]

The other three younger men were all single when they came to the USSR, but Nordwall married a Ukrainian woman shortly after being posted there and was able to take her to Britain after his expulsion.[43] They were all more than 10 years younger than the senior MVEEC men and were employed in the actual installation and erection of the elec-

---

37 Ibid., p. 108-12.

38 Ibid.

39 Thornton, Foreign Office Deposition, 20 July 1933.

40 The ages are given as of 1933. See the Supreme Court of the USSR verbatim report, *The Case of N.P. Vitvitsky, V.A. Gussev, A.W. Gregory . . . Charged with Wrecking Activities at Power Stations in the Soviet Union* (Moscow: State Law Publishing House, 1933), p. 6-11 (hereinafter cited as *The Case*).

41 Foreign Office Memo by Wylie of interviews conducted at Bush House (MVEEC main office) with Monkhouse, Cushny, Gregory, and Nordwall, 9 May 1933, FO 371/17272 N3487/1610/38 (hereinafter cited as the Bush House Interviews, 9 May 1933); and Monkhouse, *Moscow*, p. 110.

42 Bush House Interviews, 9 May 1933.

43 "Departed Britons in Poland," *Observer*, 23 April 1933, p. 12.

trical equipment.[44] With less responsibility attached to their jobs and more free time generally, these three were more active in their personal associations with Soviet citizens.

Though the testimony of Soviet acquaintances during the trial most likely was exaggerated, even British officials recognized that MacDonald in particular was a very heavy drinker and was generally considered to have the "weakest character" of the lot. His choice of associates was often suspect, and he seemed to draw to himself Soviet citizens who were very indiscreet when it came to criticizing their native land.[45] The closest relationship MacDonald developed was with his housekeeper, Riabova, and her family. Given his near constant state of ill-health, the appeal of her matronly attention was understandable. Unfortunately for both Riabova and her family, she and her two sons were arrested just prior to MacDonald himself.[46]

In general, the MVEEC policy was to maintain a conspicuous distance between its employees and the official representatives of Great Britain posted at the Moscow Embassy and the Leningrad Consulate. Though this policy was to prove ultimately risky, the firm evidently thought that they were best served by establishing close and friendly relationships with Soviet authorities and those Russians with whom they were to work as colleagues.[47] This practice was extended to include the direct employment of Soviet nationals in the offices of the MVEEC in Moscow and Leningrad. By 1930, it was found expedient for the firm's secretary, Anna Kutuzova, to take up residence with Monkhouse and Thornton (and their families) at the company compound at Perlovskaia, just north of Moscow, along the Mytishchi railway line.[48]

While it is difficult to be certain about why such men were attracted to work in the Soviet Union, some motivational factors are clear. For the younger, less established engineers, there was the attraction of higher rates of pay and one-month leaves of absence. The MVEEC contracts worked out by Monkhouse also included clauses outlining additional compensation for unduly harsh working conditions and a host of items that were to be supplied by the Soviet authorities to outfit the

44 At the time of their arrests MacDonald was 29, Nordwall was 31, and Cushny was 34 years of age.
45 Strang to Collier, 20 April 1933, FO 371/17270 N2944/1610/38.
46 MacDonald, Foreign Office Deposition, 3 July 1933, FO 371/1723 N5059/1610/38 (hereinafter cited as MacDonald, Foreign Office Deposition, 3 July 1933).
47 Strang to Collier, 20 April 1933, FO 371/17270 N2944/1610/38.
48 Thornton, Foreign Office Deposition, 20 July 1933.

engineers.[49] Certainly in the years of the Great Depression this would have been an attractive arrangement, especially for the more well-travelled of the engineers. For men such as Monkhouse, there were the additional rewards of working on the cutting edge of their industry in a society that claimed to work on the basis of rational, scientifically designed plans for economic development. Even though Monkhouse was well aware of the gap between the goals of such plans and their actual accomplishments, it was a stimulating situation for an engineer to be engaged in some of the largest electrification projects undertaken anywhere in the world at that time. Unfortunately for Monkhouse and his British and Russian colleagues, the Stalin Revolution and the First Five-Year Plan were to intervene in their work and lives in a dramatic and terrible fashion.

---

49 Chilston to Sir John Simon, 23 February 1935, FO 371/19468 N1024/1024/38. This file includes the Company's report on MVEEC's contracts and copies of some of the contracts which Monkhouse negotiated in Moscow. It was part of a large dossier concerning MVEEC's affairs in the USSR sent on 20 March 1935 by MVEEC Director, Sir Felix Pole, to Anthony Eden, just prior to the Lord Privy Seal's visit to Moscow.

2

The MVEEC and the Stalin Revolution, 1927-33

> We are fifty or a hundred years behind the advanced countries. We must make good this distance in ten years. Either we do it or we go under. — I.V. Stalin, 1931

The year 1927 was pivotal for the MVEEC and its Soviet participation, for two reasons. It was noted above that the GOELRO plan was predicated on normal relations between the USSR and the advanced capitalist states, and it was in 1927 that Anglo-Soviet relations were plunged into the abyss over the British raid on the All-Russian Cooperative Society (ARCOS), an agency which acted on behalf of Soviet trading interests in London. On the Soviet domestic front, 1927 proved to be vital, too, as it was the last full year of the NEP, and brought with it the defeat of the opposition to Stalin. On the heels of these events came the much more fullsome transformation of Soviet life in the form of the First Five-Year Plan and the Stalin Revolution.

The origins and course of the ARCOS raid are well known. In 1927 the Conservative government in Britain was deeply troubled by Soviet policy in the Far East and India, and there were allegations that ARCOS was engaged in activities incompatible with its trade status. On 26 May 1927, with Prime Minister Stanley Baldwin, Foreign Secretary Sir Austen Chamberlain, and Home Secretary William Joynson-Hicks all quoting directly from intercepted Comintern telegrams, the Conservatives were able to make their case against Soviet meddling in British politics and thereby prepare the move to sever diplomatic relations with the USSR, which followed the next day. Still, such indiscreet revelations, while serving to muster a great deal of indignant bluster, seriously injured British interests when the debate "developed into an orgy of governmental indiscretion about secret intelligence for which there is no parallel in modern parliamentary history."[1]

The costs of this parliamentary drama were extremely high. By making public the actual text of Soviet documents, Baldwin's government compromised its most valuable Secret Intelligence Service (SIS, also known as MI6), which used the non-secret Government Code and Cypher School (GC & CS) and the Passport Control Office (PCO) as its cover. Very shortly after the ARCOS debacle, the British PCO officer in Helsinki, Commander Boyce, and the espionage network he managed were exposed by the OGPU (GPU)[2]. The British would never establish a PCO in the Soviet Union in the 1930s, and it now appears that the ill-advised disclosures in the parliamentary debates of May 1927 contributed to Soviet infiltration of these services in subsequent years.[3]

Against this background of aggravated Anglo-Soviet relations, the willingness of the MVEEC to remain in the USSR was, according to Monkhouse, interpreted by Soviet officials as a sign that certain British firms disagreed with the political mood at Whitehall.[4] It is impossible to know what influence this might have had on Soviet decisions at the time, but it was after the diplomatic rupture that the MVEEC concluded a five-year contract with the Leningrad Machine Trust (Mashinostroi) to manufacture turbines on the MVEEC's design. The Trust's representatives had full access to the Company's British workshops, labs, and drawing offices as well as to all patents. Under the agreement the patent fee would be removed after the completion of the five-year contract. The MVEEC was to send engineers, mechanics, and technical personnel to train Soviet engineers and oversee the project.[5] Over the years 1923-33 the MVEEC employed about 350 British subjects in the USSR and, in addition to these, contracted many more Soviet employ-

---

1 C. Andrew, *Secret Service: The Making of the British Intelligence Community* (London: W.H. Heinemann, 1985), p. 332-33.

2 The GPU (State Political Administration) replaced the Vecheka in February 1922 and was raised to federal status in November 1923 as the OGPU (Unified State Political Administration). The acronyms were used interchangeably in the late 1920s and early 1930s. The OGPU was unified with the NKVD (People's Commissariat of Internal Affairs) in 1934. See Knight, *The KGB*, p. 323, Appendix A.

3 Andrew, *Secret Service*, p. 332-33, 407. For a contrary and less convincing point of view see H. Flory, "The ARCOS Raid and the Rupture of Anglo-Soviet Relations, 1927," *Journal of Contemporary History*, 12, 4 (1977): 707-23.

4 Monkhouse, *Moscow*, p. 226.

5 "Five Year Agreement between Leningrad Machine Trust and Metropolitan Vickers," *The Times* (London), 18 March 1927.

ees for the firm in various capacities.[6] During these years the Company also trained large numbers of Russian engineers at its Trafford Park works.[7]

With the Company's activities increasing during the early years of the First Five-Year Plan, the Commissariat of Foreign Trade offered the MVEEC the opportunity to open a technical consulting bureau in Moscow. This was a rare privilege, as there were only three European firms and one American firm accorded equal treatment by the Commissariat. The arrangement was particularly useful in cases where innovative technology was being installed. Before this accommodation was reached, all transactions had to be passed through ARCOS in London before being finalized. This had often meant long delays, even over minor revisions in plans, and the British engineers were pleased with the flexibility shown in this instance. ARCOS continued to retain its right to confirm all agreements made through the Moscow bureau, and its electrical department worked through the Electro-Import office in Moscow.[8]

Following the resumption of relations between Great Britain and the Soviet Union in 1929, Monkhouse found the Moscow bureau to be an aid to many other British firms who now made use of the MVEEC office in Moscow to facilitate their own negotiations. Monkhouse understood the importance of re-establishing the "good name of British manufacturers, particularly amongst young Soviet engineers, and others who during the most active years of 1928-29, had had their attention deliberately directed to Germany and America."[9]

The establishment of an office in Moscow[10] required additional secretarial staff as well. After some difficult negotiations with the Commissariat of Foreign Trade that lasted for several months, it was agreed that the MVEEC could employ Soviet citizens. The cost for clerical workers was high by British standards, with the Soviet salary at 250 roubles per month (36 pounds at official 1933 rates) as compared to 12 pounds per month for a British clerk. Part of the salary to such employees could be paid in foreign currency "or its equivalent," a seemingly

---

6 "The Moscow Trial, New Light on the Case of 1933," *The Times* (London), 22-25 May 1933.

7 Dummelow, *1899-1949*, p. 121.

8 Monkhouse, *Moscow*, p. 228-29.

9 Ibid., p. 230.

10 The MVEEC had opened a small office in Leningrad in 1926 to assist its work at Mashinostroi. It served to coordinate the efforts of the local erection crews but was unsuitable as a central bureau. Chilston to Simon, 1 March 1935, FO 371/19468 N1024/1024/38.

innocuous arrangement that would have grave and unforeseen consequences. Once the issue of clerical staff had been resolved, the officials at Electro-Import allowed the MVEEC to employ Soviet erectors in the field on comparable terms.[11]

Despite these signs that the MVEEC continued to remain in favour with the Soviet authorities, it is clear that the afflicted condition of Anglo-Soviet relations, in particular, and the "war scare"[12] that swept Soviet society more generally began to place a strain on the interaction between the MVEEC's engineering corps and their Soviet colleagues out in the field. Sheila Fitzpatrick has argued that such international stress undoubtedly exacerbated the tensions on the Soviet domestic scene, which saw the major defeats of Trotsky and Zinoviev, and the deepening of the grain crisis that prompted Stalin's decision to bring an end to the NEP.[13] As Thornton and Monkhouse came to understand later, it was at this point that the tide rapidly shifted against both foreign and native "bourgeois" specialists.

Prior to this, there had been relatively few incidents which suggested OGPU interest in the MVEEC's affairs. After the trial, Thornton recalled some vaguely threatening letters he received from a woman who had seen him on one of his visits to A. Simon's sister-in-law in Leningrad. Whether they were part of a blackmail scheme by their author who hoped that she, too, could receive foreign-made articles, or part of a secret-police harassment tactic meant to discourage such contacts, is very difficult to say. In any case, when Thornton showed the letters to a Soviet colleague he was warned that the woman was undoubtedly an "agent." This did not apparently make much of an impression on Thornton, who chose to forget about the incident and ignored its implications at the time.[14]

Another instance involved a warning given to Thornton by a former colleague at the Shatura Cable Works. N.P. Kushinskii told Thornton that the OGPU were trying to arrange for his return to Shatura in order to implicate him in the ongoing problems with "blowups" in the cable lines. According to Thornton's testimony later, the cable network

11 Ibid., p. 232-33.
12 See M. Reiman, *The Birth of Stalinism: The U.S.S.R. on the Eve of the "Second Revolution,"* trans. George Saunders (Bloomington: Indiana University Press, 1987), p. 14-15; A. Meyer, "The War Scare of 1927," *Soviet Union/Union Soviétique*, 5, 1 (1978): 1-25; and J. Sontag, "The Soviet War Scare of 1926-1927," *The Russian Review*, 34, 1 (1975): 66-77.
13 S. Fitzpatrick, "The Foreign Threat during the First Five Year Plan," *Soviet Union/Union Soviétique*, 5, 1 (1978): 26.
14 Thornton, Foreign Office Deposition, 20 July 1933.

still suffered from the abuses it took during the Great War and the general lack of maintenance that characterized Soviet projects at the time. After this he made a point of trying not to return to job sites he had previously worked at because of these potential difficulties.[15]

Incidents of this type, while rare in the early years of the MVEEC's involvement in the Soviet Union, now became part of the general political environment pervading the industrial sector in the country. From March 1928 until June 1931, Soviet industry was racked with the Shakhty affair, the Industrial Party Trial, and the Menshevik Trial. In each of these highly publicized trials, threats from foreign capitalists were said to be linked to the sabotage and wrecking of the First Five-Year Plan's industrialization drive. What else, so the lessons of these trials taught, could explain the unfulfilled norms, accidents, and resistance to the Party's plan in the workers' paradise?[16] According to Stalin, these assualts demonstrated that economic sabotage, as well as military attack, was part of the capitalist arsenal against the Soviet Union. Soviet citizens were warned that class warfare may have been inspired from abroad, but it had allies within Soviet society. Both the "kulaks," who resisted collectivization of agriculture, and the "bourgeois specialists," who resisted higher socialist production norms, had to be defeated by increased Party vigilance and the application of Soviet justice.[17]

As early as 1924, Monkhouse himself had been told of the coming "red" tide of young Soviet engineers by the Director of the Balakna Power Station on the Volga river. This "red" Director assured Monkhouse that within three years the universities would be turning out their first "batches" of "red" engineers and that the "technical men of old-tempering" would be removed unless they were "exceptional men whose loyalty to the Soviets was absolutely unquestionable."[18] By 1929 the tide had indeed come in and Monkhouse watched as "many chief engineers — men of long experience and men whom I [Monkhouse]

---

15 Ibid.
16 Important discussions of these trials are found in R. Conquest, *The Great Terror: Stalin's Purge of the Thirties* (New York: Macmillan, 1968), Appendix F, "Earlier Soviet Trials"; Fitzpatrick, "The Foreign Threat," p. 26-35; and Bailes, *Technology and Society*, Part 2.
17 I.V. Stalin, "O rabotakh aprel'skogo ob"edinennogo plenuma TsK i TsKK (April 1928)," in I.V. Stalin, *Sochinennia*, Vol. 11, p. 54; and Fitzpatrick, "The Foreign Threat," p. 27-28. For an important discussion of the impact such crises had on judicial practices, see P. Solomon, "Local Political Power and Soviet Criminal Justice, 1922-1941," *Soviet Studies*, 37, 3 (1985): 305-29.
18 Monkhouse, *Moscow*, p. 266-67.

believed were working loyally for the Soviet—[were] ruthlessly removed from their posts and replaced by young Party men whose theo-
retical and political training was without question excellent, but who
possessed exceedingly flimsy practical qualifications for the high positions in which they were placed."[19]

It was understandable, given these dangerous circumstances, that
Soviet engineers altered their interaction with the British engineers
during these years. Increasingly they refused to visit the flats of their
foreign associates in Leningrad, although there were Soviet citizens
from outside Leningrad who were apparently not yet aware of the risk.
The firm was advised by the OGPU to meet with Soviet colleagues at
the Europe Hotel for social occasions. Naturally this was to be at the
MVEEC's expense. At the Engineers' Club in Leningrad, where the
British engineers had previously been welcome guests, they were now
outcasts. The membership had drastically changed by 1930 as the old
intelligentsia was replaced by the "red expert."[20] Business dealings
with Soviet engineers and technical staff were also hampered, since the
uneasiness which "non-party engineers showed at being left alone
with foreigners" made the inclusion of local Communist officials necessary for subsequent negotiations.[21] Not surprisingly the number of
engineers involved in production-related jobs declined by as much as
17 percent in this period. These engineers apparently felt that the combination of difficult working conditions and very high production
norms, set on the basis of political, rather than technical considerations, was a serious obstacle to "success" as defined by the regime.
The cost of failure in an industrial culture where being "red" might
prove to be more helpful than being "expert" was too high for many.[22]

Housing for the MVEEC's employees also became a problem by
1930. Thornton claimed that the decision to build the complex at Perlovskaia, located just outside of Moscow, was at least in part due to the
fear of foreigners exhibited by Muscovites and the consequent difficulty in finding appropriate housing.[23] The arrangements for the building of the MVEEC's compound, however, revealed a willingness on
the part of the local Soviet authorities to accommodate the British firm

---

19 Ibid., p. 266.
20 Ibid., p. 145-46; and Thornton, Foreign Office Deposition, 20 July 1933.
21 Monkhouse, *Moscow*, p. 147.
22 S. Fitzpatrick, "Cultural Revolution as Class War," in S. Fitzpatrick, ed., *Cultural
    Revolution in Russia, 1928-1931* (Bloomington: Indiana University Press, 1978; Mid-
    land Book Edition, 1984), p. 22.
23 Thornton, Foreign Office Deposition, 20 July 1933.

that was in marked contrast to the situation in Moscow. Monkhouse obtained permission to get a 45-year lease on a parcel of land, and the local authorities required no special declaration on the part of this foreign *zastroishik*, or home builder. Though building supplies were in high demand in the Moscow area, payments in sterling ensured the availability of needed materials. The British firm also managed to co-ordinate their efforts with a group of peasants whom they knew from their other endeavours. These men travelled "some hundred miles" to do the work on a piecework basis. A final example of the free rein the MVEEC was allowed with this project came when they were permitted to tap a four-inch water main from the Moscow aqueduct and did so with their own crew.[24] Evidently not all branches of the Soviet bureaucracy or society were "vigilant" when it came to monitoring relations with the MVEEC.

Still, ominous signs were mounting, although to be sure their significance was much clearer in 1933. Thornton recalled later that early in 1930, Kutuzova was visited by representatives of the local soviet who tried to convince her that the MVEEC's presence was going to do her harm. Shortly after this she was summoned to be interviewed by the OGPU in Moscow. She disappeared for two days and was very distressed upon her return, but told Thornton that she had refused to become an "agent." It was at this point that Thornton advised her to become an "honest informant," but, to offer her some protection from OGPU harrassment, the MVEEC instituted a policy which required that Kutuzova was to be accompanied whenever she left the MVEEC compound or their offices.[25]

The basic trends that came to dominate the MVEEC's interaction with Soviet society intensified in the wake of the Industrial Party Trial of November-December 1930. Monkhouse later claimed that "almost every Russian engineer who had been in any contact whatever with the British engineers of the Metropolitan Vickers Electrical Company was subjected to interrogation by the OGPU and some thirty to forty of my own acquaintances were imprisoned."[26] Thornton also recalled the importance of this episode, and he included in his deposition a list of 46 former colleagues and the MVEEC's Soviet employees who had been arrested during this period. At least one of these, G.I. Efremov, was believed to have been executed after the Industrial Party Trial. Efremov had been employed as an erector by the MVEEC and had

---

24 Monkhouse, *Moscow*, p. 233-35.
25 Thornton, Foreign Office Deposition, 20 July 1933.
26 Monkhouse, *Moscow*, p. 146.

trained for six months at the Trafford Park works in Manchester. He was a very valuable man, but was "indiscreet" when criticizing Soviet authorities.[27] It is not known if this was the extent of his "criminal" behaviour.

These observations help substantiate the claims by Bailes that the number of engineers drawn into the police investigations numbered in the thousands.[28] For those involved in industry during this period there could be little doubt that the "Revolution from above" was crashing down on the heads of the technically trained specialists. Thornton apparently did not follow the Industrial Party Trial as it was unfolding, although his attention was drawn to a portion of the published confession of the key defendant, Professor L. Ramzin.[29] Ramzin "confessed" to being involved in a conspiracy with A. Simon of Vickers and a variety of other shadowy Englishmen including a "Sir Philip," a "Colonel" Lawrence, and a "Lord" Churchill. Thornton had made enquiries with the directors of his firm and found that Simon of the MVEEC (not Vickers)[30] had indeed met with Ramzin in London and introduced the Soviet representative to Sir Philip Nash, the managing director of the MVEEC, and Sir Herbert Lawrence, a director of the MVEEC and a well-known banker, with the hope of encouraging future business. Ramzin was an important figure in the Thermal Technical Institute at the time, although his eclipse was at least partly related to his opposition to plans which were overly reliant on gigantic enterprises.[31] As for "Lord" Churchill and his hopes for naval exercises in the Black Sea — such errors in detail were further evidence, in Thornton's view, that the whole confession "reeked" of OGPU "dictation." Moreover, the

---

27 Thornton, Foreign Office Deposition, 20 July 1933.

28 Bailes, *Technology and Society*, p. 70 and chap. 4, "The Industrial Party Affair."

29 See the Soviet published version of the trial in Andrew Rothstein, ed., *Wreckers on Trial: A Record of the Trial of the Industrial Party Held in Moscow, November-December 1930* (New York: Workers' Library Publishing, 1931).

30 By 1927 Douglas Vickers had decided that the price he paid for the Metropolitan Company, including its electrical interests, had been too high indeed. Vickers sold the controlling interest of the MVEEC to GEC in 1927. In 1928, Dudley Docker regained control of the MVEEC, and the firm was incorporated with British Thomson-Houston, the Edison Swan Electric Company, and Ferguson, Pailin Limited under the "Associated Electrical Industries" rubric during this period of British rationalization in industry. Vickers did continue to hold stock in the MVEEC throughout these years, and the structure of the MVEEC on the ground in the USSR remained intact. MVEEC also retained five of its former Directors and became part of the new Associated Electrical Industries Limited, which employed some 30 000 people. In subsequent years GEC once again assumed control, and the MVEEC is now known as GEC Switchgear Ltd. See Scott, *Vickers*, p. 167; and Dummelow, *1899-1949*, p. 119.

31 Bailes, *Technology and Society*, p. 113.

notion that Simon, who had initiated the MVEEC's Russian venture in 1922, and to a certain extent staked his reputation on its success, would want to destabilize Soviet Russia was, Thornton thought, "absurd."[32]

Despite what would later be seen as obvious danger signals, the engineers remained essentially oblivious to the potential problems they might face themselves. With some remorse Thornton later recalled:

> I had not the slightest idea that the G.P.U. contemplated any arrests. I had always been given to understand by my informants that no arrests or searches would ever be made as the Soviet Government were afraid of counter measures abroad. I realize now [July 1933] that this information was "put across." If I had understood the situation, which I entirely misgauged, I think I could have got Mr. Cushny and the erectors . . . out of the country without prejudicing the Company's business here.[33]

Thornton's comments here reveal common features of the engineers' thinking that help explain their errors in judgement. In several instances they were told by various Soviet citizens employed by the MVEEC that the OGPU had forced the unfortunate Russians to become informants. Invariably the response of Thornton and Monkhouse was to advise these people to tell the police whatever they needed to know. They later claimed that they had nothing to hide and seemed genuinely concerned that the Company not cause any more trouble for their Soviet employees if, for example, the MVEEC engineers simply dismissed them. The engineers were also aware that one of the typists and their secretary had been "ordered" by the police to seduce Cushny, Monkhouse, and Thornton himself.[34] In one instance, Monkhouse was followed by an attractive OGPU "blondinka" who made it clear that she was to pay rather close personal attention to the British engineer while he was travelling to and from Baku.[35]

It is still not clear why the MVEEC personnel stationed in the Soviet Union waited until the actual detention of their Soviet personnel had begun before they decided to take up such issues with the management of the firm in the UK. Up until that point (January 1933) they may have felt the individual incidents were too trivial or commonplace in the current Soviet context to be of consequence. Certainly they were aware of the periodic *chistki* or Party "sweeps" that characterized the

---

32 Thornton, Foreign Office Deposition, 20 July 1933.
33 Ibid.
34 Ibid.
35 Monkhouse, *Moscow*, p. 259-62.

period and thought that their own troubles were part of that process.[36] They also thought that complaints against such action could only injure MVEEC's business and, from their perspective, the tactics of the OGPU did not appear to be directed specifically against the MVEEC in any case.[37]

Another feature of their thinking was the high opinion held by the senior men, Thornton and Monkhouse, of the efficiency of the security forces of the USSR. Many foreign travellers,[38] including the British engineers, had had occasion to seek OGPU assistance, and its reputation was therefore not simply one of a repressive force. Indeed, Monkhouse held that the OGPU intentionally spread fantastic rumours and tales of torture and punishment which apparently added credibility to its function in Soviet society.[39] It was also difficult for the MVEEC engineers to fathom why a company with the reputation of long and faithful service to the Soviet Union should be the object of an attack now. Thornton observed, "the G.P.U. [OGPU] would have acted before now if they had intended to do anything at all and not wait eight years, that is allowing us two years to incriminate ourselves."[40]

Thornton's comment, made in 1933, needs some clarification. It has been suggested that the period from 1924-27 was relatively free of interference, while the rash of incidents after 1927 seemed to be part of a concerted policy of "specialist" harassment. This continued until spring of 1931, and the aftermath of the Menshevik Trial, when the mood in the Stalinist leadership once again began to swing in favour of the industrial specialists. Thornton had also observed that the OGPU's interest in the MVEEC declined in the later part of 1931 and 1932.[41] Thornton's reference to a two-year period "in which to incriminate ourselves" is particularly tantalizing because 1931 was the year that the formal structure of the Industrial Intelligence Centre was established — but that is getting ahead of ourselves.

The overall impression that can be gained from the depositions of the MVEEC cadre is consistent with the position held by Bailes and others and suggests that Stalin had been won over by those in the Central Committee and the head of VSNKh, G. Ordzhonikidze, to the view

36 MacDonald, Foreign Office Deposition, 3 July 1933.
37 Thornton, Foreign Office Deposition, 20 July 1933.
38 See the account of the American asbestos engineer, Walter Rukeseyer, *Working for the Soviets: An American Engineer in Russia* (New York: Covici-Freide Publishers, 1932), p. 31.
39 Monkhouse, *Moscow*, p. 262-63.
40 Thornton, Foreign Office Deposition, 20 July 1933.
41 Ibid.

that the industrial sector had been secured from danger by the series of investigations and trials that had recently been undertaken from 1928-31.[42] The Soviet press increasingly carried the new line. *Pravda* announced in June 1931, that the "wrecking organizations had been smashed."[43] The following month the head of the OGPU, V. Menzhinskii, published an article in *Pravda* dedicated to the fifth anniversary of the death of Dzerzhinskii, his predecessor. The OGPU chief echoed the new approach to technical specialists when he reminded readers that Dzerzhinskii had "used the G.P.U. to protect specialists from all kinds of oppression."[44] To news of this type on 20 August 1931, the engineering journal, *Inzhenenernyi Trud*, proclaimed that "Specialist Baiting is outlawed!"[45]

This benign situation began to erode only in September 1932 when Kutuzova once again began to be periodically summoned by the OGPU. Other members of the MVEEC staff were also questioned about the "living arrangements" at Perlovskaia and Kutuzova's relationship with the British engineers. By this point, Thornton knew that Kutuzova was reporting to the OGPU on the amount of *torgsin* roubles being spent by the MVEEC. These roubles were used for goods in restricted supply — a kind of official black market.[46] That these events were only a foretaste of what was to come became all too apparent in January 1933, when a number of the MVEEC's Soviet employees suddenly disappeared.

In spite of all these indications, it certainly appears that the MVEEC found it difficult to see that the winds of change were upon them. Early in January, at the joint plenum of the Central Committee and Central Control Commission, Stalin, Chairman of the Council of People's Commissars V. Molotov, Secretary of the Central Committee and the Moscow Party organization L. Kaganovich, and People's Commissar for Heavy Industry G. Ordzhonikidze had all come out with severe criticism of industrial managers.[47] Stalin, speaking about the threat from the remnant of the "moribund" bourgeoisie, warned:

---

42 Bailes, *Technology and Society*, p. 150-51; Kuromiya, *Stalin's Industrial Revolution*, p. 272-76; and S. Fitzpatrick, "Ordzhonikidze's Takeover of Vesenkha: A Case Study in Soviet Bureaucratic Politics," *Soviet Studies*, 37, 2 (1985): 164-65.
43 Fitzpatrick, "The Foreign Threat," p. 33. "Po-novomu robatat,' po-novomu rukovodit,'" *Pravda*, 25 June 1931, p. 1.
44 Quoted in Kuromiya, *Stalin's Industrial Revolution*, p. 276.
45 Ibid.
46 Thornton, Foreign Office Deposition, 20 July 1933.
47 Kuromiya, *Stalin's Industrial Revolution*, p. 292-93.

These gentlemen are no longer able to launch a frontal assault against
the Soviet regime. They and their classes made such attacks several
times, but they were routed and dispersed. Hence, the only thing left
them is to do mischief and harm to the workers, to the collective
farmers, to the Soviet regime and to the Party. And they are doing as
much mischief as they can, acting on the sly. They set fire to ware-
houses and wreck machines. They organize sabotage.[48]

The echo of Stalin's speech would be heard time and again in the
Metro-Vickers trial of April 1933 but, for now, the MVEEC staff in the
USSR were simply confused by the renewed interest Soviet authorities
were showing in Company affairs.

The MVEEC itself was the subject of an investigation by the Commissariat of Heavy Industry in January, but according to later testimony by Cushny, this failed to cause much concern, since the Company's equipment passed this preliminary examination.[49] In general,
the MVEEC had confidence in its relationship with those at the summit
of Soviet industry such as Ordzhonikidze and the related bureaucratic
interests of the Commissariat of Foreign Trade. It was hard for either
the MVEEC directors in London or Monkhouse and Thornton in the
USSR to understand how any of these concerns could benefit from a
crisis in Anglo-Soviet trade.

The first disturbing sign that a crisis of unforeseen proportions was
upon those associated with the Company was recognized on 6 January
when MacDonald's housekeeper, Riabova, vanished. Despite inquiries
with the local police and the OGPU, the young engineer could not find
out what had become of her. When MacDonald informed Thornton of
his housekeeper's disappearance, however, Thornton "had little doubt
that she had been arrested by the G.P.U. [OGPU] for some civil offense
such as hoarding gold, insulting communists or anti-Soviet speeches. I
did not think that it could have any connection with us at the time."[50]
MacDonald's concern grew on 26 January, when he opened a letter
from Riabova's daughter in search of some information about the missing woman and found that her two sons had also been arrested. It was
now clear to MacDonald that this was no ordinary passport verifica-
tion (*proverka*), or *chistka*.[51]

Though in early January Thornton had not sensed any change in
the temper of OGPU operations, it soon became evident that the net

48 Stalin, "The Results of the First Five-Year Plan," 7 January 1933, *Works*, p. 211-12.
49 See Cushny's account in *The Times* (London), 23 May 1933, p. 15-16.
50 Thornton, Foreign Office Deposition, 20 July 1933.
51 MacDonald, Foreign Office Deposition, 3 July 1933.

cast around MacDonald's household was similarly being drawn about the Perlovskaia compound. On 25 January, Kutuzova received a call at the MVEEC's bureau in Moscow from her estranged husband, who lived in Leningrad, but was unexpectedly now in Moscow. She was reluctant to take the call, but did manage a very short conversation. About a half-hour after this she asked to leave to see her husband. This was a marked departure from the standing practice which had been instituted in 1932, a practice that made sure Kutuzova was escorted by another MVEEC employee whenever she left the firm's bureau or compound. Once in the street, the folly of her action became clear as she was "literally dragged" into a Ford coupe waiting nearby and taken to the OGPU headquarters at the Lubianka prison.

That evening Monkhouse decided that he had to break with past practices and contact the MVEEC's office in London about the whole affair. He was later told that his call was instrumental in gaining the release of Kutuzova the following day.[52] Richards, upon hearing of these disturbing developments, asked Monkhouse to return to London where he would arrange a meeting with the Soviet trade representative there, Ozerskii. When Monkhouse met with Richards and Ozerskii in London early in February, Ozerskii claimed that he had twice contacted Menzhinskii, the ailing head of the OGPU, and was rather unconvincingly told that "Kutuzova's arrest had been the work of a Department of the O.G.P.U. unknown to its chiefs." The OGPU had nothing against the MVEEC or any of its engineers and the matter was allowed to drop there.[53]

While Ozerskii's statement might appear to be little more than a ruse, there is important circumstantial evidence that the economic section of the OGPU was acting independently of other governmental institutions if not, as Ozerskii suggested, acting independently of overall OGPU direction. Monkhouse himself came to believe that Ozerskii had been intentionally misled by the OGPU after the British engineer had seen the way the secret police had reacted to his own account of the meeting with the Soviet trade representative. Beyond this, it was almost certainly the case that when the axe finally fell on the British subjects themselves, Maxim Litvinov, the Commissar of Foreign Affairs, did not know about the impending Anglo-Soviet crisis.[54] If such was the case, and this issue will be subsequently explored in some depth, it would be a marked departure from the only previous precedent, the Shakhty Trial, in which German citizens were involved and the diplo-

52 Monkhouse, *Moscow*, p. 272-73.
53 Ibid., p. 274-75.
54 Ovey to Vansittart, 13 March 1933, FO 371/17265 N1650/1610/38.

matic apparatus headed by Litvinov's predecessor, Chicherin, coordinated its actions with those of the secret police.[55]

Further evidence that the Soviet trade organizations were not apprised of the impending action against the British MVEEC can be
found in the archives of Vickers, the armament company which had
held a controlling interest in the MVEEC until 1927, and continued to
hold substantial stock. From February 10 to 22, a Soviet trade mission
of ARCOS officials and Red Army officers toured various Vickers
works on what was the first military-technical mission to Vickers since
the Revolution. According to General Noel Birch, a Vickers director,
the Soviets were very keen to purchase the latest array of artillery and
ballistic devices and were well informed about the "secret list" of items
that the Department of Overseas Trade recommended against selling
to the Red Army.[56] Since the MVEEC and Vickers had a long-standing,
if diminishing connection, it seems unlikely that a coordinated Soviet
attack on the MVEEC would have coincided with continued purchases
from a closely related British company. This point is further strengthened when it is recognized that during the interrogation of the arrested
engineers, Soviet authorities showed some confusion about the actual
relationship of the former parent company, Vickers, and the MVEEC.
That such a problem developed was certainly understandable, since
British officials themselves often used the short form "Vickers" when
they were referring to the MVEEC. It seems likely, then, that the OGPU
preferred to pursue its own investigations outside the realm of the
Commissariat of Foreign Trade, the Commissariat of Heavy Industry,
or the Narkomindel, and thereby sought to produce a fait accompli
where the MVEEC was concerned.

At about same time as Ozerskii was trying to convince the MVEEC
management in London that no concerted effort was being mounted
against the Company, Thornton went to the office of Electro-Import in
Moscow through which the MVEEC arranged its affairs with the Commissariat of Foreign Trade. He met with A. N. Dolgov, a man who was
associated with Vinter's work in the electrification industry and had
been hitherto very helpful when it came to employing Soviet personnel
in the MVEEC's work.[57] When Thornton told him of Kutuzova's arrest,

55 See G. Hilger and A. Meyer, *The Incompatible Allies: A Memoir History of German-
Soviet Relations, 1918-1941* (New York: Macmillan, 1953), p. 217-18; and H. Dyck, *The
Soviet Union and Weimar Germany* (London: Chatto & Windus, 1966), p. 129-30.

56 Report by General Sir Noel Birch (Director) 22 February 1933, K 616, Papers of Vickers Ltd.

57 Rassweiler, *The Generation of Power*, p. 72-73; and Thornton, Foreign Office Deposition, 20 July 1933.

Dolgov "almost fainted." In a very agitated manner he claimed it was "criminal" to have Soviet citizens in foreign employ and that he was withdrawing his "support from our scheme of employing Russian erectors absolutely."[58] This rapid reversal suggests that Electro-Import was not advised of the OGPU plans for the MVEEC either and that Dolgov was very quick to realize the potential implications of these recent events. Dolgov was not seen in his office for the next three days and would later hold the distinction of being the only witness at the engineers' trial, aside from technical advisers, not to be charged with any crime despite the fact that Thornton had allegedly bribed him. He would be portrayed by defenders of the British engineers as an agent provocateur during the trial, and in contrast to his previous record of support and involvement with foreign firms, it appears that he had aided the OGPU for some time.[59] Shortly after the arrests of the MVEEC's personnel, Dolgov was demoted to his old job in the Central Department of Electro-Import, thereby removing him from responsibilities relating to the British firm. This suggests that Dolgov may have been an unwilling agent in the service of the secret police.[60]

More was learned about the implications of Kutuzova's arrest when the unfortunate woman returned to the MVEEC's office in Moscow on the morning of 26 January. She was near hysteria and completely exhausted. Her hands were covered with ink and she told Monkhouse and Thornton that she was forced, under threats to her entire family, "to write that we were engaged in spying and bribing and being in close contact with the Consulate and Embassy. She further said that she had been forced to write 'disgustful' things in relation to myself [Thornton] and Mr. Monkhouse."[61] Her interrogators tried to convince her that such testimony could never be used, but that it was useful to have when "bargaining" with the British. In what was almost certainly a reference to the impending end of the Anglo-Soviet Commercial Agreement, she had been told that the most dangerous time would be in April — the treaty was to lapse on 16 April — when "the Governments would quarrel."[62]

From the interrogation she had undergone throughout the entire evening, Kutuzova gained the impression that the OGPU had a near-

58 Thornton, Foreign Office Deposition, 20 July 1933.

59 See British Acting-Counsellor William Strang's comment in Strang, *Home and Abroad* (London: Andre Deutsch, 1956), p. 97.

60 Thornton, Foreign Office Deposition, 20 July 1933.

61 Ibid.

62 Ibid.

complete knowledge of the MVEEC's men, their nicknames, character-istics, and weaknesses.[63] This information was consistent with that learned by Monkhouse over the next two days which indicated that "a careful watch was being made of [his] own movements and those of several of our engineers."[64] It was also learned that one Soviet erector, Oleinik, had "disappeared" after finishing his last assignment.[65]

As for MacDonald, he had been generously provided with a re-placement for Riabova by the Soviet authorities he was assisting, but the new woman had an annoying habit of letting unknown visitors into his apartment. MacDonald also recalled after the trial that one Or-lov, an engineer who had never shown much interest in the young Briton prior to Riabova's disappearance, now had become very friendly and had invited himself over to MacDonald's flat several times. Further evidence of this type of informal surveillance occurred on 1 March, when MacDonald was at a party at the Astoriia hotel, and was, as usual, enjoying perhaps too much drink. He did not make it home that night and he received close attention from "several men" who were not friends, yet wanted to talk to him at great length. In re-sponse to a query by another MVEEC engineer about the reason for his failure to appear at work on 2 March, MacDonald denied that he had been arrested that night, but admitted he "may have been under infor-mal examination."[66]

Over the next week the MVEEC engineers were unaware of any new developments. As it turned out this was indeed the quiet before the storm. It would later become known that the OGPU gained en-trance to the MVEEC compound on 9 March, by pressuring and threatening the Russian servants.[67] On 11 March 1933, the OGPU co-ordinated four raids at the premises of the MVEEC engineers. At the Perlovskaia compound, Monkhouse and Thornton were interrupted during a business dinner by a large OGPU force of about 80 men. The premises were searched and they were presented with warrants for their arrest. John Cushny and MacDonald were picked up at Cushny's flat in Moscow where MacDonald was temporarily staying. It was soon learned that in Moscow the MVEEC bureau office next to Electro-

63 Ibid.

64 Monkhouse, *Moscow*, p. 274.

65 Thornton, Foreign Office Deposition, 20 July 1933.

66 This account was provided by MacDonald in response to Tearle's account which as-serted that MacDonald had been arrested 1 March. See Richards to Collier, 20 July 1933, FO 371/17274 N5682/1610/38.

67 Strang to Simon, 13 May 1933, FO 371/17272 N3829/1610/38 contains a report by MVEEC employee Buckell on this revelation.

Import had been searched and the MVEEC office in Leningrad was also raided. In this later instance, however, the British clerk was left at liberty while four of the Soviet staff were detained. The OGPU force in Leningrad included about 20 secret police and two engineers who could speak some English. The importance of these last two was made clear when the group searched the premises and removed hundreds of MVEEC letters and pieces of personal correspondence.[68] Charles Nordwall and Albert Gregory were picked up over the next few days, as were a number of Soviet erectors, among them Oleinik. It was now learned that he had been missing from his home in Poltava since 24 February. In short order then, these six British engineers and a large, but undetermined number of their Soviet associates found themselves under interrogation at the Lubianka prison in Moscow.

On 12 March, the first moves were made by the MVEEC to seek the support of the British government. Two British employees of the firm, Buckell and Burke, who were at Perlovskaia the previous evening, had witnessed the arrests. Early the next day they urgently sought a meeting with the embassy staff in Moscow. The news of the Leningrad raid was quickly confirmed with the British Consul-General there, Bullard, and the Ambassador, Sir Esmond Ovey, was brought into the proceedings.[69] Further aggravating the mood of the diplomats, who were rapidly to assume the role of defenders of the MVEEC's employees, was the announcement in *Izvestiia* that day that 35 Russians had been executed by the OGPU without trial for "wrecking" in the Ukraine under new powers that had been granted to the secret police.[70] It was against this backdrop of increasing tensions and violence within the Soviet domestic domain that the Metro-Vickers affair rapidly developed into a serious international crisis.

---

68 Ovey to Vansittart, 12 March 1933, FO 371/17265 N1610/1610/38; ibid., 13 March 1933, FO 371/17265 N1638/1610/38; and Richards to Collier, 26 May 1933, FO 371/17272/1610/38.

69 Bullard to Vansittart, 12 March 1933, FO 371/17265 N1612/1610/38, 12 March 1933.

70 *Izvestiia*, 12 March 1933, p. 2 carries the names of the 35 executed as well as the names of 22 others sentenced to 10 years imprisonment and 18 more sentenced to 8 years imprisonment. Ovey to Vansittart, 13 March 1933, FO 371/17265 N1649/1610/38; "35 Shot Without Trial," *The Times* (London), 13 March 1933, p. 14; and S. Wolin and R. Slusser, *The Soviet Secret Police* (New York: Frederick A. Praeger, 1957), p. 16.

3

The Politics of Crisis Diplomacy

> I felt that nothing but absolute and earliest possible
> realisation by these people of their folly could prevent
> them from drifting into a position from which with-
> drawal would be still more difficult for them.
> — Sir Esmond Ovey, British Ambassador, Moscow 1933

> Concretely and practically the claims of the Ambassador
> in this case reduce themselves to a proposal for the ex-
> emption from Soviet jurisdiction of all British subjects
> granting them immunity for any crime or delinquency . . .
> as soon as his [Ovey's] government express a conviction
> of their innocence.   — Tass, 16 March 1933

While the turmoil of Soviet domestic politics was a key element in the
process that enveloped the MVEEC engineers and encouraged their arrest, it soon became clear that the struggle over their fate would have a
decidedly international dimension. The day after the arrests, the British Ambassador, Sir Esmond Ovey, relayed news of the OGPU action
to the Permanent Under-Secretary at the Foreign Office, Sir Robert
Vansittart.[1] With both the Prime Minister of the National Government,

---

1 FO 371/17265 N1611/1610/38, 12 March 1933. Previous studies of this event include Donald Lammers, "The Engineers' Trial (Moscow 1933) and Anglo-Soviet Relations," *South Atlantic Quarterly*, 62 (1963): 256-67; Gail Owen, "The Metro-Vickers
 Crisis: Anglo-Soviet Relations between Trade Agreements, 1932-1934," *Slavonic and
 East European Review*, 44 (1971): 92-112; Jonathan Haslam, *The Soviet Union and the
 Struggle for Collective Security in Europe, 1933-1939* (New York: St. Martin's Press,
 1984), chap. 2.; and Gordon Morrell, "Britain Confronts the Stalin Revolution: The

Ramsay MacDonald, and the Foreign Secretary, Sir John Simon, at the Geneva Disarmament Conference, it would be Ovey and Vansittart who would shape British policy in the initial weeks of the confrontation. From the beginning, Ovey's hard-line recommendations were meant to convince the Soviets of the damage to Anglo-Soviet relations that would be incurred if they insisted on a trial. Ovey also pressed the urgency of the situation on his own superiors in London. Vansittart was content in the early going to rely on his Ambassador in Moscow, the "man on the spot," but it gradually became apparent that less severe measures than those proposed by Ovey would be the course pursued by the British government. Since Ovey was to play a central role in the early course of events, it is important to gain some understanding of his approach to diplomacy and his working assessment of Stalin's Russia.

There was a certain irony that Ovey, a man who had hitherto been considered by Vansittart to be "an apostle of moderation,"[2] was faced with a situation which prompted him to advocate measures that would ultimately bring an end to his tenure in Moscow. Ovey had been sent to Moscow in 1929, as part of the second Labour government's attempt to normalize relations with the Soviet Union following their suspension that was prompted by the ARCOS raid of 1927. Although there is no direct evidence that it played an immediate role in Labour's decision, the renewal of relations was important to the British foreign policy establishment for another reason. By 1929, the transformation of the USSR from its "leninist" to "stalinist"[3] foundations was underway. This process would involve massive state intervention into all spheres of Soviet life in what was undoubtedly the most important of all the totalitarian experiments of the twentieth century. It would also serve as

Metro-Vickers Trial and Anglo-Soviet Relations, 1933" (Ph.D. Dissertation, Michigan State University, 1990).

2 Memo by Vansittart, 19 March 1933, FO 371/17265 N1850/1610/38.

3 As usual, the use of such terms is fraught with danger. The term "leninist" is used here to differentiate the society formed out of the October Revolution, the Russian Civil War, and New Economic Policy period (1921-28) from the "stalinist" world of of the First Five-Year Plan with its forced collectivization, rapid industrialization, dekulakization, and the cultural revolution which accompanied these changes. While there is an ongoing debate among students of the period regarding the relationship between the "Stalin Revolution" and its Bolshevik roots, nearly all historians would agree that "stalinism" represented a significant transformation of the USSR, though some see it as a break with the past while other see it as the logical culmination. For a recent and engaging examination of this period, see Lewis Siegelbaum's, *Soviet State and Society between Revolutions, 1918-1929* (Cambridge: Cambridge University Press, 1992).

the foundation upon which Stalin built the USSR into a superpower. For the British foreign policy establishment, assessing the nature of this rapidly changing society, and responding to it, was to prove a major intellectual, moral, and physical challenge. By establishing a diplomatic mission in the USSR, the British were once again in a position to gain some day-to-day insight into the development of the Soviet experiment.[4]

Once the decision to resume relations had been made and the negotiations completed, the task fell to Labour's Foreign Secretary, Arthur Henderson, to appoint Britain's first ambassador to the USSR. Hugh Dalton, Henderson's nephew and Parliamentary Under-secretary, recalled later that there "were many aspirants to be ambassador in Moscow, including a number of Labour M.P.'s ... [Henderson] made up his mind in favour of appointing a professional diplomat who could speak Russian. Finally the choice fell on Sir Esmond Ovey. He began well but ran into difficulties later."[5]

Ovey was born 23 July 1879 in Oxfordshire, the youngest son of a family of the minor landed gentry.[6] Like most British diplomats of his generation, Ovey was educated at Eton, but he did not proceed to university.[7] Instead, he gained valuable experience by travelling abroad. In 1900 he visited Moscow, the Caucasus region of the Russian empire, and the Crimea in what proved to be his only visit to Russia prior to his appointment to Moscow 29 years later. In 1902 he was nominated an attaché and completed the competitive exams for the diplomatic service in March 1903. Over the next couple of years Ovey was given junior posts at Tangier and Stockholm (1904), Paris (1906), and Washington (1908) as a second secretary. During this time he passed an examination in public law and achieved proficiency in Arabic. While in Washington, Ovey met and married the daughter of Rear-Admiral W.H. Emory of the United States Navy.[8] The nationality of Ovey's wife

---

4 Of course British intelligence had continued its activities following the breach of 1927 and had run agents into the USSR via its Baltic "window" in Helsinki. The best account of this exercise is found in Andrew, *Secret Service*, p. 333-34.

5 Hugh Dalton, *Call Back Yesterday: Memoirs, 1887-1931* (London: F. Mueller, 1953), vol. 1, p. 232.

6 For a penetrating examination of the experience of the British gentry and aristocracy in the Victorian period and after see David Cannadine, *The Decline and Fall of the British Aristocracy* (New York: Anchor Books, 1990).

7 Ovey was one of 37 attachés recruited between 1900 and 1907. Of this group, only 15 (40%) had attended university. See Raymond A. Jones, *The British Diplomatic Service, 1815-1914* (Waterloo: Wilfrid Laurier University Press, 1983), p. 168.

8 Ovey's first wife died in 1924; in 1930 he married Marie Armande, widow of Senor de Barrios of Mexico, and daughter of Réné Vignat of Paris.

proved helpful at the outbreak of the Great War when Ovey, posted since 1913 at Constantinople, was stricken with typhoid fever and was too ill to be evacuated with Sir Louis Mallet and the rest of the Embassy staff. He was moved to the American Embassy where, despite the protests of the German Ambassador, Wangenheim, he was given protection and allowed to recover.

Although it is unlikely that any posting could have introduced Ovey to a situation patterned closely on the Soviet Union of 1929, several of his previous appointments may have served Ovey well in this regard. He was posted in various capacities at Sofia (1912), Constantinople (1913-14), Rome (1925), and Mexico (1925-29). While all these were distinct societies to be sure, they had each experienced significant social and political turmoil in recent years, and this exposed Ovey to the challenges changing societies posed for British diplomats raised in the late Victorian period. Ovey's ability to find his way to an understanding of Stalin's Soviet experiment may well have owed something to his previous tour of duty.

When not abroad, Ovey was posted in the Northern Section of the Foreign Office (1920-24). Here, along with William Strang, who would join Ovey in 1931 as his Counsellor in the Moscow Embassy, Ovey dealt with issues of diplomacy which concerned a broad range of countries, including Soviet Russia. At the same time, Frank Ashton-Gwatkin and E.A. Walker, Ovey's future Acting-Counsellor (1930) and First Secretary (1930-33), worked in the Foreign Office. Since the personnel which made up Ovey's staff did not include anyone with previous "Soviet" experience, such contact as close proximity in the Foreign Office provided may have helped to create familiarity among those who found themselves in the diplomatic compound of Stalin's Russia in the 1930s.

The announcement of Ovey's appointment to Moscow as Britain's first diplomat of ambassadorial rank to the USSR came on 13 November 1929 and marked both an end to a very hostile period in Anglo-Soviet relations and an abrupt change in Ovey's own career. A few months prior to the announcement, Ovey had been bound for Brazil, having just completed his term as Britain's Minister to Mexico. Apparently Ovey had been chosen for the Mexico post by Austen Chamberlain precisely because of his reputation as a reliable, level-headed representative, who could handle difficult assignments — qualities that would be severely tested at the end of his mission to Moscow.[9]

---

9 See Ovey's obituary, "Sir Esmond Ovey: A Wide Diplomatic Career," *The Times* (London), 31 May 1963, p. 16.

As the first British diplomat of ambassadorial rank to be posted to the USSR he had been largely successful in minimizing the effects of the anti-Soviet campaigns that arose in Britain around the charges of dumping, religious persecution, the use of forced labour, and the like, and had shown a sympathetically critical eye when evaluating the relative merits and promise of the Soviet experiment.[10]

It should be borne in mind that Ovey's task was not only intrinsically difficult, but, given the two-year hiatus in relations and the very small staff[11] Ovey took with him to Moscow, conditions were far from ideal. Beyond this there was the problem of geographic isolation — Ovey and his staff were rarely outside of Moscow and since so much of the dislocation, violence, and construction of the First Five-Year Plan took place in the countryside, they were often reduced to seeing the ripple effect of these events rather than the events themselves.

Another problematic aspect of the task faced by Ovey and his staff was the difficulty of wading through the various accounts of the current conditions, which Ovey found ranged "from the ultra-pessimistic to the ultra-optimistic. The unsympathetically disposed observer perceives nothing but privation and inefficiency wherever he goes, while the 'Red' sympathizer sees in the broad plains of Russia the asphodel meadows of earthly paradise."[12] Ovey's inclination as an "objectively minded" observer was to seek many points of view in an effort to reach his conclusions about often confusing and illusive subjects.

Early in 1930, Ovey sent an extensive analysis of the First Five-Year plan to Henderson. Arguing that the purpose of the plan was to make the USSR economically self-sufficient, Ovey cautioned that Soviet promises of increased trade were "doubtless prepared for the purpose of producing a good effect" and were only likely to yield short-term dividends in any case.[13] He then turned to a discussion of the major facets of the Soviet strategy for economic development. The premise

---

10 The best account of Labour's decision to re-establish diplomatic relations with the Soviet Union is D. Lammers' article, "The Second Labour Government and the Restoration of Relations with Soviet Russia (1929)," *Bulletin of the Institute of Historical Research*, 37 (May 1964): 60-72. The only study examining Ovey's perceptions of the Soviet Union is G. Morrell, "Sir Esmond Ovey: Britain's First Ambassador to Soviet Russia, 1929-1933" (M.A. thesis, University of Waterloo, 1985).

11 Prior to 1920, the British routinely posted 65-70 diplomats, consular officials and military attachés. The number steadily declined as posts across the territory of the former Russian empire were closed. In 1930, Ovey had 8 members on his staff. In 1931, a consulate was opened in Leningrad and the number grew to 13. This was the general size of the British mission in the USSR throughout the 1930s.

12 Ovey to Henderson, 1 June 1931, *DBFP*, #137.

13 Ibid., 4 January 1930, *DBFP*, #52.

that the USSR could finance the massive industrialization campaign solely on the basis of the export of raw materials seemed "somewhat utopian" to Ovey. Although the 1929 harvest of grain had been good, the current year, with its focus on the collectivization drive, was critical to the strategy. Ovey noted that the peasants who held small plots and who were referred to by the Communist Party as "kulaks," were hostile to the regime's grain taxes and forced collectivization. These people, "when recalcitrant, were bullied out of existence by the imposition of grain taxes in excess of their actual production."[14]

All was not negative in the countryside, however. One unnamed source told Ovey that the "country generally is . . . safer, including the wild mountain districts of the south, than at any period during the Imperial regime."[15] Still, with the problem of famine occurring in some regions, and growing evidence of tension between the regime and the peasantry generally, the situation was serious. For the moment, Ovey had no illusions about the willingness of the Soviet authorities to continue to use force to enact its program and estimated that "in the ruthless prosecution of their ideals, [the regime] could be counted on not to be deflected by the deaths of even hundreds of thousands of peasants in a given district."[16]

A fine illustration of the manner in which Ovey and his staff gained insight into this grim aspect of the Soviet "experiment" was provided in a Chancery memo to Ovey from C.H. Hardy, the assistant archivist in the Moscow Embassy. In April 1930, Hardy and three other members of the staff were walking around the Belokamenaya train station in Moscow. A train guarded by troops with fixed bayonets attracted their attention and they strolled closer to investigate. As they drew nearer they saw that

> each of the wagons had been converted into a prison van; the small ventilators near the roof had been barred over, and the doors were fastened by the hasp, so that they were open to the extent of about six inches. . . .
>
> At many of the ventilators were to be seen the faces of from three to five children, while the narrow opening was occupied from top to bottom by faces of men and women. . . . There would appear to have been from thirty to forty in each wagon — men, women, and children. All we could see were of the typical peasant type, and were evidently some of the so-called kulaks on their way to the great concen-

---

14 Ibid.
15 Ibid.
16 Ibid.

tration camp at Vologda, and the forced labour in the Archangel Province.[17]

Strong testimony of the quality of these reports, which over the next three years would examine the ongoing tragedy of collectivization and the winter famine of 1932-33, can be found in the fact that historians such as Robert Conquest and others base some of their historical analysis on the British Embassy coverage of this process.[18] To some extent, however, the use that has been made of these reports by these historians has been misleading, especially in the case of famine which swept Ukraine—but not only Ukraine—in the winter of 1932. Most often this is cited as evidence of anti-Ukrainian intent on the part of the leadership, and the Ukrainian "genocide" is a term used in this context as well. What is clear from Ovey's reports and those of his staff is that he tended to see the campaign as a campaign against peasants—not against Ukrainians or any other nationality. That most Ukrainians were peasants was no doubt true, but other non-Ukrainian peasants starved because of the policy as well. The Communist Party in this context talked in terms of "liquidating the 'kulaks' as a class," not in terms of anti-nationalism, and Ovey's characterization of this horrifying epoch accurately reflects this feature of the campaign.[19]

The energies of Ovey and his staff were also devoted to the completion of a kremlinological study of the leading personalities of the Communist Party that had been initiated by the Chargé, R.M. Hodgson, in the mid-1920s.[20] The Embassy study left no doubt that at the centre of the Communist Party's current campaign to transform the USSR was Joseph Stalin. His primacy in Soviet politics was apparently secure.

> Stalin is said to be a man of extraordinary force and character and ability. He has certainly been remarkably successful in removing any possible rival from his path, his greatest triumph being the downfall of Trotsky. . . .

17 Ovey to Henderson, enclosure by Hardy, 21 April 1930, DBFP, #81.
18 See Robert Conquest, The Harvest of Sorrow: Soviet Collectivization and the Terror-Famine (New York: Oxford University Press, 1986) and Marco Carynnyk, Lubomyr Luciuk, and Bodhan Kordan, eds., The Foreign Office and the Famine: British Documents on Ukraine and the Great Famine of 1932-1933 (Kingston, ON: Limestone Press, 1988), especially the Foreword by Michael Marrus.
19 See Sheila Fitzpatrick's discussion of the use of "class war" in the "cultural" revolution that was a central part of the "Stalin Revolution" in The Russian Revolution, 1917-1932 (Oxford: Oxford University Press, 1984), p. 129-34.
20 A copy of the complete project can be found in Ovey to Henderson, 11 May 1931, FO 371/15616 N3456/794/38.

... By surrounding himself with mediocrities, and by the employment of iron discipline aided partly by luck and by the natural apathy of the Russian people, he has reached a position of absolute despotism, such as no Rosas or Mussolini ever attained to.[21]

Ovey's mention of "mediocrities" and the "natural apathy" of the Russian was a recurring theme in his writing on the subject of Russian political culture. While most Russians, he claimed, were "passive," "docile," and "helpless in the face of authority,"[22] "the only people who are exceptional in Russia are those people from whom the Bolsheviks are sprung, and who for years suffered imprisonment, and the risks of expulsion and death from hands of an incompetent regime. The incompetence of the rest of the population is the trump card of Bolshevism."[23] The critical issue upon which the whole fate of the Five-Year Plan hinged was Stalin's continued ability and willingness to pay the price of unpopularity with large segments of Soviet society in the near term. As Ovey saw the situation, "can Stalin win the economic war or are the defeatists right? This, to my mind, as a new and untrained observer of the greatest industrial experiment ever tried by mankind, is the kernel of the problem."[24]

For the moment, the enthusiasm of the Party, the gradual increase in literacy which aided the task of propaganda and increased mobility for the young, and the dominance of the urban workers were factors which ameliorated some of the very sizable costs associated with the Five-Year Plan. The continued use of coercion, especially if it was required over a long period and did not yield significant improvements in the quality of life for the Soviet populace, involved great risks for Stalin's regime.

If, however, Stalin is right and is ruthless and strong enough, the improvement of the machinery, the cheapness of labour (the relative inefficiency of which is easy to exaggerate) and the immensity of mass production should tend to produce a state of affairs which would gradually increase the standard of living of the people. If Stalin is wrong and the standard of living finally fails to react in an upward

---

21 Ibid.

22 Social historian Moshe Lewin has contributed much to our understanding of Russian political culture on this issue. He characterizes Russians as having a "janus-like" face — obedient when facing authority figures — tyrannical when looking down on less-powerful people. See Moshe Lewin, *The Making of the Soviet System: Essays in the Social History of Interwar Russia* (New York: Pantheon Books, 1985), especially chap. 11, "The Social Background of Stalinism."

23 Ovey to Henderson, 3 June 1930, *DBFP*, #88.

24 Ibid., 4 January 1930, *DBFP*, #52.

sense, the experiment must fail when years of empty promises of improved conditions have resulted in continued disillusionment.[25]

By June 1930, Ovey had sufficiently developed his view of the Soviet domestic scene to characterize it here as his "working" assessment for the duration of his tenure. He dismissed the idea, heard now only in "extreme" circles, that "the Soviet industrial and social experiment is an entirely Utopian and impossible Dream."[26] The significance for British policy was to recognize that the USSR was here to stay, and Ovey counselled that

> we are face to face with a "going concern." If we are to trade with them we must trade with them as they are. One cannot destroy the cake of Bolshevism and still have the cake of trade with Russia. Evolution can only be gradual, and can only result in the lopping off of such exaggerations as, in practice, prove to be superfluous and harmful. . . . If this is the case, and Bolshevism has come to stay, it will gradually be considered as calmly as Mahometanism, not to be fought tooth and nail, but as a fact with which one must reckon, and against which one must defend oneself quietly and confidently.[27]

Ovey went on to argue that any expression of fear about the menace of Bolshevism on the part of European powers only flattered the regime and served its domestic agenda. This would only make the Soviets more difficult to deal with, and, since there was no credible threat of Bolshevism in Britain anyway, Ovey argued that such protests would only be counter-productive.[28]

This moderate tone prevailed when Ovey turned his attention to two other aspects of the "Stalin Revolution" which aggravated Anglo-Soviet relations at this time — the issues of "dumping" and religious persecution. Throughout 1930, the international community pressed the Soviets about the volume of their grain exports, exports which were necessary to finance the industrial portion of the First Five-Year Plan. While France was the leading voice in this campaign,[29] questions arose in Britain about the economic impact of the Soviet scheme. Contrary to claims made by the conservative press, the price of grain had

---

25 Ibid. Given the events of the 1990s, when the last of the old Stalinists passed from the scene in the Soviet Union, Ovey's observations here seem to have had a lot of run in them.

26 Ovey to Henderson, 3 June 1930, *DBFP*, #88.

27 Ibid.

28 Ibid.

29 See J. Haslam, *Soviet Foreign Policy, 1930-1933: The Impact of the Depression* (New York: St. Martin's Press, 1983), chap. 4, "The USSR Faces a Campaign against Dumping."

been falling steadily throughout the 1920s, that is, before the Soviet plan took effect.[30] In an unhappy coincidence, the low price of grain meant that the Soviets would have to export more to pay for industrial goods. This turned out to be bad for farmers in Europe and America during the Depression and very bad for peasants in Ukraine and elsewhere in the USSR. As far as Ovey was concerned, he stressed that the problem of "dumping" was exaggerated and was not part of any plot to undermine Western capitalism. Rather, the cheap prices and the increased volume — which at their high point in 1931, rose to just over half of the Tsarist exports of 1913[31] — was a temporary phase of the overall economic strategy.[32]

The issue of religious persecution occurred simultaneously with that of "dumping" and proved to be a more tiresome and troublesome problem for Anglo-Soviet relations at the time. As more details of alleged and actual persecution became known, as they did through the efforts of newspaper correspondents in traditionally anti-Soviet posts such as Riga and the lobbying of White Russian emigré populations throughout Europe, pressure mounted on European governments to defend the faithful in the USSR. The Labour government in Britain, though not itself overly concerned about the issue, was not immune to this public pressure, and Ovey was required to supply a considerable amount of information on the subject to help inform Labour's response to this pressure. This became a more formal problem when the British clergy, including the Suffragan Bishop of Fulham, applied to the Foreign Office for assistance in obtaining entrance visas for British clergy who wanted to visit the USSR and see things first-hand.[33]

Ovey's first reports on the religious situation dealt directly with the complications involved for the foreign diplomat once an issue of internal affairs became the focus of international attention. Any attempt on his part to secure the visas requested would have to be done by respecting "scrupulously the undoubted right of a State to order its own

---

30 For a rebuttal to conservative opinion at the time which recaptures the tenor of the debate, see the sympathetic account offered by W.P. Coates and Z. Coates, *A History of Anglo-Soviet Relations* (London: Lawrence & Wishart and Pilot Press, 1945), p. 360-61.

31 In 1913 the Tsarist regime exported just over nine million tons of grain. The figure for Soviet exports in 1931 was five million tons of grain. See Appendix D for related data.

32 Ovey to Henderson, 4 March 1930, *DBFP*, #71.

33 Ibid., 18 January 1930, FO 371/14848 N500/23/38.

life within its own jurisdiction in its own way."[34] Ovey was already aware of Soviet sensitivity to criticism about their campaign against religious practices and felt that any official requests or investigations which would "interfere against the march of their Marxian theories would certainly be deeply resented."[35] The only course open to him was informal representations to Litvinov on behalf of the British clergy.

Ovey proceeded to outline his perceptions of the Soviet campaign against what the Soviets saw as religious superstition. "There is no doubt whatsoever as to the determination of the Soviet Government eventually to substitute Marxian atheism for belief in the tenets of the Orthodox Church, and great efforts are being made to train not only the new but the present generation to disbelief in Christianity by propaganda and other means."[36] These "other means" did entail, in certain circumstances, the actual destruction of churches, or, as was the case with St. Isaac's Cathedral in Leningrad, their conversion to secular uses.[37] Ovey thought it likely in such conflict that priests had been imprisoned and even shot during the anti-religious campaign, but this occurred only because the priest became a political enemy of the state.[38]

In characteristic fashion Ovey saw similarities between the Soviet situation and that which he had witnessed in Mexico following the Mexican Revolution.[39] At other times he saw similarities with the situation in France before the Great War[40] or the reforms instituted by Henry VIII in England.[41] This approach, which saw precedents for Soviet action in the behaviour of France, Mexico, and England, may well have served to minimize the importance of the issue.

This view found support with the dominant view on the issue in the Foreign Office. Laurence Collier, First Secretary in the Northern Department, noted that Soviet policy differed in degree, and not in kind, from restrictions on non-Catholics in Spain and non-Moslems in Moslem states. He argued that it is "the method of its administration, rather than in its provisions themselves, that the actual persecution, as distinct from legal restriction, can be said to exist."[42] What this meant

---

34 Ibid.
35 Ibid.
36 Ibid.
37 Ibid. Ovey noted, for instance, that the bronze church bells were melted down and their value was a "considerable asset to the nation."
38 Ibid., 31 January 1930, FO 371/14840 N630/23/38.
39 Ibid.
40 Ibid., FO 371/14840 N631/23/38.
41 Ibid., 3 March 1930, CAB 23/63 C[abinet] P[aper] 74(30).
42 Memo by Collier, 17 January 1930, FO 371/14840 N286/23/38.

for British policy was that no formal initiative seemed necessary or well advised at an official level. On 12 February, the Cabinet decided that the best it could do was to allow Ovey to pursue his quiet diplomacy as "His Majesty's Government could not interfere in the internal affairs of a foreign state."[43] The Cabinet also undercut the Christian Protest Movement, which had been so active in raising the issue, by refusing to allow mention of Russian subjects in services held by the Army and Admiralty on 16 March—the day the Archbishop of Canterbury held a special Intercessory Service for the Church in the USSR.[44]

As the debate continued in Britain, Ovey pursued his talks with Litvinov and, by the middle of February, visas were granted for the British chaplain in Helsinki to come to Moscow and conduct services in Leningrad and Moscow periodically.[45] While this result was undoubtedly partly possible because of the skill and tact that Ovey and Litvinov exercised behind the scenes, the hue and cry of the British press may have convinced the Soviets that some small concession on this point would prove useful.

With the issue of chaplain services now resolved, Ovey refrained from any general requests for additional information from Litvinov regarding the alleged religious persecution. The Soviet authorities were irritated and puzzled by the European outburst, which characteristically "they attribute to some organized plan of attack against themselves—'why should this particular moment be chosen?'—they ask."[46] Ovey speculated to Henderson that if "agitation were to be dropped now or shortly without any foreign government trying to intervene it might conceivably result in some temporary cessation of the anti-religious campaign by the Communist Party."[47] This was the best outcome foreign powers could hope for given the Soviet commitment to undermine the Church. Ovey also cautioned that a breach of relations over this issue, which the Christian Protest Movement in Britain favoured, would only insure that the faithful in Russia would be treated badly.[48]

---

43 See the conclusions in CAB 23/65, 12 February 1930.

44 See Coates, *A History of Anglo-Soviet Relations*, p. 344-45.

45 Sir Lancelot Oliphant (Assistant Under-Secretary of State, Foreign Office) to Wigam (Paris), 18 February 1930, FO 371/14841 N871/23/38.

46 Ovey to Henderson, 20 February 1930, FO 371/1481 N1139/23/38.

47 Ibid.

48 Ibid.

Early in March, the British Cabinet took up the whole issue again. Henderson presented Ovey's most recent detailed report which, the Foreign Secretary warned, must be kept secret lest Ovey be declared persona non grata in the USSR.[49] In the report Ovey stressed his conviction, which had been confirmed by discussions with other foreign diplomats and journalists,[50] that there was "no evidence of any general shootings of priests as priests, or massacres of religious congregations. There has been no return to the thumbscrew-and-rack period of religious persecution."[51] Drawing on the work of Bernard Pares, the liberal historian who had been at the forefront of Russian and Soviet studies in Britain for the past decade,[52] Ovey pointed out that since the Orthodox Church was hitherto an instrument that legitimized the Tsarist autocracy, it was logical for the Bolsheviks to assail it as the last remaining institution of the old order.[53] His reference to Pares' work, *A History of Russia*,[54] was not an isolated one. Ovey periodically tried to ground his reports in the context of what he considered to be the best scholarly literature of his day.

Ovey's comment that priests were not shot "as priests" came out of his conviction that

> the real objective of the new campaign in Russia is the kulak, not the priest; but since the priest is often the friend of the kulak some of the blows of the Communist drive inevitably fall upon his shoulders. When kulaks are shot for opposing the Government's policy, it may be that priests are shot too; but in such a case they would be suffering for their political errors and their economic fallacies rather than for their religious faith.[55]

Ovey achieved an almost chillingly dispassionate "objectivity" about the fate of such people in these reports that was, for good or ill, in the

---

49 Ibid., 3 March 1930, FO 371/14842 N1390/23/38 and CAB 23/63 CP 74(30), 3 March 1930. Horace Seymour, the Head of the Northern Department, minuted that Ovey should be specially commended for his excellent work on a delicate issue.

50 See his comments on the diplomatic community's view of the issue in Ovey to Henderson, 20 February 1930, FO 371/14841 N1139/23/38.

51 CAB 23/63 CP 74(30), 3 March 1930.

52 Interestingly enough, prior to the revolution, Pares had counselled Sir Arthur Nicolson in person about the viability of a Duma-led Russia, but Nicolson had remained unconvinced by Pares' pro-Duma stance. See Keith Neilson, "'My Beloved Russians': Sir Arthur Nicolson and Russia, 1906-1916," *The International History Review*, 9, 4 (1987): 517-688.

53 Ibid.

54 Bernard Pares, *A History of Russia* (London: J. Cape, 1926), p. 394, 490.

55 CAB 23/63 CP 74(30), 3 March 1930.

best tradition of a diplomat treading close to matters involving the internal affairs of a sovereign state.

Ovey also thought it wise to underline the fact that a sizable number of people, though the number was often overstated by the authorities, supported the secularization of Soviet society. The regime's program against the Church had a long-term agenda the success of which Ovey could not "prophesy." He did see signs that the youth of Russia were being affected by the campaign and related that a member of his staff had overheard the remark of a young child who commented "on the number of icons in the room of one of the women in a neighbouring house: 'Why does she want them' he said, 'everyone knows there is no God!' "[56]

It should be noted, however, that there were many who remained faithful to their beliefs. E.M. Yaroslavskii, the leader of the regime's anti-church campaign and head of the League of the Militant Godless, or the *bezbozhniki*, estimated that some two-thirds of the peasantry were still believers at the end of the 1930s.[57] This raises an important point about Ovey's perspective on and analysis of the collectivization drive and the anti-church campaign. The first of these was clearly directed against a peasantry that was geographically removed from Ovey's embassy in Moscow and culturally remote from the British diplomat's world. As has been noted above, the general Russian population, made up chiefly of the peasantry, was "unexceptional" in Ovey's view — "passive," "apathetic," and "docile" are not terms of endearment in this context. From his writing about Stalin's relationship to the people, it is clear that he found the peasant "mentality" hard to understand.

> It is hard to say in what light the peasantry regard him [Stalin]. It is said that when he ordered that collectivization should be enforced less crudely in the beginning of 1930, "Little Father Stalin" was prayed for before many an icon; while his name and the Pope's were coupled together when there was some slacking-off in the so-called religious persecution later in the year.[58]

Ovey's comments about the "alliance" between "kulaks" and priests suggests that Orthodox priests, too, were not men with whom Ovey would feel any special connection and this, coupled with Ovey's

56 Ibid.

57 Moshe Lewin, "Society, State, and Ideology," in Sheila Fitzpatrick, ed., *Cultural Revolution in Russia, 1928-1931* (Bloomington: University of Indiana Press, 1978), p. 63.

58 Ovey to Henderson, 11 May 1931, FO 371/15616 N3456/794/38.

liberal-secularist approach to his work, may help explain the distance he was able to achieve in his reports about the violence and cruelty of these campaigns.

Still, there is something more that may have been at work here. The contrast between Ovey's interest in, and even enthusiasm about, what was being built by the Stalin Revolution, as against what was being destroyed, recalls the approach taken by E.H. Carr, the famous diplomat-historian of the interwar period, who is well known for his refusal to pose as a "hanging judge" of the Soviet experiment.[59] As with Carr, Ovey was most interested in what might be termed the "constructive" aspects of Soviet policy. Elements such as the massive industrialization campaign of the First Five-Year Plan and the near utopian attempts to organize the economic, social, cultural, and political life of the Soviet realm were central to his analysis. It is also likely that he thought them the most significant for British policy since arguably the industrial strength of the USSR could have consequences for Soviet foreign policy and hence for Anglo-Soviet relations. To this extent, then, Ovey reveals himself as a "realist" concerned with the growing potential of the USSR.

Ovey's focus is even more significant when it is recalled that the British government was becoming increasingly interested in analysis of this type. At the same time that Ovey was offering these reports, plans were underway to create the Industrial Intelligence Centre (IIC) which would operate as a sub-committee of the Committee of Imperial Defence (CID). The formal structure was not in place until 1931, but its Director, Major Desmond Morton, had been active since the late 1920s in developing a capacity to evaluate the "total" power potential of foreign powers — economic, military, and political power were all part of the assessment.[60] The first state to be targetted by the IIC was the

---

59 See E.H. Carr, *What Is History?* (New York: Vintage Books, 1961) and his multi-volume history, *Foundations of a Planned Economy, 1926-1929* (London: Macmillan, 1969). For an examination of E.H. Carr's approach to the study and evaluation of the Soviet experiment, see Walter Laqueur, *The Fate of the Revolution: Interpretation of Soviet History from 1917 to the Present*, rev. ed. (New York: Charles Scribners' Sons, 1987), chap. 6, "E.H. Carr."

60 See R. Young, "Spokesmen for Economic Warfare: The Industrial Intelligence Centre in the 1930s," *European Studies Review*, 6 (1976): 473-89; F. Hinsley, *British Intelligence in the Second World War: Its Influence on Strategy and Operations* (London: Her Majesty's Stationary Office, 1979), vol. 1, p. 30-32; W. Wark, "British Military and Economic Intelligence: Assessments of Nazi Germany before the Second World War," in C. Andrew and D. Dilks, eds., *The Missing Dimension: Governments and Intelligence Communities in the Twentieth Century* (London: Macmillan, 1984), p. 264 n.71; and W. Wark, *The Ultimate Enemy: British Intelligence and Nazi Germany, 1933-1939* (Ithaca: Cornell University Press, 1985), especially chap. 7.

USSR. Though the records of the IIC for the period prior to 1933 are still mainly closed,[61] the later reports reveal the same interest in, and respect for, the planned economy of the USSR that Ovey exhibited. For example, in December 1933, E.F. Crowe, IIC member and Comptroller General for the Department of Overseas Trade (DOT), reported that while problems with transportation and skilled labour were still very serious, the USSR "possesses a thorough organisation for planning industrial mobilisation" and "full advantage is taken of state ownership and centralised control."[62] There will be more to say about the activities of the IIC later. For now it is enough to note that Ovey and the CID were involved in assessing assets that were created by the Stalin Revolution and would prove vital to waging total war in the twentieth century.

Beyond Ovey's concern with Soviet power, however, it is evident that these issues were the most intellectually attractive features of Soviet life, and were, Soviet rhetoric aside, the most progressive aspects of the Stalin Revolution. Ovey was impressed by the energy and effort being expended to transform backward Russia, and while he was able to see the large human costs involved, one gets the sense that he thought it would be worth the price if the goals of the Stalin Revolution were obtained. Having said this is not to place Ovey in the camp of the "fellow traveller," however, and at times his interest in Soviet projects seems very close to that exhibited by Allan Monkhouse. Like Monkhouse, Ovey was not ignorant of the human suffering, and he made sure to report on its causes and effects as he saw them. Moreover, as he told Henderson, "we shall never wish to be Bolsheviks, nor will they probably wish to be a capitalistic country."[63]

Ovey's professional estimation of the Soviet Union was reinforced by the relatively close contact the British diplomatic community had with the Commissar of Foreign Affairs, Maxim Litvinov, and his British-born wife, Ivy (née Low). The Soviet couple's relationship with British diplomats went back to pre-revolutionary days when Rex Leeper, a Foreign Office official, introduced them to one another in 1914 and later served as the official witness at their wedding in 1917.[64]

---

61 Unfortunately, one of the potentially most useful IIC records, CAB 48/3, which contains the memoranda for the period June 1929 to March 1933, has not yet been released to the Public Record Office in Kew.

62 Memo by E.F. Crowe (DOT) for Chiefs of Staff on Industrial Mobilisation of USSR, 14 December 1933, CAB 48/4 Foreign Countries Intelligence (FCI) 45.

63 Ovey to Henderson, 3 June 1930, *DBFP*, #88.

64 A. Pope, *Maxim Litvinoff* (New York: L. Fischer Press, 1947), p. 111. For a discussion of Ivy Litvinov's work on the introduction of Basic English in the USSR see John Carswell, *The Exile: A Life of Ivy Litvinov* (London: Faber and Faber, 1983). For a re-

Ivy Litvinov was particularly close to William Strang's wife, being treated as "family" in the British Counsellor's residence in Moscow. She moved freely in the diplomatic community during this period and was a part of the social set which sought refuge from the struggles of everyday life in the more cosmopolitan milieu of Moscow's foreign embassies.[65] While it is difficult to assess the exact impact such personal familiarity had on the course of Anglo-Soviet relations, it doubtless came as a shock when Ovey's normally cordial relationship with Litvinov deteriorated completely in the heated exchanges which ensued over the arrests of the British engineers.

Events in 1932 had already foreshadowed a dimunition of goodwill in formal Anglo-Soviet relations. After the signing of the Ottawa Agreements with the Dominions of the Commonwealth in the summer of 1932, Britain was obliged to abandon the Anglo-Soviet trade agreement of 1930. This decision, prompted primarily by pressure from the Canadian wheat and timber lobby, was announced on 17 October 1932. From the British point of view, the decision was not meant to stop all trade with the Soviets, as the Canadians had hoped, but rather to renegotiate the terms of that trade. The British were well aware that they needed continued Soviet purchases to service the considerable commercial credits that had been extended to the USSR under the old trade agreement. In giving the required six months notice of their desire to terminate the 1930 trade agreement, the British also made clear their intention to open trade talks with representatives of the USSR [66] The Soviets, if the number of anti-British articles in the Soviet press is any indication, were not at all pleased with the British decision. There were repeated accounts of "Riga Agency forgeries," "Flood gates of anti-Soviet propaganda," and "English agents in U.S.S.R."[67] Ovey found that the Narkomindel

> approved of this anti-English press campaign inasmuch as they justified appearance of such articles in "Izvestiya" and would do nothing to stop them until apparently His Majesty's Government had abolished the liberty of the press in Great Britain. In Great Britain the

cent examination of Litvinov's career, see Hugh Philips', *Between the Revolution and the West: A Political Biography of Maxim M. Litvinov* (Boulder: Westview Press, 1992).

65 H. Von Herwarth, *Against Two Evils* (New York: Rawson Wade, 1981), p. 53.

66 I. Drummond, "Empire Trade and Russian Trade: Economic Diplomacy in the Nineteen-Thirties," *Canadian Journal of Economics/Revue canadienne d'économique*, 5, 1 (1972): 40-42.

67 See Ovey's report on the Soviet press, Ovey to Simon, 14 November 1932, *DBFP*, #178.

press was free to attack everybody including the Government itself; here it was allowed only to attack foreigners.[68]

The temper of relations remained difficult throughout much of the remainder of 1932. Ovey repeatedly made representations in the "strongest terms possible" and he was concerned that his own personal position, "or that of any successor of mine who may be sent out here will be quite intolerable."[69]

It is generally thought that the Soviet leadership was engaged in serious internal disputes at this time and that Stalin was trying to win over the Central Committee to his view that Party "discipline," even when it involved members of the Politburo, should be enforced by the OGPU and not by the Party Central Control Commission. Opposition to Stalin, apparently led by Rudzutak, Kirov, Kuibishev, and Ordzhonikidze, formed within the Politburo and this created a momentary paralysis at the summit of the Soviet leadership.[70] By the end of November, however, the anti-British press campaign had subsided and, with the arrival of the new Soviet Ambassador in London, Ivan Maisky, there were signs that a less aggravated relationship was possible.

In one of his first meetings with Foreign Secretary Simon, Maisky came close to offering a retraction of the recent *Izvestiia* barrage. He told Simon that the offensive sentences should be seen as "conditional and hypothetical and should not be read as absolute assertions."[71] Simon, apparently not easily convinced of the offered interpretation of the Soviet press, warned Maisky that any continuance of the attitudes presented over the past several weeks would jeopardize the manner in which trade talks were normally conducted between two "friendly nations." The British government required an apology if relations were to be returned to an agreeable footing and found it impossible to proceed

---

68 Ibid., #180.
69 Ibid., 21 November 1932, *DBFP*, #188.
70 Conquest, *The Great Terror*, p. 52-54; and L. Schapiro, *The Communist Party of the Soviet Union* (New York: Random House, 1960), p. 392-93. Much of the evidence about this apparent struggle came from Bukharin through the medium of the emigré Menshevik, Boris Nicolaevsky. In his excellent biography of Stalin, Robert H. McNeal points out that Bukharin, himself expelled from the Politburo in 1929, may not have been a reliable source for information about conversations among its members after his expulsion. In the midst of all these other difficulties Stalin's wife, Nadezhda, committed suicide 8 November 1932. According to McNeal, Stalin was badly shaken by her death and seems to have convinced himself that it was indeed a suicide. See R. McNeal, *Stalin: Man and Ruler* (New York: New York University Press, 1988), p. 146, 164-65.
71 Simon to Ovey, 28 November 1932, *DBFP*, #193.

to trade negotiations unless there was Soviet compliance with that request.[72]

Simon's rough handling of Maisky and Ovey's representations in Moscow were intended to impress upon the Soviets the fact that the British were quite willing to use the leverage of trade talks in this particular dispute. Maisky met with the Permanent Under-Secretary at the Foreign Office in early December, and the new Soviet Ambassador finally managed to bring an end to the affair which had beset him from the moment he had arrived in London. He told Vansittart that he had discussed the issue with the editor of *Izvestiia*, who complained that he had been "misled" by one of his correspondents and that he was now willing to apologize for having published such inaccurate information.[73] On the same day the Soviets announced their willingness to begin negotiations for a new trade settlement.[74] Before a new agreement could be hammered out, however, the Metro-Vickers crisis erupted.

While there is little doubt that the events of 11 March 1933 took Ovey and his embassy staff by surprise, it must be borne in mind that they had almost no previous contact with the MVEEC engineers in the Soviet Union.[75] It was only after the two MVEEC employees, Buckell and Burke, sought the aid of the Embassy that Ovey was made aware of the crisis which rapidly developed into a full-blown confrontation. By relying on the account of Buckell and Burke, and with no clarification from the Soviet authorities or Whitehall, Ovey came to the conclusion that while there "may be insignificant douceurs, tipping or presents," there was no real substance for any criminal charges against the engineers.[76] For the remainder of his tenure in Moscow the British Ambassador rigidly defended this interpretation.

Ovey's immediate concern was that the present conditions in the Soviet Union, which he characterized as a "reign of terror," offered no grounds for confidence if the arrested engineers were not immediately released. The execution without trial of "wreckers and saboteurs" by the OGPU announced in the Soviet press the previous day undoubt-

---

72 Ibid.
73 Ibid., 8 December 1932, *DBFP*, #200.
74 Ibid.
75 Gail Owen seems too harsh in her criticism of British officials who were not in contact with the MVEEC's representatives as a matter of company policy (see Owen, "The Metro-Vickers Crisis," p. 97). The Acting-Counsellor, William Strang, claimed later that he had met Thornton prior to the arrests, but had seen Monkhouse only once during a rare visit to the Embassy by a director of the MVEEC, C.S. Richards (see Strang, *Home and Abroad*, p. 79).
76 Ovey to Vansittart, 12 March 1933, FO 371/17265 N1611/1610/38.

edly heightened the Ambassador's anxiety. In such a situation Ovey had no compunction about recommending the threat of severing relations with the USSR since the legal remedies of Soviet courts, and the "excessive zeal" of the police, were quite capable of the "trumping up of frivolous and fantastic accusations against a friendly and reputable British Company."[77] In an effort to impress the Soviets with Britain's resolve, Ovey advised Vansittart that he, Ovey, ought to be recalled immediately.[78]

The response from the Foreign Office in London similarly took the line that "any suggestions implicating them [the engineers] in any 'plot' or illegal activities will command no credence whatever here."[79] Vansittart connected the pursuit of a new trade agreement with an early and satisfactory resolution of the entire matter. The trade talks that had been proceeding slowly since December 1932 were immediately suspended.[80] He did not agree with Ovey, however, that the issue of the continuance of diplomatic relations arose at present. Ovey was ordered to find out what the exact nature of the charges was, where the arrested persons were being held, and whether it was possible to communicate with the detained MVEEC engineers.[81] Since these tasks had already been anticipated by Ovey — Strang had been sent to the Narkomindel that day — the British officials awaited a Soviet response.

The British press took up the MVEEC story the same day, with *The Times* placing news of the engineers' arrest alongside an article from its Riga correspondent on the recent OGPU executions.[82] The following day a Reuter's report emphasized that the foreign circles in Moscow were at a loss to explain the OGPU attack on the MVEEC. Company officials released statements complaining that some mistake must have been made, since it was MVEEC policy to have nothing to do with political matters in the Soviet Union.[83]

In Moscow, Ovey was having difficulty getting anywhere with Litvinov and the Narkomindel officials. He thought it likely, and most students of the affair agree, that the diplomatic apparatus had been kept out of the decision to proceed with the arrests and Litvinov's "somewhat discourteous refusal to see me today, may conceivably be

---

77 Ibid.
78 Vansittart to Baldwin, 14 March 1933, Baldwin MSS, Foreign Affairs B, vol. 120.
79 Vansittart to Ovey, 13 March 1933, FO 371/17265 N1610/1610/38.
80 CAB 23/75, 18(33)2, 13 March 1933.
81 Ibid.
82 *The Times* (London), 13 March 1933, p. 14.
83 Ibid., 14 March 1933, p. 14.

indication that serious political aspect is being considered."[84] Ovey thought it unlikely that Litvinov could overturn the police action by appealing to Stalin on grounds of foreign policy. In the end this proved only partially correct, and a number of issues which will be treated below suggest that while Litvinov could not stop the investigation and trial from proceeding, he was able to make special arrangements for the British defendants before and during the trial.

With Litvinov unavailable, Ovey took the opportunity to express the "British" position, as he saw it in any case, to Krestinskii, the First Deputy-Commissar of the Narkomindel. The British Ambassador pressed his view that public opinion was rapidly hardening in Britain and would be unable to understand why commercial negotiations should be pursued with the same authorities which arrest "well-known honourable British subjects on what could only be a criminal charge."[85] Ovey told Krestinskii that he continued to hope that it would be found "a mistake had been made."[86]

Ovey's diplomatic foray takes on greater significance when it is noted that he embarked upon this course of action before receiving instructions from Vansittart on the advisability of connecting the MVEEC case to commercial relations or diplomatic relations. For the time being, Ovey thought he could anticipate instructions, and his conversation with Krestinskii bears this out. As the course of the diplomatic engagement went on, however, Ovey became increasingly frustrated with the unwillingness of his government to go beyond economic sanctions and threaten the severance of diplomatic relations as well.[87]

Soviet silence on the reasons for the arrests was finally broken just after midnight on 14 March. The deputy department head in the Narkomindel, Guelfand, telephoned Strang with the official Soviet communiqué. It outlined the charges of criminal wrecking at various electrical enterprises in the USSR that were now to be brought against more than 20 Soviet citizens and the six British engineers. The Soviet diplomat also revealed that Monkhouse and Nordwall had been released and that arrangements were underway for Embassy personnel to visit the remaining British prisoners.[88] The late hour of the call, and the accommodations included in the Soviet communiqué regarding the

84 Ovey to Vansittart, 13 March 1933, FO 371/17265 N1650/1610/38.

85 Ibid., 13 March 1933, FO 371/17265 N1649/1610/38.

86 Ibid.

87 This is confirmed by William Strang's account in *Home and Abroad*, p. 84 and by the discussion below.

88 Ovey to Simon, 14 March 1933, FO 371/17265 N1658/1610/38.

release of two engineers and early contact with the Embassy staff for the others, suggest that the Narkomindel[89] had been trying to get concessions that would ease the pressure of the situation. Since the order for the release of the two prisoners came from Menzhinskii, there is little doubt that the Metro-Vickers affair had now become an issue that was being dealt with at the highest levels.[90]

Given the lack of documentary evidence on the Soviet side it is hard to know exactly what they hoped to gain by the early release of Monkhouse and Nordwall. The investigating authorities may have genuinely felt these two to be less involved, although both were found guilty in the trial which followed. Conversely, the OGPU might have thought that the two engineers would seek out other members of their "criminal" group and further expose the hostile "anti-Soviet wreckers." In any case, the immediate result of their release was that the two men went directly to the British Embassy where the first in a series of discussions occurred which finally gave the diplomats in Moscow some first-hand information about the case.

While there is no reason to question Stalin's overall primacy in the management of the Metro-Vickers crisis, the exact nature of his role remains unclear. Shortly after the resolution of the affair the British learned from a "reliable source" that "Stalin expressed to one of his chief colleagues (probably Kalinin or Voroshilov) his annoyance at having been brought to sanction the action in Metro-Vickers case without having been warned by those whose duty it was to know of the risk of the serious repercussions on world opinion."[91] The notion that the OGPU had pursued its investigation of the MVEEC engineers on its own and, having found the makings of a "case," brought the evidence forward to Stalin without consulting with the Narkomindel is substantiated by other pieces of evidence that will be discussed below.

Back in London, the British were gaining additional insight into possible Soviet motives from C.S. Richards, one of the directors of Metro-Vickers. He told Laurence Collier that it was likely the OGPU felt it was on to something since the breakdown of turbines, machines whose capacities could not be tested to the breaking point prior to their

---

89 The same day the British Embassy staff was told by the Narkomindel that Litvinov had made the arrangements for a visit with the remaining prisoners at the Lubianka prison. Ovey to Vansittart, 14 March 1933, FO 371/17265 1704/1610/38.

90 Ovey to Simon, 14 March 1933, FO 371/17265 N1658/1610/38.

91 Strang to Simon, 20 June 1933, *DBFP*, # 502. It is hard to agree with Owen's contention that it was Stalin who had initiated events, since she cites the same dispatch and does not explain how "sanction" can mean that Stalin "put them up to it" (see Owen, "The Metro-Vickers Crisis," p. 97).

installation, was a problem poorly understood by the non-technically trained secret police. Several tragedies had already occurred, Richards explained. One "first class disaster" had seen the breakdown of turbines at an installation in Kuznetsk and resulted in an explosion that blew the roof off one of the largest plants in the world.[92] Such episodes, in his opinion, were largely the result of the "inefficiency of Russian workmen," and the problems were not limited to "Vickers" turbines but extended to other firms as well. Richards thought it possible that the OGPU, "in their self-confidence have acted without reference to Stalin." This hypothesis was lent some substance when he had picked up hints from Ozerskii and Kahan, both of the Commissariat of Heavy Industry, that they might try to get Stalin to prevail on the OGPU to drop the case. Richards himself was going to remind Ordzhonikidze, the Commissar of Heavy Industry and a Politburo member, of the MVEEC's outstanding contribution to Soviet electrification. The Metro-Vickers Director feared that contracts might go to Germany if the crisis became worse.[93]

While information about the charges against the engineers in Moscow became better known, at the Foreign Office questions continued to be raised about such issues as Thornton's alleged bribe to Dolgov, his opposite number in Electro-Import in Moscow. Richards wrote a "secret and confidential" letter to Collier which underscored the close relationship Dolgov had had with the MVEEC and Thornton in particular. When Thornton approached Richards about a "loan" to Dolgov, who needed the money for a deposit on a flat or house, Richards had agreed on the grounds that similar arrangements were made by the MVEEC for its own employees from time to time. The MVEEC director claimed that the Company was always concerned about the potential problems of bribery and if "Dolgov had been in a position to influence orders in any way I would never have approved this transaction."[94] It is difficult to see how Dolgov could remain unaffected by such treatment, and while one cannot establish any direct connection between the "loan" and Dolgov's behaviour following the transaction, the decision to treat Dolgov as if he were an MVEEC employee highlights the imprudent behaviour of the MVEEC management at the time.

Richards was also called upon to clarify the MVEEC's participation in the "International Price Arrangements Committee," a cartel-like structure formed in Germany in October 1930, which undertook to

---

92 Foreign Office Minute by Collier, 14 March 1933, FO 371/17265 N1801/1610/38.
93 Ibid.
94 Richards to Collier, 21 March 1933, FO 371/17265 N1802/1610/38.

keep prices for machinery sold in the Soviet Union from falling to uneconomic levels. There was wide participation in this body by all the important firms from Germany, Switzerland, Italy, France, the United States, Sweden, and Austria, as well as Great Britain.[95] When queried by the Foreign Office about the activities of the cartel, Richards claimed that he had warned the German companies that the number of participants was too large and that leaks were ever more likely. The Soviets, according to Richards, knew that all the important electrical companies that operated in the Soviet Union pooled information in the Price Arrangements Committee, but it appears he had only a vague idea of exactly how much the Soviets knew about the full extent of the Committee's activities.[96] That Soviet intelligence did take an interest in the deliberations of these companies became evident during Monkhouse's pre-trial interrogation when he was shown minutes from a 1932 meeting where Richards reported on conditions in the Soviet Union.[97]

It now seems clear that the Soviet claim at the time, that companies associated with such cartels operated as part of the economic intelligence services of their respective countries, had some foundation, at least in the British case. As we have seen, by 1931 the British Committee of Imperial Defence (CID) had formed an Industrial Intelligence Centre (IIC)[98] which, under the directorship of Major Desmond Morton, recruited British businessmen to collect economic intelligence, particularly in countries such as the Soviet Union, where British military attachés were absent. Morton, on the instructions of Prime Minister Ramsay MacDonald, regularly passed his information on to his close friend and neighbour Winston Churchill.[99] The head of the IIC also had strong backing from the Secretary of the CID and Cabinet Secretary,

---

95 Ibid.

96 Foreign Office minute by Collier, 17 March 1933, FO 371/17265 N1827/1610/38.

97 Ibid; Monkhouse to Richards, 14 March 1933, FO 371/17265 N1719/1610/38; and Haslam, *The Soviet Union and the Struggle for Collective Security*, p. 17-18.

98 While some records of the IIC held in CAB 48 are now open, the record CAB 43/3, which contains memoranda for the period June 1929 to March 1933, has not yet been made available at the PRO. Also see Haslam, *The Soviet Union and the Struggle for Collective Security*, p. 242 n. 54, and Wark, "British Military and Economic Intelligence," p. 264 n. 71.

99 It would be wrong to think that Morton's only role during Churchill's years "in the wilderness" was that of a purveyor of intelligence on Nazi Germany. Churchill also requested Morton's well-informed views on matters pertaining to British agents operating in the Soviet Union. See Churchill to Morton, 31 October 1930, Churchill papers 2/169, in M. Gilbert, ed., *Winston S. Churchill*, Vol. 5 Companion Part 2: *Documents: The Wilderness Years, 1929-1933* (London: Heinemann, 1981), p. 216 and n. 1.

Maurice Hankey.[100] Thus, despite the fact that the IIC did not get the serious attention of a Cabinet minister until Sir Philip Cuncliffe-Lister became the Secretary of State for Air in 1935,[101] the economic intelligence it collected found its way into both the formal and informal circles of the government.

The place of the MVEEC in this formal and informal intelligence network has also been clarified in recent years. Vickers, the British armament company of which Metro-Vickers was a subsidiary for much of the 1920s, is known to have had some of its employees act as SIS station chiefs. According to Andrew and Trebilcock, during this same period Richards routinely asked the MVEEC engineers resident in the Soviet Union for "general information" on the Soviet economy which was made available to the parent Vickers company as well. This information ranged from the "state of the harvest to the progress of heavy industry" and was "almost certainly" passed on to the IIC and SIS.[102] Wesley Wark has argued that information collected by the IIC became part of the British Chiefs of Staff assessment of the Red Army threat to India's North-Western frontier in the late 1920s and contributed to an appraisal of Soviet military strength in 1934 which put it beneath that of the first-rate European powers.[103]

Although most of this type of "intelligence" would hardly qualify as "secret" outside the Soviet context, Thornton's deposition makes it clear that the MVEEC engineers, at least by 1932, took special care when passing along such information. Thornton, Monkhouse, and Cushny developed a rather crude code to transmit their assessment of the stability of Soviet society. Such reports, Thornton claimed, were found necessary because of the long-term credits which the Soviets had with the firm. Situation "A" signified a general decline in the economic stability of the regime over the past year; situation "B" signified that the OGPU was increasing its activities around the MVEEC's operations.[104] These codes were used in communications with Richards in London, a fact which belied his consistent and disingenuous denials

---

100 Morton conveyed this information to Hankey's biographer, Steven Roskill. See Steven Roskill, *Hankey: Man of Secrets*, Vol. 3: *1931-1963* (London: Collins, 1974), p. 22 and n. 6; and R.W. Thompson, *Churchill and Morton* (London: Hodder and Stoughton, 1976), p. 20-21, 148.

101 Andrew, *Secret Service*, p. 355-56.

102 Ibid., p. 355-57, and chap. 11, n. 74, 75.

103 Wark, "British Military and Economic Intelligence," p. 94; and W. Wark, "British Military and Economic Intelligence on Nazi Germany," p. 234, quoted in Andrew, *Secret Service*, p. 356-57.

104 Thornton, Foreign Office Deposition, 20 July 1933.

that he had never received any information at all from engineers in the field concerning the general situation of the Soviet Union.[105]

A less verifiable connection of the MVEEC to the IIC can be found in Thorton's bewilderment in his 1933 deposition about why the OGPU waited two years before moving in on the MVEEC engineers — an interval which coincides with the formation of the IIC.[106] Since the OGPU files are not open it is impossible to trace the connection, but Thornton's testimony after his release raises the possibility that the Soviets, too, found the "coincidence" problematic.

Of course the possibility of an MVEEC role in the gathering of economic "intelligence" in the USSR was not given much credence in the public discussion in Britain at the time. Rather, it was widely held that it was the OGPU which was the misguided provocateur of the crisis. In the week following the arrests, in a development that encouraged Ovey to hope that the OGPU might yet be forced to abandon the case, Soviet censorship of foreign press correspondents softened enough to allow transmission of opinions of the type that the " 'OGPU had made an outrageous blunder,' deleting only the word outrageous."[107] Such reports found their way into a number of editorials in British papers such as the *Observer*, the *Economist*, and *The Times* and comparisons were quickly drawn between the MVEEC arrests and the trials of 1928, 1929, and 1930. The *Observer* offered dour warnings to the Soviet government that the British people had an "instinct for underlying principles and a way of hardening unpleasantly against those who commit injustice upon British subjects."[108] Moreover, since the engineers were "unquestionably innocent," the actions of the OGPU and Litvinov's inability to reply to questions about the case only served to inflame diplomatic and commercial relations.[109]

This view contrasted with that offered in the more classically liberal *Economist* which cautioned the British government to keep its head over this "stupid incident" and not be stampeded into foolish action by anti-Soviet public opinion. What was needed was more trade with the Soviet Union, not a return to the mood of 1927.[110] At the same time, during the annual meeting of the Association of British Chambers of Commerce, groups such as the Manchester Chamber of Commerce

105 Foreign Office Memorandum by Sir L. Oliphant, 15 April 1933, *DBFP*, # 409.
106 Thornton, Foreign Office Deposition, 20 July 1933.
107 Ovey to Vansittart, 19 March 1933, FO 371/17265 N1817/1610/38.
108 *Observer*, 19 March 1933, p.16.
109 Ibid., p. 17.
110 *Economist*, 18 March 1933, p. 575-76.

were promoting the rapid negotiation of a trade agreement with the Soviet government. The current "state of delay and uncertainty is having an adverse effect on Anglo-Russian trade," the association argued.[111]

The first press articles which speculated on the actual nature of the arrests and the plausibility of the Soviet charges were provided by a young recruit to the Reuters news agency, Ian Fleming. Using a Riga dateline that was picked up by a number of major papers in Britain, Fleming connected the MVEEC arrests with recent troubles at the Dneprostroi hydroelectric project and speculated that the engineers were going to be accused of actions which resulted in the corrosion of the blades on the turbines.[112] Fleming's account received widespread attention when the BBC aired a broadcast based on Fleming's article, without consulting the MVEEC first, and almost immediately the young man, who would spend much of his later life in the world of Cold War fiction and film, was embroiled in a debate over the merits of his first report on the MVEEC affair. The MVEEC naturally decried the report of corrosion as nothing short of fantastic and argued that it would take millions of gallons of acid or sand to produce the condition that Soviet sources now alleged afflicted the turbines.[113]

Fleming was now called upon to account for his story and did so in a memorandum to his editor, Rickatson-Hatt. In order to assess more accurately the Soviet allegations Fleming had consulted Gerald Coke of Industrial Steels Ltd., which was part of the Vickers combine, and Coke, who had direct information from Anthony Vickers on the Soviet charges, told Fleming that while the Soviet charges were indeed "fantastic" they were not "mechanically impossible." According to Fleming's biographer, Zeiger, Fleming's memo makes it clear that the Foreign Office had seen a draft of the article before it went to press as well. Rickatson-Hatt thought it significant that the Soviet news agency Tass, which normally disavowed Reuters coverage from Riga, had not issued any statement on Fleming's theory and this lent "colour to the

---

111 *Manchester Guardian*, 14 March 1933, p. 13.

112 See the articles carried in the *Observer* ("Moscow's British Prisoners," 19 March 1933, p. 17) and *The Times* (London) ("Indignation at the B.B.C. Broadcast," 20 March 1933, p. 12). The best biographical sketches of Fleming's first encounters with the Soviet Union are by Zeiger, *Ian Fleming*, p. 38-58 and Pearson, *The Life of Ian Fleming*, p. 46-64.

113 See the MVEEC response in "Indignation at B.B.C. Broadcast," p. 12.

supposition that the Soviet authorities may actually be bringing these charges against the British engineers."[114]

A couple of days after the acrimony over the arrests had erupted in the British press the Foreign Office received a private letter from one Denis McQueen Potter that addressed itself to the technical possibility of the corrosion of the turbines. McQueen Potter was the son of a stainless steel expert of Brown, Bayley's Steel Works in Sheffield, and his father had worked as a consultant for the MVEEC on a number of stainless steel turbines. Imploring Collier to keep his information very secret, McQueen Potter provided the Foreign Office with a technical summary of the problems such turbines encountered when operated at anything other than a very precise temperature. In any other conditions the stainless steel broke down as if the blades were made from bad steel or had been abused by acid. He knew from his father that even in Manchester, where one could reasonably expect the levels of technical skill and maintenance to be superior to those in the Soviet Union, numerous difficulties had plagued the blades of the turbines when these turbines were first put to the test. The description he had gleaned from Fleming's article immediately brought to mind the many problems his father had encountered at the Trafford Park works.[115]

The officials at the Foreign Office apparently raised such possibilities with the MVEEC, but there is no record of anything resulting from such conversations. What is clear is that there were good reasons for the MVEEC at least to consider the possibility of problems with their equipment that might have been the result of British design as well as Soviet negligence. In contrast to the confident public disavowals by MVEEC officials, there did appear to be some plausible technical grounds for the Soviet allegations which were never given full consideration in the discussions of the day. Since the Foreign Office knew of such possibilities and chose not to condition its recommendations accordingly, one can state that both the British government and the MVEEC thought it helpful to their cause to keep some important material from surfacing at the time.

In the Commons strong statements of support for the British engineers and outrage against the Soviet Union heightened the tension of the situation. In response to Baldwin's assurances of 15 March, that the Soviet government had no grounds for its police action, Sir N. Grattan Doyle was prompted to call for the immediate release of the en-

---

114 Zeiger, *Ian Fleming*, p. 42.
115 Denis McQueen Potter to Collier, 23 March 1933, FO 371/17266 N2077/1610/38.

gineers.[116] By 19 March the contours of Labour's critique of the government could be seen in its parliamentary leader's public address in Birmingham. Arguing that "Russia is a sovereign State, and those who go there must live under the laws that govern that State," George Lansbury insisted that "scare headlines" and the statements of Baldwin and the Dominions Secretary, J.H. Thomas, "will not help in the solution of a very difficult situation."[117] Instead of prejudging the issue, Lansbury cautioned, the government was best advised to work to secure the "fairest trial possible."[118]

As awareness about the Metro-Vickers affair was growing in Britain the pace of diplomatic efforts in Moscow quickened as well. Finally finding Litvinov available for discussion on 16 March, Ovey initiated the first of a series of conversations with the Soviet Commissar which resulted in the complete erosion of their formerly cordial relationship and ended with Ovey's recall to London for "consultation." Throughout the Ovey-Litvinov talks, the British Ambassador repeatedly pressed his instructions from the Foreign Office to their extreme, at times anticipating such instructions and even overstepping them in spirit if not in fact.

From the outset Ovey pressured Litvinov for Soviet cooperation in defusing the crisis. Over the Commissar's objections the British Ambassador reiterated his concern over the summary executions and recently increased powers of the OGPU. Ovey claimed that the issue was not "one of sovereign rights but rather of whether the British public and His Majesty's Government could continue to consider Russia a country in which it was possible for an Englishman to live and trade with, or with which His Majesty's Government could maintain relations."[119] Ovey suggested that public opinion and pressure from the

---

116 *Parliamentary Debates: House of Commons, 5th Series*, Vol. 275, col. 1945, 15 March 1933. [Hereinafter cited as *H.C. Deb. 5 s.*]

117 *Manchester Guardian*, 20 March 1933, p. 9.

118 Ibid.

119 Ovey to Vansittart, 16 March 1933, FO 371/17265 N1760/1610/38. The only diplomatic papers available on the Metro-Vickers affair are the records of the Ovey-Litvinov conversations for this two-week period. The Soviet records are found in Ministerstvo Inostrannykh del SSSR, *Dokumenty Vneshnei Politiki SSSR*, vol. 16 (Moscow: Izdatel'stvo Politicheskoi Literaturi, 1970), "Soobshchenie sovetskoi pechati o besedakh Narodnovo Komissara Inostrannykh Del SSSR M. M. Litvinova c Poslom Velikobritanii b SSSR Oviem, 16-28 Marta," p. 233-40. These short excerpts are virtually verbatim the records released by the British in the *Documents of British Foreign Policy, 1919-1939*, 2nd series, vol. 7, published in 1958.

Commons might bring "irresistible forces" to bear on the government to break off relations with the Soviet Union.[120]

For his part, Litvinov insisted that Britain was making "too much noise" and was speaking in "too strong terms" about an issue which was an internal Soviet matter. Such pressure, the Commissar for Foreign Affairs added, would only strengthen Soviet resolve. Litvinov argued that there was a public opinion in the Soviet Union as well, and that if foreigners received preferential treatment the effect on such opinion would be "deplorable." To this Ovey retorted that "people were simply more terrorized than ever before by the fact that not only Russians but foreigners were now being arrested." The situation, in Ovey's view was "fraught with danger."[121]

The same day Litvinov struck back in the Tass release cited earlier, claiming that Ovey's arguments "reduced themselves to a proposal for the exemption from Soviet jurisdiction of all British subjects granting them immunity for any crime or delinquency. . . . as soon as his [Ovey's] government expressed a conviction of their innocence."[122] The statement focussed on Ovey, rather than the British government, and initiated a largely successful attempt on Litvinov's part to paint the British Ambassador as a somewhat "hysterical" diplomat acting beyond his instructions. For the remainder of his mission to Moscow Ovey's recommendations were tempered and toned down for public consumption and Cabinet deliberation by the Foreign Office, and Litvinov did his best to take advantage of Ovey's position.

Ovey's dogged pursuit of Litvinov was part of his overall strategy to engage the Soviet Commissar more fully in the extrication of the engineers. Reflecting on his first meeting with Litvinov, Ovey reported to Vansittart that:

> my attitude was that of one who spoke rather in sorrow than in anger. This method is best in my opinion for dealing with this irritable and in some respects good natured boor. . . . The author of non-aggression pacts and curator of foreign relations, although today he was forced to play the game, in his innermost heart disapproves, I feel, the orders which he has been given.[123]

Ovey believed, and the Narkomindel accommodations for the prisoners confirmed his viewpoint, that the largely Jewish "bourgeois" Nar-

---

120 Ibid.
121 Ibid.
122 The Tass statement of 16 March 1933 was included in Ovey to Vansittart, 18 March 1933, FO 371/17265 N1804/1610/38.
123 Ibid., 17 March 1933, FO 371/17265 N1778/1610/38.

komindel might prove to be useful allies for the British. Though the situation was not dangerous enough for these "rats yet to make a move to safety," few in the Narkomindel agreed with Stalin's recent course. Events over the next several days would add substance to the notion that Litvinov was in a position to soften the blows being dealt to Anglo-Soviet relations.

Along with these reflections on the Soviet political scene, Ovey included a draft of a formula which he thought might provide a means to end the affair without a trial or further jeopardy to Anglo-Soviet relations. In rather high-handed language, which reflected his confidence that the Soviets might yet yield to pressure, Ovey's formula required that the prisoners be released immediately "in view of the fact that insufficient evidence has been found," and that, if such action were forthcoming on the part of the Soviets, His Majesty's Government would consider the incident closed. Any recurrence of a "similar incident," however, would be interpreted by Britain as a sign that the Soviet government no longer attached any importance to continued friendly relations between the two countries.[124] This last clause of the formula virtually assured that the Soviet authorities would reject it as a basis for dismissing the case — accepting it would mean any subsequent arrests of British subjects in the Soviet Union could be attacked along the lines that might be set by such a Metro-Vickers precedent. Ovey added a note to his formula requesting that no public reference should be made to the Soviet's intention to hold a trial because such publicity would make it very difficult for it to step down. This went some way to modify the features of "diktat" implied by his recommendations, but when the Soviets were presented with the formula it was dismissed in an all-too-predictable manner.

Vansittart responded the same day to Ovey's formula, and his comments suggest that he was less optimistic than the British Ambassador in Moscow that the affair could be defused without a trial. The Permanent Under-Secretary authorized Ovey to present an amended formula to the Soviets in an effort to give them "one last chance" to close the incident. He cautioned that any mention of a Soviet apology in the British formula would make Britain's primary objective, the release of the prisoners, more difficult. He also emphasized to Ovey that, whenever possible, the Ambassador should stress the damage already done to Anglo-Soviet relations irrespective of the resolution of the affair now. It

---

124 Ibid.

was here that Vansittart's pessimism[125] was revealed most clearly since this last tactic offered little reward to the Soviets if they did release the prisoners. He also stressed that if the Soviets did not release the prisoners, then pressure should be applied to gain genuine legal assistance for them and, failing that, it had to be demonstrable that all possible efforts had been made to that end.[126]

Armed with Vansittart's authorization, Ovey set about redrafting his formula, which he presented to Rubinin during breakfast on 18 March. Ovey stretched Vansittart's mandate when he included a clause requiring a Soviet expression of "sincere regret" to His Majesty's Government, and the final version of the amended formula retained the provision that any further arrests of British subjects "on grounds proved by subsequent inquiry to be insufficient" would be interpreted by the British as a sign that the Soviet Union had an inadequate commitment to continued good relations. Since Rubinin was not authorized to respond to Ovey's formula, Ovey had to wait until he could meet with Litvinov to get an official reply.[127]

The tone and contents of the Ovey formula proved a concern to the Foreign Office as well as the Narkomindel. Sir Lancelot Oliphant, Assistant Secretary of State for Foreign Affairs, telephoned Ovey on 18 March, as soon as he received a copy of the amended formula, and criticized the Ambassador for ignoring the Foreign Office warning against requiring a Soviet apology. While Oliphant's action is understandable, the means he chose might well have compromised Ovey's position in the Soviet eyes. It is very likely that such conversations were being monitored by Soviet authorities. Later on in the crisis the British took the precaution to speak in prearranged codes to guard against such intercepts.[128] Oliphant also contacted Vansittart about Ovey's personal diplomatic strategy and received the dejected reply that in any case, the "Russians appear to be in no mood for a formula."[129]

---

125 Vansittart's recollection of his divergence with Ovey is mentioned in his memoir, *The Mist Procession* (London: Hutchinson, 1958), p. 461, but understates Ovey's frustration with the "half-measures" recommended by the Foreign Office and adopted by the Cabinet.

126 Vansittart to Ovey, 17 March 1933, FO 371/17265 N1780/1610/38.

127 Ovey to Vansittart, 18 March 1933, FO 371/17265 N1798/1610/38.

128 Ibid., 21 March 1933, FO 371/17265 N1924/1610/38, includes the observation "You will see from my telegram No. 89 how, M. Litvinov, who was probably already aware of your views from my telephonic conversation with Sir L. Oliphant. . . ."

129 Sir Lancelot Oliphant to Ovey; Oliphant to Vansittart; and Vansittart to Oliphant, 18 March 1933, FO 371/17265 N1798/1610/38.

The next Ovey-Litvinov meeting took place on 19 March, despite Ovey's attempts to see the Commissar earlier. Ovey was surprised by the mild manner that Litvinov exhibited when faced with the latest version of the "formula." After listening carefully to Ovey, Litvinov took up his own claim that he had already done much to ease the situation, but that these efforts had been sabotaged by Baldwin's statement in the House, and by the language used by Vansittart and Ovey himself. On the issue of the prisoners' release, Litvinov replied that he could not be hopeful about such an occurrence. The case had just been passed to the Prosecutor's Department of the Russian Soviet Federated Socialist Republic (RSFSR) and this meant that the OGPU investigations were now complete. It was now up to the Prosecutor, Andrei Vyshinskii, to decide whether there was sufficient evidence for a trial; if there was not "sufficient evidence," then the release of the prisoners would become a possibility. Litvinov told Ovey that he was "totally unable to exercise influence on this incorruptible official." He was able to inform the British Ambassador that on Litvinov's own initiative arrangements had been made for an Embassy visit to the prisoners for that evening. He also asked Ovey to enquire about the possibility of the MVEEC posting bail for the prisoners. Such an arrangement would secure their release for the moment at least.[130]

Ovey interpreted the tone and substance of this exchange of views with Litvinov in the most optimistic terms. The arrangements Litvinov had made for another Embassy visit, the unprecedented possibility of posting bail for prisoners in a Soviet jail, the easing of press censorship on the arrests, and the fact that the OGPU had turned the proceedings over to the Public Prosecutor — who could now dismiss the case — added up, in Ovey's mind, to a window of opportunity for a successful end to the conflict. His recommendation to Vansittart was that "only a delicate but emphatic push" was now required to gain the immediate release of the engineers and "that this push be given in London to the Soviet Ambassador, perhaps in the form of a hint, almost an 'indiscretion voulue' of what was certainly coming to them should the prosecutor's 'conscience' be considered as more important than the maintenance of relations."[131]

Not content to let matters rest with the Foreign Office without the benefit of his additional input, Ovey telegraphed a more detailed outline of what he considered an "emphatic push" later the same day. Pre-

---

130 Ovey to Vansittart, 19 March 1933, FO 371/17265 N1816/1610/38.
131 Ibid.

facing his three-point plan with the observation that "any breach of relations to be followed perhaps in a few years by a second resumption would be undesirable and even undignified," Ovey insisted that continued relations with the Soviet Union had diminishing value unless a "radical change supervenes." His three recommendations included a warning to Maisky that unless the prisoners were released immediately, a trade embargo would begin after 17 April,[132] Soviet trade representatives would be asked to return home, and no trade deal would thereafter be entertained. If, after a short interval, such a warning went unheeded by the Soviets, then Ovey argued that both he and the Soviet Ambassador should be asked to return to their respective countries. Finally, if the above demonstrations of British will did not convince the Soviets to step down and they proceeded to hold a trial and find any British subject guilty, then all relations should be severed at once. Such a procedure, in Ovey's view, got progressively stronger and provided the Soviet government with two separate occasions to yield before the final act of rupture.[133] The key was to step up the measures being applied and press for full satisfaction, for "the enemy are in full retreat. They have got to yield somewhere. The sooner the better. If we do not follow up the battle of Marne we may still drift into the trench warfare of long and humiliating inactivity."[134]

Ovey's proposal was not well received at the Foreign Office. Vansittart minuted that "Sir E. Ovey is going too far too fast" with the suggestion of his recall or diplomatic rupture. The Soviets could still retreat at this late date and it was still possible that the prisoners might be tried and acquitted. Anthony Eden, the Parliamentary Under-Secretary of State, agreed with Vansittart on the inadvisability of considering a threat to diplomatic relations and minuted that Ovey's remarks concerning the threat to Soviet trade were more valuable at this stage since it was trade that "the Soviets fear to lose."[135]

The notion that the Soviets were vulnerable to trade sanctions, despite its currency among British officials, may have been overstated. While the foreign trade figures for the Soviet Union confirm the view that Soviet purchases abroad were declining rapidly as the Second Five-Year Plan got underway, it was not only the pressures on Soviet cash reserves that produced the trend. Rather, many sectors of Soviet

---

132 The date the Anglo-Soviet trade agreement would formally expire.

133 Ovey to Vansittart, 19 March 1933, FO 371/17265 N1850/1610/38.

134 Ovey added these comments "after night's reflections" (ibid., 20 March 1933, FO 371/17265 N1844/1610/38).

135 Ibid.

heavy industry were now able to meet the needs of the centralized command economy, which thereby diminished the need for foreign imports. It was this capacity that would produce a favourable Soviet trade balance for the first time since 1929.[136] The First Five-Year Plan had set out to develop such a capability and, at terrific human costs, the fulfillment of much of the Plan had provided a substantial portion of the infrastructure necessary for modern industry.

While Britain was not the only nation to assume that the Soviet industrial market was theirs to be exploited — many Americans also clung to the same erroneous conception — it is ironic that the weapon they hoped to wield in the MVEEC crisis would miss its mark. Undoubtedly Ovey's calculations were based on the evidence of the 1931 and 1932, years which featured a declining growth rate in industry and an absolute decline in agriculture production.[137] While Ovey could not have predicted future developments, these years turned out to be exceptionally bad, and it is likely, as Owen suggests, that on this count the Soviets had more accurate information about the current state of their economy than did foreign analysts. Indeed, the first news the Foreign Office received on Anglo-Soviet trade in the first quarter of 1933 came from Soviet press releases at the end of April.[138] In this instance, though British policy may have been a thoughtfully considered one, it nonetheless was based in part on an illusion.

The Metro-Vickers affair was thrust back into the public arena in Britain by Eden's address to the Commons on 20 March. With Ovey's recent dispatches in mind and a number of parliamentary questions to be answered, Eden provoked a heated debate in the House over concerns about the Soviet legal process with his announcement that British legal counsel could not represent the arrested engineers in a Soviet trial. Lansbury waded into the discussion but was shouted down and interrupted by Churchill, among others, when the senior statesman for Labour reminded fellow parliamentarians that Soviet legal counsel was not allowed in British courts either. Eden made sure to keep his responses as formulaic and general as possible. He recounted the general direction of Ovey's diplomacy in Moscow without making any

---

136 See Appendix B, "Soviet Foreign Trade, 1913-1940," particularly the years 1930-37, which demonstrate this trend.

137 See Appendix E, "Soviet Gross Production." Michael Dohan has examined the impact of the world trade and credit situation on the First Five-Year Plan in "The Economic Origins of Soviet Autarky, 1927/28-1934," *Slavic Review*, 35, 4 (December 1976): 603-35.

138 Owen, "The Metro-Vickers Crisis," p. 98; Strang to Simon, 22 April 1933, *DBFP*, #440; and ibid., 30 April 1933, *DBFP*, #470.

specific reference to the possible levers that Ovey proposed. Most importantly, Eden made no reference to any provisions for a trade embargo at this time. It was publicly admitted, however, that trade negotiations had been suspended.[139]

Ovey was relatively pleased with the way Eden's statement was drafted. The tone of Eden's explanations and Vansittart's permission to explain to Litvinov the British motive for not going public with the threat of an embargo retained the latitude for secret diplomacy that Ovey hoped would resolve the affair. On this basis Ovey instructed Strang, who was preparing for a meeting with Krestinskii, that the Commons' speech had "expressly omitted" such a reference in order that the Soviets might now have the chance to release the prisoners without appearing to bow to British pressure.[140]

Beyond this, however, Ovey found the entire situation "extremely disquieting" and was keen to underscore his view that the "half measures" to date had not achieved the end of securing the release of the prisoners. He felt unable to approach Litvinov again unless he was authorized to threaten to break off relations if the British were not given full satisfaction. If His Majesty's Government were forced to suffer the humiliation "of permitting Soviets to hold a trial of any kind whatever," his own position would be untenable and the Soviets would have gained an important victory.[141] Since Ovey was aware that Vansittart was preparing a memo for an important Cabinet meeting on the subject of the MVEEC affair, his very strong language was undoubtedly meant to energize the proceedings in London. Rather despondently he concluded his remarks by proposing his immediate recall if the Cabinet came to any other decisions than those which he had recommended.[142]

As Strang wrote in his memoir, Ovey's course "did not recommend itself to London."[143] Vansittart's memo for the Cabinet meeting of 22 March outlined the political objections to Ovey's plan to threaten a breach of relations. Thus far, Vansittart counselled, His Majesty' Government had gained "considerable credit" for the firm and balanced character of its diplomacy. Vansittart also thought it possible that, even if a trial were held, the engineers might yet be released due to the economic pressure that would be applied against the Soviet state via an

139 H.C. Deb. 5 s., 276, col. 17-20, 20 March 1933.
140 Ovey to Vansittart, 21 March 1933, FO 371/17265 N1924/1610/38.
141 Ibid.
142 Ibid.
143 Strang, Home and Abroad, p. 84.

embargo. Staying with the current course was Vansittart's recommendation when the Cabinet met to discuss its options.[144]

On 22 March Vansittart gave his views to the Cabinet, which promoted a graduated response to a range of possible Soviet actions. In the "unlikely event" of the engineers being executed, Vansittart recommended breaking off all relations and bringing Ovey home. In the "still more unlikely event" of the prisoners being released before a trial, the British should "drive an even harder commercial bargain than we should otherwise have attempted." The most "probable event" was, in the Permanent Under-Secretary's opinion, that a trial would be held, that an adverse verdict would be pronounced, and that the release or light sentencing of some or all of the engineers would ensue. In such an instance, and indeed this was basically the scenario which would occur in April, Vansittart submitted that the British should refuse altogether to resume commercial negotiations.[145]

Vansittart was also concerned about the state of British public opinion. A Reuters telephone message to Moscow intercepted by the British authorities gave the impression that interest in the current dispute was waning in some quarters. Simon had "corrected" the impression by intervening with Sir R. Jones of Reuters and asking that the news from Moscow continue to be reported in the British press in full.[146]

In the Cabinet discussion which followed Simon took the view that any threat to diplomatic relations would be ineffective in the present instance and would set an awkward precedent for relations with other nations "where it was less applicable." On the issue of trade measures, however, it was decided that an embargo bill should be drafted, and a committee comprised of MacDonald, Baldwin, and Simon was charged with that task. The President of the Board of Trade, Walter Runciman, pointed out that he had already told companies to be slow in fulfilling their contracts with Soviet Russia. This economic irritant would now be increased with a decision to draft an imports prohibition bill.[147]

While the Cabinet deliberated on stepping up British pressure, Foreign Office legal advisers were examining the legal ramifications of imposing a trade embargo or severing diplomatic relations before the Soviet legal process had run its course. The Second Legal Adviser, Wil-

---

144 Vansittart, Memo to Cabinet, 22 March 1933, CAB 23/75, 20(33)11, C.P. 78(33); and Vansittart to Ovey, 21 March 1933, FO 371/17265 N1951/1610/38.
145 CAB 23/75, 20(33)11, C.P. 78(33), 22 March 1933.
146 Ibid.; and Simon to Ovey, 22 March 1933, *DBFP* # 266, note 4.
147 CAB 23/75, 21(33)1, 22 March 1933.

liam Bennett, cautioned that in terms of international law the Soviets had the right to present whatever evidence they had and only then could a British trade or diplomatic reprisal be justified. He also warned that premature action by Britain would set a bad precedent for recipro- cal action when Soviet citizens were arrested in the United Kingdom by British authorities.[148] The Third Legal Adviser, Gerald Fitzmaurice, concurred with Bennett's view of the legal situation. He admitted that while there might be good tactical reasons for threatening the Soviet government privately as to what would happen, "to threaten that these things will happen (e.g., an embargo on Soviet goods or the rup- ture of diplomatic relations) if the prisoners are brought to trial at all, and failing their immediate and unconditional release before the trial, will undoubtedly put us in the wrong technically."[149]

Fitzmaurice pointed out that questions were already being asked as to why similar action was not taken against Germany and, "though such cases may not be parallel, it is awkward."[150] As events would evolve, the British government managed to avoid public transgression of these tenets of international law, although the private pressure they applied violated the spirit, by arranging for an embargo to take effect from 18 April — after the Soviet trial was held.

Events in Moscow were lending more substance to the notion that the Narkomindel was doing its best to minimize the damage to Anglo- Soviet relations. After a second consecutive postponement of a foreign policy communiqué there had come the announcement that Gregory Sokolnikov, the former Soviet Ambassador to Great Britain, had been appointed to the Collegium of the Narkomindel. Ovey interpreted the move as another part of the Soviet strategy to impress upon those circles in Britain who knew the former Ambassador that someone who understood the British perspective was in a position of importance in the foreign policy establishment. In addition to these signals, there had been a "feeler" sent through the International News Services's *Daily Express* correspondent in Moscow which raised the possibility of bail for the MVEEC engineers if the British company were to approach the Public Prosecutor with an official request.[151]

Ovey believed that, taken together, the most recent Soviet moves were "signs of retreat." He strongly advised against any idea of pursu-

---

148 Foreign Office Minute by William Bennett (Second Legal Adviser), 22 March 1933,
     FO 371/17266, N2082/1610/38.
149 Fitzmaurice to Collier, 23 March 1933, FO 371/17266 N2038/1610/38.
150 Ibid.
151 Ovey to Simon, 22 March 1933, FO 371/17265 N1976/1610/38.

ing the prospect of bail since, in a country where no individual can leave without permission, the idea was a "farce." If the Soviets got wind of any real interest in posting bail either by His Majesty's Government, the MVEEC itself, or through stories in the Press, they would be that much harder to deal with, in Ovey's view.[152]

Though Ovey had serious reservations about discussing bail, the MVEEC officials in London felt obliged to explore the possibility. Richards met with Simon at the Foreign Office and reviewed Vyshinskii's recent offer[153] of bail for Thornton at 25 000 roubles and for Cushny and Gregory at 15 000 roubles each.[154] With Monkhouse and Nordwall already at liberty in Moscow, this would leave only the hapless William MacDonald and the MVEEC's Soviet employees in the Lubianka prison.

Richards was anxious to avoid sanctioning the arrests and possible trial of MVEEC employees and was told by the legal counsel at the Foreign Office that posting bail would not imply approval of Soviet proceedings. The Company also had reservations about posting bail for only some of the prisoners and wanted to get Ovey's opinion on the merits of offering bail for both British and Soviet employees of the MVEEC. Ovey had an opportunity to gauge the intent of Vyshinskii's offer when he visited the MVEEC prisoners in the evening of 23 March and found the Public Prosecutor present at the Lubianka prison. It became apparent to Ovey that the offer of bail was by no means standard procedure in the Soviet Union — indeed Vyshinskii could not provide any specific details about previous offers of bail at all. The prisoners had not yet been advised of the specific charges against them, but Vyshinskii explained to Ovey that the Soviet investigation would be complete within a day or two. The overall impression was that the offer was being made in this instance to "show that Soviet law differed in no essential respect from Western European law."[155] On the basis of this conversation, Ovey telephoned Simon, using a prearranged code, and reaffirmed his previous conviction that while posting bail did not imply approval of the arrests, such an act by the MVEEC would embolden the Soviet authorities. His opinion was forwarded to the MVEEC and it was at this point that the Company authorized Monk-

152 Ibid., 23 March 1933, FO 371/17265 N1998/1610/38.
153 This offer was made through Maisky to MVEEC Director, Sir Felix Pole. Simon to Ovey, 23 March 1933, FO 371/17265 N1998/1610/38.
154 According to Strang in *Home and Abroad* (p. 85), these sums worked out to £2 650 and £1 590 at the official rate of exchange.
155 Ovey to Simon, 24 March 1933, FO 371/17266 N2065/1610/38.

house to offer bail for all employees in prison, both British and Russian, on the understanding that this did not imply acceptance of the Soviet police action.[156]

Whatever hopes the British still entertained that the crisis might be defused without a public test of strength were dashed by a communiqué from Vyshinskii published in *Izvestiia* the same day. Vyshinskii announced that a trial would be held early in April in an open session of the Supreme Court, and the British accused, "as in the majority of other countries," would have to use defence counsel from the national legal bar. The MVEEC employees and certain other Russian engineers would be charged under articles 58-6, 58-7, 58-9, and 58-11 of the Criminal Code of the RSFSR for the crimes of gathering secret information of State and Military importance, committing acts of diversion and wrecking, and offering or accepting bribes for the above crimes.[157] Vyshinskii challenged any rumours of "third degree" methods and insisted that only those enemies who were trying adversely to affect the Soviet Union's relations with other countries could maintain such "absurd" opinions. The Public Prosecutor's comments concerning the British prisoners still held in Soviet custody revealed their unique status as foreigners:

> With regard to the further fate of the accused and in particular of the British engineers in the present case, it is already clear from course of investigation that possibility of a partial change of measures of prevention is not excluded. Possibility of liberation from custody on bail of three engineers whose examination is on the point of completion is not excluded.[158]

Despite this serious setback Ovey's view from Moscow remained that the Soviet authorities might yet be turned from their apparent course by British pressure. Though officials in the Narkomindel were informing the diplomatic community that an embargo might cause some economic hardship, they were certain the Soviet Union would gain prestige by "making haughty English who have humiliated us in the past swallow this trial." Such Soviet conviction had been encouraged, the British Ambassador pointed out, by the absence of an unequivocal public warning from His Majesty's Government and was furthered

---

156 Richards to Collier, 24 March 1933, FO 371/17266 N2054/1610/38 and enclosed telegram #32, Vansittart to Ovey, 24 March 1933.

157 Ibid.; and Verbatim Report of Supreme Court of the USSR, *The Case of . . . Charged with Wrecking Activities in the Soviet Union*, p. 72-73.

158 *Izvestiia*, 24 March 1933, p. 1; and Ovey to Simon, 24 March 1933, FO 371/17266 N2053/1610/38.

strengthened when the MVEEC showed interest in the idea of bail. Ovey now recommended an immediate declaration in the Commons which would both threaten an embargo and intimate a subsequent rupture of relations if the whole affair were not brought to a swift end.[159]

Ovey's insistence on a clear and strongly worded response to the Soviet announcement that there would be a trial, particularly his repetition of his long-held view that the threat to diplomatic relations should become part of the British arsenal, was important because it implied that the more cautious approach favoured by Vansittart and Simon was a misguided failure. While it is not clear what meaningful distinction Ovey thought existed in international law between an avowed respect for sovereign rights and a vehement refusal to endorse the exercise of those rights in light of Vyshinskii's announcement, Ovey once again insisted that the hard line was the only line.

It fell to Vansittart to draft a memorandum for the Cabinet on the recent turn of events and Ovey's interpretation of the new situation. The Permanent Under-Secretary noted Ovey's recommendation that a direct threat to commercial and diplomatic relations should now be made by Britain in a last attempt to prevent the trial altogether, but he once again argued that such a policy would be ill advised at this juncture. Though an acquittal in a Soviet court would be "unprecedented," the proper course was to

> proceed without further delay to state publicly our intention to take action against Soviet imports. . . . It seems undesirable to declare in Parliament that we will in fact take action in this if the prisoners are condemned, as this might be held by the Opposition to prejudge the question whether such evidence as may be produced at the trial may justify condemnation, and would make it more difficult for the Soviet Government to order an acquittal without undue loss of face.[160]

Vansittart's recommendations had the political advantage that, by avoiding a public statement which would connect the trade embargo to the outcome of the trial, the British government could try to minimize the criticism voiced in certain sectors of the press and from Opposition politicians that they were meddling in the judicial process of a foreign power. At the same time it could be argued that resolute action had been taken. Vansittart still strongly objected to any threat to diplo-

---

159 Ibid., 24 March 1933, FO 371/17266 N2066/1610/38.
160 Memorandum by Vansittart, 24 March 1933, FO 371/17266 N2106/1810/38 which was discussed in Cabinet on 29 March 1933, CAB23/75, 22(33)2.

matic relations — the most extreme of Ovey's recommendations — but he wanted to authorize Ovey to inform his hosts that any conviction whatsoever would result in the embargo taking place after 17 April.[161]

While British officials deliberated their options, the Soviet press, having announced that a trial would definitely be held, attacked the British position vigorously. *Izvestiia* carried articles that ridiculed the "arrogance" of the British imperialists who sought to treat the Soviet Union as a colonial possession by dismissing Soviet sovereign rights. There were also objections raised against the posture of the MVEEC regarding the posting of bail: "The English firm finds it necessary to state that if they go bail, that in no way implies approval of a trial. 'Who asked for the approval' the *Izvestiya* enquires, 'and how is this necessary to a Soviet court?' "[162]

Consistent with the belligerency of the Soviet press was the confidence exhibited by the Narkomindel's Press Department. Ovey reported that these Soviet officials were convinced that the British were now interested only in a fair trial and proper treatment of the prisoners. In a thinly disguised critique of the lack of support he had hitherto received from His Majesty's Government, Ovey speculated that the absence of a Commons declaration had further encouraged Soviet resolve, but he advised that it was still possible "through a skilfully worded, yet unequivocal form of declaration, accompanied by exact definition of what alone will satisfy us, to dictate to Soviet government where and how this final surrender shall take place."[163] Not only were Ovey's terms in this "diktat" extremely harsh and amazingly optimistic, but his continued inability or unwillingness to concede that the Soviets had a "right" to hold a trial, as he had been informed previously by both British and Soviet officials, was striking indeed. It marked yet another instance in which recommendations emanating from the British Ambassador in Moscow differed markedly from policy as it was understood by those in London.

On 28 March Ovey met with Litvinov. Though they did not realize it at the time, this was to be Ovey's final representation to the Soviet government. The details of their final encounter reflect the substantial decline their relationship had undergone as a result of the MVEEC affair. Ovey was armed with the strongest authorization he was to receive from London. The day before, Vansittart had told him that he

---

161 Ibid.
162 *Izvestiia* 26 March 1933, p. 1; and Ovey to Simon, 26 March 1933, FO 371/17266
     N2102/1610/38.
163 Ibid.

was to inform Litvinov that embargo powers would be in place in time for the trial unless Ovey supplied "good news" in the meantime.[164] Litvinov, with his usual gruffness, told Ovey that the Public Prosecutor's evidence on the engineers was thought to be "sufficient" to hold a trial. When confronted with Ovey's communication concerning a British embargo, Litvinov retorted, "you cannot employ such methods with U.S.S.R. as with Mexico." This last remark, which was reported in the Soviet press the same day, was a direct personal insult to Ovey, who had been posted to Mexico prior to his tenure in Moscow. It brought the stormy session to an abrupt halt and convinced both Ovey and his superiors in London that his personal involvement in the MVEEC affair should come to an end.[165] The following day, Ovey was instructed to return to London "for consultation," and the Embassy was left under the capable direction of the Chargé d' Affaires, William Strang.[166] Litvinov's confrontational rebuttal of Ovey's communication and the public remonstrances against British policy to date in the MVEEC case strongly suggest that, while the Soviet authorities had not initiated the arrest of the British engineers with a coordinated policy, they had now arrived at one.

The Cabinet met on 29 March, and adopted, without amendment, Vansittart's more moderate recommendations that focussed on the trade embargo rather than diplomatic relations. In general it was thought that a trade embargo could not now prevent a trial, but that the extent of the enforcement of the powers to restrict Soviet exports to Britain might be directly connected to the treatment of the prisoners and the result of the trial. Runciman submitted a draft of a possible embargo bill and an accompanying commentary on the possible effects that such a bill might have on Britain and the Soviet Union.[167] He highlighted the costs to consumers that would be incurred by restricting the entry of cheap Russian goods into Britain. The most heavily hit sectors would be those involved in the building industry and textiles. Such restrictions would also increase the costs of consumer goods such as furs and fish. Additional damage would be done to British creditors who had outstanding accounts with the Soviet Union. According to Runciman, these totalled, along with British government credits, in the order of 15 million pounds. The private creditors might have to be compen-

164 Vansittart to Ovey, 27 March 1933, FO 371/17266 N2101/1610/38.
165 Ovey to Simon, 28 March 1933, FO 371/17266 N2140/1610/38.
166 Simon to Ovey, 29 March 1933, FO 371/17266 N2204/1610/38.
167 Draft Russian Goods (Import Prohibition) Bill, C.P. 85(33) and C.P. 86(33) by Runciman were discussed by Cabinet on 29 March 1933, CAB 23/75, 22(33)2.

sated once the bill was introduced and, without credits, it was likely that Soviet trade would go elsewhere.

A British embargo also the raised the danger of Soviet retaliation. Though Soviet purchases in Britain were relatively small, certain industries, most notably the machine industries sector of which the MVEEC was a part, had found the growth in the Soviet market an important exception to the otherwise depressed condition of world trade. Runciman also warned that the Soviets might deliberately try to undercut Britain in eastern European markets as an act of retaliation. The President of the Board of Trade tried to cast a promising light on the British strategy by reminding the Cabinet that it was unlikely that Soviet gold reserves could compensate, over the longer term, for the lack of the foreign exchange created by a British boycott. Runciman did raise the issue that Soviet imports were likely to decline over the next years in any case, but the discussion contained in the Cabinet conclusions did not resolve or even address the apparent contradiction that, if the Soviets needed fewer imports, they needed fewer export markets to pay for the imports as well. With these reservations it was decided to proceed with the drafting of the Russian Goods (Import Prohibition) Bill.[168]

On 3 April the National Government revealed its intention to seek embargo powers against Soviet trade in the Commons.[169] The urgency of the measure, MacDonald insisted, required that the Russian Import Prohibition Bill should receive speedy passage within the next two days. Undoubtedly opposition Liberal and Labour opinion would have been resistant to such a rapid transaction on this subject in any case, but the vague justifications and unclear intent of the embargo powers quickly inflamed opposition opinion. Lansbury challenged the government to justify why the cooperation of the House should be forthcoming when it had not been apprised of all the facts of the case. Since neither the details of the proposed legislation nor the details of the correspondence and conversations that had taken place between Ovey and the government were yet public, Lansbury recommended that a White Paper be provided before any legislation was considered.

MacDonald's response to this and similar objections was not very reassuring to those who feared a hidden agenda which would see a long-term anti-Soviet slant to British policy developing out of the specific measure now proposed. The Prime Minister refused to clarify the

---

168 Ibid.
169 *H.C. Deb. 5 s.*, col. 1431-37.

exact intent of the embargo bill and sought to portray the forthcoming bill as a simple enabling act without describing what, in fact, it would finally "enable." He lamely told the House that since the Anglo-Soviet trade agreement was to expire by 17 April something had to be done in any case about trade relations, but this line of argument was both misleading and unconvincing. Both Lansbury and the leading Liberal critic Sir Herbert Samuel pursued MacDonald throughout the question period, and in the midst of the debate the frustrated MacDonald demanded that what he had "announced must be accepted by the House of Commons."[170] Given the overwhelming majority enjoyed by the National Government this claim was undoubtedly true, but in the heated climate of the Commons, pointing out such a truth was indeed unwise. Those members of the Commons who were already predisposed to resist now became still more indignant and those who were inclined to an anti-Soviet posture had their die-hard hopes raised even further.[171] In the debates that were to come over the next couple of days, the government had to endure a protracted if futile assault from the opposition members in an increasingly combative Commons.

It was perhaps to alleviate some of the concerns voiced in the question period of 3 April that, by 5 April, the day of the second reading of the Import Prohibition Bill, the House was provided with a White Paper[172] containing selected diplomatic correspondence that had passed between Moscow and London. In a lengthy summary of the contents of the White Paper and its bearing on the swift passage of the Bill,[173] Foreign Secretary Simon drew a portrait of a totalitarian regime engaged in a reign of terror which had wrongly, but characteristically, drawn a "great British company" into its web of proletarian justice and third-degree methods. He claimed that there was no direct or immediate connection between the Bill and the proceedings in Moscow, but that by passing the Bill at this time the Soviet state might yet come to understand the "real gravity of the situation."[174]

It fell to Sir Stafford Cripps to launch the opposition of the Labour minority. In his view the very tendentious picture of events that Simon's commentary outlined and the incomplete set of documents provided in the White Paper — they covered the affair only up to March 16 — disclosed "no adequate ground for the demand made by

---

170 Ibid., col. 1436.
171 Lammers, "The Engineers' Trial," p. 262.
172 Command Paper 4286.
173 *H.C. Deb. 5 s.*, 276, cols. 1767-1890.
174 Ibid., col. 1783.

His Majesty's Government for the liberation of the employees of the Metropolitan-Vickers Company at Moscow without trial."[175] Moreover, the arguments put forth by the British government did not, in Cripps' opinion, establish a credible case for the imposition of a trade embargo.

Having attacked the evidence upon which the government claims were made, Cripps set about developing a critique of the legal basis for the proposed "intervention" into Soviet domestic politics. While acknowledging that in such instances the Foreign Office had every right to be informed by the Soviet authorities of the ongoing judicial process, he argued, as had the legal counsel at the Foreign Office previously,[176] that international precedent demanded that no objection could rightly be raised until the local courts had made a final decision. Cripps cited three instances from international law which he maintained upheld his view. These examples ranged from an eighteenth-century letter of the Duke of Newcastle to the King of Prussia, and an 1828 letter by the United States Secretary of State, Henry Clay, which discussed similar problems in South America. Perhaps more pointedly Cripps referred to the views of the eminent British Justice, Sir Robert Phillimore, who argued in *Commentaries on International Law*[177] that:

> The State to which the foreigner belongs may interfere for his protection when he has received positive maltreatment, or when he has been denied ordinary justice in the foreign country.... The State must be satisfied that its citizen has exhausted the means of legal redress afforded by the tribunals of the country in which he has been injured.... It is only after those propositions have been irrefragably proved that the State of a foreigner can demand reparation.[178]

A key element in Cripps' analysis of this aspect of international law was his judgement that once Britain had recognized the Soviet regime as the government of the USSR, the precept of international law, as outlined above, was operative. Given this "truth," Cripps went on to contend that no real facts had arisen to suggest that the British engineers were not going to receive justice as it was meted out in the So-

---

175 Ibid., col. 1784.
176 See the views of Bennett and Fitzmaurice outlined above.
177 Published in 1889. Sir Robert Phillimore was a Justice of the High Court of the Admiralty and is not to be confused with his son, Sir Walter George Frank Phillimore, who was also specialist in international law and Lord Justice of Appeal from 1913 to 1916. The latter served as British legal counsel at the drafting of the Treaty of Versailles and edited the third edition of his father's *Phillimore's International Law: Three Centuries of Peace and Their Teachings*, vol. 4 (1917).
178 H.C. Deb. 5 s., 276, cols. 1786-89.

viet Union; and, hence, no rightful objection could be raised until the Soviet courts had arrived at a conclusion. On the contrary, it seemed to Cripps that the British engineers were receiving exceptionally good treatment since five of the six were already out on bail.[179]

There was no shortage of Conservative members who wished to refute Cripps' dissertation on the Metro-Vickers affair. Throughout his speech he had been interrupted by angry shouts and objections. When Major Hills embarked on his rebuttal, he did so on the same grounds as Cripps had chosen to base his case — that of international law. Quoting from a work by the widely known Cambridge scholar, Francis Oppenheim, Hills stressed that "corrupt administration of the law against natives is no excuse for the same against aliens, and no Government can cloak itself with the judgement of corrupt judges."[180] Hills also returned to the source of Cripps's authority on international law, Phillimore, and drawing on a passage subsequent to that quoted by Cripps, countered that, "a plain violation of the substance of natural justice, e.g., refusing to hear the party or to allow him to call witnesses, would amount to the same thing as an absolute denial of justice."[181]

It was here that the principal root of disagreement, aside from whatever political opportunism existed in the debates, was revealed. Conservative opinion did not accept that international recognition of the Soviet Union carried with it a recognition of the legitimacy of its domestic order. For them, international "equality" and hence, international law, did not really apply to the Soviet case, since the very nature of Soviet political life precluded justice as that term was normally understood by members of the comity of nations. Ironically, the Soviets themselves repeatedly argued that they were opposed to "bourgeois justice" as practised by other states, but of course for citizens of the proletarian state this was supposed to be a merit rather than a flaw. For those on the British Left, however, it was easy to see that the Soviet Union was one of a number of political "experiments" that were operating in the troubled years of the Depression, but it was clear to

---

179 Ibid., cols. 1790-98. *The Times* (London), 5 April, p. 5, reported that on the previous evening Thornton, Cushny, and Gregory had been released on bail though MacDonald remained in prison.

180 Ibid., col. 1802. Oppenheim held the Whelwell Chair of International Law at Cambridge prior to the Great War and was the author of *International Law: A Treatise*, published in two volumes in 1905 and 1906. He was a regular consultant to the Foreign Office during these years and part of the "positivist" school of international law which held that such laws were derived from custom and the "quasi-legislation" of international convention.

181 Ibid.

them that it was not the worst of these, given the fascist menace in Italy and Germany. If the National Government applied different standards to the Soviet Union than it did to fascist powers, it did so, in the view of its Labour critics, for political rather than humanitarian reasons.

In the long debates of April 5 and 6, variations on these themes came through in bitter challenges and rebuttals over the proposed Russian Goods (Import Prohibition) Bill. In the event, nothing could be done to stop its passage, although the heat of the debate may have tempered the government's resolve such that it promised to use the Bill only in connection with the case of the engineers and agreed to limit its powers to three months. At that time it would once again be subject to parliamentary approval.[182] The passage of the Bill set the stage for an Anglo-Soviet confrontation in the event of a trial being held and any adverse verdict being rendered. The powers included in the Bill enabled action against about 80 percent of Soviet imports for three months, beginning on 18 April.[183] By delaying the enactment of the prohibitions until after the trial would be completed the National Government technically avoided transgressing international law by delaying their intervention until the Soviet judicial process had run its course, but there could be little doubt that in passing the legislation before the trial was begun the British government hoped to influence the tenor of the show trial that would begin 12 April.

Lammers has suggested that it was likely that the "National government's response would have been more restrained had the incident occurred in any other country, even one under Fascist rule," and that the "ultimate objection is not that the National government was 'discriminating' against Soviet Russia, but that it did not sufficiently 'discriminate' against Nazi Germany and Fascist Italy."[184] It would be easier to accept such a verdict as a whole if it were not for the evidence against the engineers outlined above, particularly the role the MVEEC apparently played with the IIC. On the basis of current evidence it is hard to maintain the image of a stalwart National Government rising to the defence of innocent victims of a communist-totalitarian regime who were guilty of no real "crimes," but had the misfortune of labouring for a spiteful regime in a deeply paranoid society. In this instance at least the Soviets appeared to have something to be "paranoid" about, and the arrest of the British engineers was not a completely bogus, po-

---

182 *H.C. Deb. 5 s.*, 276, cols. 1933-2032, 6 April 1933.
183 CAB 23/75, 27(33)1, 12 April 1933, Russian Goods (Import Prohibition) Act, C.P. 101(33).
184 Lammers, "The Engineers' Trial," p. 263.

litically inspired frame-up. That the Soviet authorities could, and did, deem it necessary to turn the public show trial, which resulted from the MVEEC arrests, into a Stalinist "morality play" replete with dubious "confessions" and transparent political "lessons" for the consumption of Soviet citizens, had much to do with the role of the judiciary and the place of the Metro-Vickers trial in the development of Soviet political culture in the 1930s.

4

In the Bowels of the Lubianka

> Wherever the law exists, crime can be found.
> — Aleksander Solzhenitsyn, *The Gulag Archipelago*

For the student of the Metro-Vickers trial, the existence of both Soviet and British documentary evidence provides a unique opportunity to examine the methods of the OGPU during the pre-trial interrogation and to assess the manner in which "evidence" and "confessions" were produced. In contrast to the other show trials of this period, where the defendants or "victims" were Soviet citizens who failed to leave a record of their experience — usually because of immediate "liquidation" or imprisonment in labour camps — the memoir literature, press coverage, Foreign Office depositions and interviews, and the 800-page Soviet trial transcript make it possible to reconstruct many facets of this event from the perspective of both the accused and accusers.

While it is clear that the recollections of the arrested engineers after their arrest and sentencing were tendentiously shaped by the tribulations they had recently undergone, the corroborating detail regarding past events and persons makes these sources a rich store of information about the years leading up to the debacle of 1933. It also seems likely that their ability to produce detailed accounts of such experiences was "aided" by the rigorous interrogation of Soviet officials, who directed such sessions by using Thornton's diary and notebooks as keys to their investigation.

As with most *post factum* accounts of potentially embarrassing or incriminating events there remains the possibility that those involved might consciously conceal or distort the critical facts. In the cases of the depositions of Thornton and MacDonald,[1] which were produced three months after their arrest, trial, and imprisonment, this concern is perhaps the greatest, but there are a number of reasons to believe that any conscious distortion of the events which led to their arrests was minimal. In the first instance, both men knew that the Foreign Office officials and the MVEEC officials had questioned the other four engineers about the whole affair, and since most of the important observations and episodes were shared by more than one engineer, Thornton and MacDonald, had they chosen to, could not misrepresent events without directly contradicting the testimony of the others. There is no evidence that either the Foreign Office officials or the directors of the MVEEC found many fundamental discrepancies in the testimony of the six engineers.

A further factor adding strength to this line of reasoning, and making it unlikely that any devious strategy was mapped out by the engineers in concert, is that the six engineers did not all work together as a group, but were usually scattered across the USSR at their various postings. Once the crisis enveloped them, conditions did not lend themselves to developing a strategy which would enable them to get their "story" straight if they thought it necessary to do so. They were kept apart while in prison, and in conversations with embassy staff during the diplomats' periodic visits to the Lubianka prison, they were prevented from raising issues relating to their arrest. Just prior to the trial it is possible that five of the six met after all, but since MacDonald still was not released on bail it was impossible to produce a unified strategy for the trial. Those at liberty did confer at the British Embassy in the days leading up to the trial, but by this time Thornton, at least, showed signs of depression and despondency and was generally reluctant to discuss what had happened. Since he and the imprisoned MacDonald were the only two who had signed damaging "confessions" which incriminated both British and Soviet citizens, such a state of mind is understandable.[2] At the trial these two men repeatedly changed their position from admitting guilt to claiming innocence. The reasons for their actions will be discussed later, but for now it is enough to point out that such shifts were greeted with surprise by the other engineers and British officials.[3] This strongly suggests that these

---

1 See the Introduction, n.16 for the citations.

2 MacDonald, Foreign Office Deposition, 3 July 1933; Bush House Interviews, 9 May 1933; Strang, *Home and Abroad*, p. 92-93.

3 See Monkhouse's testimony to Wylie in the Bush House Interviews, 9 May 1933 and Strang's complaints about Monkhouse's trial testimony in Strang to Collier, 28 April 1933, PRO MacDonald MSS PREM 1/137.

two engineers felt it necessary to pursue their own strategy and, while British officials had made recommendations for the engineers' conduct during the trial, there was no generally agreed-upon line of action in operation. Taken as a whole, such circumstances make the possibility of a carefully coordinated and sanitized coverup exceedingly remote, if not impossible.

In the case of Allan Monkhouse's memoir account, *Moscow, 1911-33*, the considerations which apply to the depositions cited above hold true in at least as strong a measure. Monkhouse kept notes on various business transactions and, as the senior MVEEC official in the Soviet Union, had access to Company records to help reconstruct his portrait of past events in that country. He also selected material for his book from the articles he authored for the British press, and in particular, the *Manchester Guardian*, immediately following his expulsion from the Soviet Union. The conversations he had with British diplomats during the crisis, as recorded in the Foreign Office correspondence, are accurately reflected in his memoir account. Since Monkhouse was among the least threatened by the Soviet charges and his memoir account can be substantiated by the testimony of the British diplomatic corps, there is little reason to believe he was deliberately trying to mislead readers in his account of the affair.

At least as important as the conscious manipulation of past events are the subconscious or unspoken assumptions which are revealed in the testimony of these sources. Though there are uneven amounts of material available for all the MVEEC personnel involved, it is possible to develop some outlines of individual and general features of their thinking about living and working in the Soviet Union which proved to be important during their interrogation.

It must be said that Monkhouse's account of the Soviet "experiment" was very sympathetic even after his arrest and trial, and his continued interest in Soviet electrification after his expulsion suggests that one factor which motivated him was a keen interest in the innovative technological and economic strategy of the USSR in this period. Joan Hoff Wilson has raised this point concerning the technically oriented sponsors of American recognition of the Soviet Union — often engineers — who were enthralled with the prospects of gigantic planned projects that were often on the cutting edge of technology.[4]

---

4 Joan Hoff Wilson, *Ideology and Economics: U.S Relations with the Soviet Union, 1918-1933* (Columbia: University of Missouri Press, 1974), p. 118-19. An example of an American engineer's view of this issue is presented by Walter Rukeseyer, "Do Our Engineers in Russia Damage America?," *Scribner's Magazine*, 10 (1931), p. 521-24.

Certainly this characteristic surfaces in the MVEEC employees in general, and the accused engineers often stressed the purely practical nature of their work while many around them — sadly many of the company's own Soviet employees and their Soviet engineering colleagues — were paying a political price for their association with the British firm.

There is, however, more in Monkhouse's view of the Soviet Union than mere excitement about electrification projects. Perhaps more than any of the other British engineers stationed there, Monkhouse, as the acting-manager of the MVEEC in Moscow, was not simply an engineer with technical skills, but also possessed qualities that made him comfortable in high-level contract negotiations as well as the formal engagements with leading Soviet officials that he attended as the MVEEC representative. This contact with the upper levels of Soviet society was coupled with an extensive knowledge of, and concern for, the varied Soviet citizenry which Monkhouse knew from his wide travels throughout the country. However involuntary the role of the common citizen might be in the Soviet "experiment," Monkhouse thought that the Soviet government would overcome the difficulties it faced.[5] He was in a unique position to have access to the problems which faced both the state and society. Indeed, it would later be suggested that it was just such knowledge that made the MVEEC, in particular, a target for OGPU action.[6]

Before turning to the experience of interrogation, some insights into the OGPU action can be gained by considering their behaviour during the arrests of 11 March. It has already been noted that the OGPU conducted simultaneous arrests in Leningrad and Moscow that evening. Monkhouse's memoir provides a revealing account of the OGPU personnel involved and their apparent purpose. The force which arrested him and Thornton at the MVEEC compound were in general appearance and "smartness . . . about the best group of men" Monkhouse had seen in the USSR.[7] They came well armed and were led by one Feldman, a deputy-chief in the EKU section of the OGPU, who had warrants to search the premises, an activity which took almost five hours.

During the search a couple of key qualities of the OGPU struck Monkhouse. While they were thorough and dogged in their search, those who knew any English at all handled the language badly, and

---

5 Monkhouse, *Moscow*, p. 331.
6 Strang to Collier, 20 April 1933, FO 371/17270 N2944/1610/38.
7 Monkhouse, *Moscow*, p. 289.

Monkhouse sensed that many of them were out of their depth. In one instance, Monkhouse was asked to account for his child's drawing of a "puffer" fish — Feldman was concerned that it was a drawing of some Soviet installation. In another case it was discovered that Monkhouse's income tax correspondence was on letterhead that included the words "On His Britannic Majesty's Service," and these documents were immediately seized upon as probable evidence that Monkhouse was a spy. Yet, when Monkhouse's Union Jack and his portraits of the British sovereigns were found, Feldman dismissed these with the words, "that is all right — that is understandable," and carefully wrapped up the portraits himself! Still more curious was the fact that when the OGPU discovered the large blueprint drawings of electrical installations the engineers did have in their possession and were clearly the most likely evidence of "industrial intelligence" gathering, they were completely ignored. Monkhouse judged from this that the OGPU team was poorly educated or inadequately briefed on technical matters.[8]

Monkhouse's observations about the type of men the OGPU used in their operations against the MVEEC recalls the character "Gletkin" from Arthur Koestler's *Darkness at Noon*. Born in peasant or working-class surroundings, with little education and experience of Western life, these "red" loyalists formed the raw machinery of the Stalinist state and were clear winners during the Stalin Revolution. Monkhouse's view of the OGPU was reinforced by his first experience with a Soviet interrogator, one Belogorskii, who was apparently well known for his ferocious demeanour. Monkhouse described him as a man who was "capable of making his strong personality and will felt in dealings with his victims, he was, however, not a man of any education, and was certainly not well-informed beyond his own particular sphere."[9]

This point is more strongly made by contrasting this characterization with the portrait Monkhouse offered of Andrei Vyshinskii and his assistant, Roginskii. Vyshinskii was by far the most educated man Monkhouse met during the case and was "a very different type from the OGPU investigators." Monkhouse noted that he saw Vyshinskii reading *The Times* (London) and other foreign newspapers, and he imagined that "outside the Moscow Court he would prove to be a well-informed and cultured man of the old-intelligentzia, but on the other hand he is a man of extreme political views who has thrown himself heart and soul into the Communist cause, thus winning for himself the high position in the

---

8 Ibid., p. 290-91.
9 Ibid., p. 294.

State which he occupies."[10] The younger man, Roginskii, was typical of the other men Monkhouse had met in the OGPU, but he lacked even that bit of politeness which most of the others exhibited. "He has the face and manner of a bully, and his methods during my examination and in Court did not belie his appearance," Monkhouse observed.[11]

Another factor that needs to be included in any account of arrest and imprisonment is the role of fear. From the accounts of Monkhouse, Thornton, and MacDonald it is evident that their fear grew as the seriousness of the OGPU purpose became clearer and as the ordeal dragged on and on. The first real signs of fear and disorientation following the arrests are found in Monkhouse's account of his first hours in the Lubianka prison, and he claims that his feelings were shared by the other MVEEC men as well. Upon arriving at the prison at around 2 a.m., Monkhouse caught a glimpse of Thornton, who had been taken in a separate vehicle, and he also saw Kutuzova in a corridor. This was the first confirmation that she had been arrested and heightened his sense that the case was enveloping the whole firm. Monkhouse was then escorted up five flights of stairs and asked to wait. An hour later he was ushered into a small lift which proceeded to descend five floors.

> I subsequently found that my colleagues were similarly impressed by this small sheet-iron box into which one was locked alone, and relatively slowly lowered five floors. Perhaps our alarm was because we had none of us realized we were on the fifth floor to start with, and imagined we were being lowered into one of the subterranean dungeons with which rumours accredit the dreaded Lubianka.[12]

Once arriving at the first floor, Monkhouse had to ascend four more flights to the prisoner-receiving room which was kept at the temperature of a "turkish bath." Here he was asked to strip naked, and anything that might be used for suicidal purposes was removed from him.[13] Finally he was taken to his cell, #96, which was clean and very sparsely furnished, but was the fairly large size of 14 feet by 9 feet. It was hard for Monkhouse to relax and collect himself with a bright light burning continuously and the guards opening the peep-hole every 10 minutes or so.[14] Fortunately for Monkhouse, he would only have to endure this regime for the next two days, until he and Nordwall were unexpectedly released. For three of the four remaining engineers this

---

10 Ibid., p. 307.
11 Ibid.
12 Ibid., p. 292.
13 Ibid., p. 293.
14 Ibid.

ordeal of solitary confinement would continue until 5 April when Gregory, Cushny, and Thornton were released on bail. Only MacDonald remained in custody for the duration of the affair.

Since the confessions of Thornton and MacDonald, and indeed, the use of "confessions" generally in show trials of this type were critical to the case made against the accused, it is necessary to consider the characteristics of this type of "evidence" and its usage in the MVEEC case. While no methods of the "third degree" were employed by the Soviet interrogators, the lengthy sessions of repeated questioning which included tiresome debates over precise wording that might appear harmless, and sometimes petty to a weary British engineer, but had very specific qualities in the minds of Soviet officials, took its toll on the accused. Even more stressful were the multiple "confrontations" that Thornton and MacDonald experienced. In such instances, a shabbily dressed Soviet associate was brought into the room and asked to report on "criminal" activities which invariably implicated one of the British engineers. The tendency of both Thornton and MacDonald was to think themselves in a more secure position than that of their Soviet codefendants, and therefore they could not bring themselves to dispute the claims made by people who had clearly been threatened with great ills if they did not confess to depositions which were sometimes drafted by the Soviet authorities themselves.[15] The net result of facing as many as 60 broken souls and wading through a similar number of written confessions from others accused was to make Thornton and MacDonald look for ways to bend, if not break, under the psychological pressure and physical exhaustion.

Although threats to their own family members were not effective against the British defendants, the two-man interrogation teams did make sure to warn MacDonald and Thornton of the consequences that would befall MacDonald's housekeeper, Riabova, and the MVEEC secretary, Kutuzova, if the engineers did not cooperate. Thornton was warned that Kutuzova's testimony concerning the alleged intimacy of their living arrangements would be made public if he, at any time, repudiated his own confession. It is curious that no action was taken during the trial along these lines, but the threat served its purpose in any event by helping to make Thornton more pliable. It may be that, in the end, the Soviet authorities decided to avoid a scene where Vyshinskii proceeded to brow-beat a humiliated Kutuzova into making public

15 This tactic of drafting the text for the accused was experienced by the British engineers as well. See Monkhouse, *Moscow*, p. 282, 294-95.

statements on this subject. Since they had her confession, why create a scene that might backfire with the foreign audience?

The Soviet authorities were also adept at playing one British engineer off against another. MacDonald claimed that he gave in once he was shown a written confession that Thornton had apparently provided the OGPU. Weary and feeling helpless, MacDonald seized on a slender hope. As he put it, "I thought: 'Well, Thornton has got something up his sleeve; so if he has done that, I can agree with it.' So I said, 'Since you have got all that, I suppose it is so.' "[16] MacDonald's testimony here seems a little strange, since it was only after he himself had confessed and was then involved in a confrontation with Thornton the following day that Thornton finally signed the first of two confessions.[17] The issue can be clarified, however, because one of the standard tactics used in these interrogations was to give a dictated statement to a British accused and have him translate it in his own hand into English. The statement that MacDonald saw in Thornton's handwriting, from the description of its contents, was not one of the confessions used during the trial and was likely one of those statements which Thornton refused to sign, but which he did translate. It was a simple matter to take this document and present it to a worn-down MacDonald as a genuine "confession." This produced the desired result with him and also encouraged Thornton's own capitulation. Given this scenario, it was understandable that relations between the two during the trial were decidedly cool.

Their growing awareness of the seriousness of the situation also contributed to the decline of their morale. Both men claimed in their depositions that they gradually came to fear for their own lives once the scope of the charges and the details of the case became clear to them. One of the factors that increased this sense of vulnerability and helplessness was the amount of information, sometimes dating back 10 years, that the authorities trotted out when needed. This enhanced the sense that nothing had been missed, and that there was no way of avoiding the outcome that the interrogators wanted to see fulfilled.[18]

It was here that the long-standing practice of the close involvement of the MVEEC staff with their Soviet environment was shown to be very risky. Many of the people whom MacDonald and Thornton faced in confrontations had obviously been drawn into the OGPU net of informants many years earlier and could accurately report the whereabouts and contacts of the British engineers over the past several years.

---

16 MacDonald, Foreign Office Deposition, 3 July 1933.
17 Thornton, Foreign Office Deposition, 20 July 1933.
18 Ibid.; and MacDonald, Foreign Office Deposition, 3 July 1933.

It is likely that the the MVEEC's habit of giving gifts to special col-leagues at Electro-Import, including Dolgov,[19] supplementing the salaries of Soviet engineers when the Soviet authorities were late in paying them, or paying extra wages for excellent service[20] created jealousies and enemies as well as loyal friends. It must also be ad-mitted that MacDonald, at least, was given to excessive drinking[21] and, in his associations with Soviet citizens, was drawn to those men who openly criticized their government and thereby drew attention to themselves.[22] As Strang observed after the trial had ended, "when in the company of foreigners the ordinary non-party Russian has an in-curable habit of engaging in anti-Soviet talk."[23] In such a working en-vironment it must have been easy to recruit informants to report on the activities of the foreigners.

Monkhouse captured the dilemma of the prisoner in his memoir account of his own struggle with the interrogator, Belogorskii. Initially Monkhouse fought and clawed against the suggested wording of the statement he was required to make. He sought to rewrite passages from Russian into English in a way that would both protect the MVEEC and would somehow satisfy his interrogator. For Belogorskii, patience was the key. Gradually the hours took their toll and "after midnight I [Monkhouse] felt my nerve was going. I was dead tired. . . . My lips twitched in a way they had never done before. It was a hard mental effort to resist writing exactly what Belogorski [sic] dictated, and, in any case . . . I wrote one or two paragraphs which I greatly re-gret having consented to write."[24] Fortunately for Monkhouse he was able, after much argument, to convince Vyshinskii that these para-graphs could not be true and that he had written them under consider-able strain.[25] It is likely that Vyshinskii allowed the more damning pas-sages to be withdrawn from Monkhouse's statement because the Pros-ecutor knew he had gained enough for his case from the still more pli-able pair, Thornton and MacDonald.

---

19 In discussion with the Foreign Office prior to the trial, Richards was particularly fear-ful that this practice might well be "misunderstood." See Foreign Office minute by Fitzmaurice, 25 March 1933, FO 371/17266 N2094/1610/38.
20 MacDonald admitted this during his interrogation, and this practice appears gener-ally consistent with the MVEEC's policy towards their Soviet associates. See Mac-Donald, Foreign Office Deposition, 3 July 1933.
21 Strang to Simon, 2 April 1933, FO 371/17267 N2289/1610/38.
22 Bush House Interviews, 9 May 1933.
23 Foreign Office Memo by Strang, 20 April 1933, FO 371/17270 N2944/1610/38.
24 Monkhouse, *Moscow*, p. 282-83.
25 Ibid.

Of course once the first "lie" had been granted by Thornton or Mac-Donald, then the next came rather more readily and their instinct was that, having incriminated themselves already, they might as well continue to do so if that meant they could clear someone else. This was the explanation Monkhouse gave about Thornton's rather lengthy confession which outlined an elaborate, if fanciful, MVEEC spy ring. Thornton told Monkhouse that "he had cleared Cushny" with this statement.[26] Cushny, it turned out, had been approached by Soviet intelligence in May 1932, when an inspector of the Commissariat of Foreign Trade suggested to him that the Soviet would pay Cushny for industrial intelligence involving British firms. Cushny's impression was that "the idea was to start me off with some fairly innocent work and gradually lead me deeper into something which might possibly be secret service work."[27]

This suggests some "mirror imaging" on the part of the Soviet authorities, which was not, as the MVEEC association with the IIC suggests, misplaced. All of the engineers were grilled about their knowledge of Soviet production capabilities, particularly their knowledge of the location and capacity of war production installations. Here the British defendants suffered badly from their lack of knowledge of Soviet law — and little good advice was available to them on this count until after their release — and they were hampered in their attempts to devise a defence strategy by the Soviet refusal to tell them specifically what the charges against them were. Despite the close personal experiences of Stalinist political culture, however, the British engineers on the whole continued to cling to the traditional Western notion that collecting general information of the type the IIC sought to gain from private business sources was not "intelligence" gathering. In Thorton's case, after his release he claimed that he did not know precisely what the Soviet definition of "economic and political spying" entailed. He absolutely denied military spying, but conceded that "If the G.P.U.'s [OGPU] definition is correct, I was certainly guilty, together with all other foreigners who were in Russia, and could get along without an interpreter."[28] MacDonald also reported that he had resisted his Soviet interrogators' claims that his reports to Thornton about airplane and munition production constituted espionage. He told the interrogators, "Oh well, if you insist that these things are spying, then theoretically I have been spying."[29]

---

26 Bush House Interviews, 9 May 1933.
27 Ibid.
28 Thornton, Foreign Office Deposition, 20 July 1933.
29 MacDonald, Foreign Office Deposition, 3 July 1933.

Since this dispute over legal definitions proved to be a central issue in the "confession" and trial of the British engineers, it is necessary to examine the parameters of the criminal charges under the infamous, even "draconian"[30] Article 58 of the Criminal Code of the RSFSR.[31] Enacted in 1926, this special section of the legal code was the centrepiece of the regime's attempt to simplify criminal law — almost reducing it to criminal policy. In practice Article 58 was applied in a manner that gave full vent to its inherently vague and ambiguous clauses. As the testimony in the MVEEC trial would make clear, a "criminal" thought, word, or deed[32] was each sufficient individually to produce a guilty verdict in a Soviet court at the time. This came at a time when the Soviet definition of "criminality" included any intentional or even "accidental" act which could be depicted as damaging to the state.

The specific nuances of the charges which faced the accused in the MVEEC trial are instructive in this regard as well. Article 58-6 pertained to espionage, and, in view of the evidence produced above on the apparent link between the MVEEC and the Industrial Intelligence Centre, one might expect that the Prosecution would have produced substantial evidence which demonstrated the real threat posed by MVEEC engineers who possessed a wide-ranging knowledge of the Soviet Union and had passed such information on to British intelligence services. This did not happen at the trial, and many observers felt that the real Soviet case was kept hidden from view.[33] The most convincing reason for the absence of revelations about British intelligence gathering would seem to be that the Soviets, unlike their British counterparts during the ARCOS crisis of 1927, chose not to reveal how much they knew about British intelligence operations for fear of revealing how they had come to know. One might add here that to the extent that the Prosecution needed hard evidence to produce a conviction, it could and did rely on the numerous confessions to the charge of "information gathering" by Soviet defendants and those of MacDonald and Thornton to obtain the desired result.

Throughout the trial those defendants who were charged under Article 58-6 were pressed to reveal what they knew about the types of

---

30 The term is from Sharlet, "Stalinism and Soviet Legal Culture," p. 164.
31 See Appendix F. For a "literary" assessment of Article 58 see A. Solzhenitsyn's *The Gulag Archipelago* (New York: Harper & Row, 1974), Vol. 1, p. 60-67.
32 This formulation is akin to the Christian doctrine of "sin" present, for example, in the Anglican *Book of Common Prayer*.
33 See Lyons, *Assignment in Utopia*, p. 365; Duranty, *I Write as I Please*, p. 323-24; and Cummings, *The Moscow Trial*, p. 257.

industrial enterprises, the relative efficiency of such enterprises, the location of military factories, and the like. Virtually all transgressions under this article came from its last clause, which dealt with "economic" intelligence that was not "an especially guarded State secret," but nonetheless, should not be transmitted to foreign powers. It was here that the basic dilemma for a private firm which operated in the Soviet Union was manifested, since it was impossible for the Prosecution to allow the kind of separation between "private" and "public" spheres which is common in a liberal, "capitalist" society. This was made even more troublesome for the British engineers, since it is possible, though in the cases of the senior men unlikely, that they knew nothing about the intelligence link between the MVEEC and the IIC.

The problems for the MVEEC's engineers were compounded because in Article 58 of the Criminal Code of the RSFSR (1927) espionage is defined in two ways. On one count the Soviet Code is very similar to Western law and involves the "transmission, theft or collection, with a view to transmission to foreign States . . . of information accounted by reason of its contents an especially guarded State secret." This appears to have been the definition that the British engineers were operating with and one that is recognizable beyond Soviet jurisdiction. In the same section of the legal code on "espionage" however, there are provisions against the

> transmission, theft or collection with a view to transmission of economic information not constituting by virtue of its contents an especially guarded State secret but not intended for divulgence to the organizations or persons enumerated above [foreign States, counter-revolutionary organizations or private persons], as the result of direct prohibition by law or by order of the heads of departments, establishments, or enterprises.[34]

This understanding of "espionage" was much more broadly cast and was widely used by the highly specialized Economic Administration section of the Secret Police in its war against "counter-revolutionary" crimes in the 1920s.[35] Such a definition made it much easier for the engineers to run afoul of Soviet law on these grounds, and it was no accident that it was the Economic Administration section of the OGPU which made the arrests of the Metro-Vickers men.

In addition to the allegations about industrial and military spying, which were buttressed by the threat to expose the allegedly "illicit" re-

---

34 Appendix F, Article 58 of the Criminal Code of the RSFSR (1927), Special Section, Counter-Revolutionary Crimes Art. 58 (vi).
35 See Knight, *The KGB*, p. 16-17.

lationship between Kutuzova and Thornton and Monkhouse, was the charge of "wrecking" brought against the British and Soviet defendants in the case. This charge came under Articles 58-7 and 58-9 which together constituted the crimes of wrecking, sabotage, and diversion. The working definition of "wrecking" (*vreditel'stvo*) that would be used time and again by the Soviet interrogators and Prosecutor Vyshinskii was very broadly cast. A "wrecker" was anyone who by either commission or omission caused, or failed to prevent, damage to state property. Clearly, in instances of deliberate acts taken to destroy a machine, motor, or turbine, cases of "wrecking" are much more simply understood in Western parlance as industrial sabotage. The OGPU investigation and the Commission of Experts that advised the Public Prosecutor claimed that there were a number of such cases that could not be "accidental" in nature. The more significant of these cases will be discussed later, though it is important to note here that the MVEEC's engineers and the British government most strenuously denied intentionally damaging or "wrecking" any Soviet machinery. For their part, Monkhouse and Thornton later claimed that, as professional engineers, they were committed to the construction and maintenance of the electrical enterprises to which they were charged, and that "wrecking" ran against their nature.[36]

During his interrogation, however, Thornton was pressed hard on this charge. In pursuit of information about "wrecking," one of Thornton's interrogators, Zhelesnikov, produced a document with Thornton's handwriting in which the British engineer asked C.S. Richards to replace him with a more "competent" person. The letter was from August 1924 and was found by the OGPU in one of Thornton's technical notebooks. Thornton claimed that it was a draft of a letter that was never sent, but it was just this sort of material, which implied that Thornton was in charge of projects that he himself felt he was unfit to complete properly, that the Soviet interrogators fastened upon.[37]

To be fair to Thornton, it seems clear from his deposition that he did try to mount some kind of strategy in the early going of his interrogation. After the first day of interrogation he realized that the case was much more serious than he ever imagined and he was already fearing that his nerves might give way under the strain. He even had thoughts

---

36 See Monkhouse's discussion of his experience as a "wrecker" during the revolutionary turmoil of 1917 in chapter 1. Thornton's attitude about the charges of wrecking can be gleaned from one of the rare moments he resisted the tendentious flow of the trial proceedings. See Thornton's cross-examination of Krasheninnikov, *The Case*, p. 449-50.

37 Thornton, Foreign Office Deposition, 20 July 1933.

that he would never escape the situation alive. He did try to steady himself, however, and decided that since it seemed that the intelligence angle was the most serious charge, if he felt himself about to give way he should implicate people outside of the country, who were beyond the immediate reach of Soviet law. Students of GULAG memoirs and literature will immediately recognize the pattern in Thornton's thought and see the real hopelessness that it reveals. After the whole affair was over, Monkhouse tried to account for Thornton's weak performance by drawing the attention of the Foreign Office to the fact that on two occasions in 1930, Thornton had nearly died. The first threat to Thornton's life resulted from an electrocution accident, the second, from the bursting of a duodenal ulcer. Thornton had never really recovered physically or mentally from these episodes and was badly burnt out by 1933.[38]

For these reasons it is easy to understand why Thornton's ability to resist was quickly broken when the confrontation with Soviet associates began, because these episodes made it clear to Thornton that people that he knew and cared about, and people that the Soviet authorities could get to, were bound up with his own fate. During the confrontations, Soviet engineers of the old stamp, that is, men associated with the early years of the GOELRO plan and were engineers first and foremost, were brought into the case, and Thornton suffered badly in these confrontations. In one telling instance, N.I. Levinson, whom Thornton had met in London in 1924, and who was very highly regarded by leading engineer-managers in the GOELRO cadre whom we have met earlier, such as Graftio and Vinter, was brought into face Thornton after having signed a confession which claimed that he, Levinson, had been paid by MVEEC manager Simon to keep quiet about the poor performance of the MVEEC switchgear equipment installed at the Volchovstroi project. Thornton claimed that Levinson was a "gentleman" and that the MVEEC would not have dreamed of bribing him, though he did admit to buying Levinson a suit of clothing and perfume for his wife on one occasion. Levinson repaid him with "scrupulous care" for these items, Thornton insisted.[39]

From this confrontation, Thornton grasped the fact that the most technically competent engineers were once again being targeted by the regime, but he also learned that there were limits to the scope of the inquiry as well. Zhelesnikov had earlier complained to Thornton about

---

38 See Monkhouse's comments to Wylie in the Bush House interviews, 9 May 1933.
39 Thornton, Foreign Office Deposition, 20 July 1933.

the MVEEC participation in the foreign cartel which effectively fixed prices for industrial goods sold to the USSR and elsewhere. He now pressed Thornton about the costs of MVEEC switchgear equipment purchased by the Soviets. Thornton attempted to rebuff this complaint with the retort that since Vinter had been the one to order the equipment, "do you think he was bribed by the firm?"[40] Zhelesnikov's immediate response was to warn Thornton never to mention Vinter's name again in the proceedings. This provides the only direct evidence that there were set limits to the sweep being carried out against the technical intelligentsia in 1933.

Over the course of the crisis, however, Strang, who headed the Embassy after Ambassador Ovey's recall, came to believe that in the Soviet electrical industry there "appeared to be a good deal of honest wrecking." This observation had been prompted in part by information from an anonymous member of the MVEEC's staff who claimed that wrecking had occurred at the Moscow electrical power station of MOGES. Such acts were prompted by the frustration of a working class that was overburdened with onerous production norms, Strang's informant had concluded.[41] Similar claims have been made by foreigners who worked as emigré labourers in the USSR during the years of the Great Depression. John Scott, an American who worked in the Soviet steel complex at Magnitogorsk, maintained that "wrecking" did occur and that such acts were often prompted by a desire for revenge against a regime that had, through its repression, created genuine anti-Soviet sentiment.[42] Another American, Andrew Smith, worked as a factory inspector in the Electrozavod works in Moscow in the early 1930s. Contrary to the view offered by Strang's informant and by Scott, Smith found that workers did "wreck" machinery at an alarming rate, but most often did so out of a desire to fulfill their production quota. In such instances the workers tended to improvise techniques and neglected simple maintenance procedures such as the regular oiling and cleaning of their machines. The result was the eventual breakdown of the machinery and even more time and money lost.[43]

---

40 Ibid.

41 Strang to Simon, 17 June 1933, FO 371/17251 N4720/113/38; and ibid., 25 July 1933, FO 371/17251 N5516/113/38.

42 See J. Scott, *Behind the Urals* (Bloomington: Indiana University Press, 1973 [1942]), p. 186-87.

43 Smith, *I Was a Soviet Worker*, p. 59-64. It is unlikely that this Andrew Smith was the same man that Thornton named in his confession of 13 March 1933 since the American Smith recounts numerous experiences on the subject of wrecking, but makes no mention whatsoever of the Metro-Vickers trial. The American Smith was a genuine

In a trial such as the Metro-Vickers trial, both Scott's and Smith's explanations for wrecking would be fused into one criminal act. The confessions of wrecking, diversion, and sabotage, given by men such as the Soviet defendants Gussev, Lobanov, Sukhoruchkin, and Zorin made a strong impression on some members of the audience at the trial, and A. Cummings, the *News Chronicle* reporter, became convinced that these men were true anti-Soviet criminals.[44] As for the charges against the British defendants, these men were to be portrayed by the Prosecutor as the manipulators of the Soviet engineers, and hence avoided in the main the charge of carrying out the wrecking themselves.

If any additional latitude was needed for the Soviet court it was provided under Article 58-11, which pertained to "any type of organizational activity" which could be shown to have a connection to the perpetration of any of the other crimes under Article 58. Alexander Solzhenitsyn has claimed, in his *Gulag Archipelago*, that this article was so broadly enforced that in practice no organization was even needed for the prosecution's case to be made.[45] In the MVEEC trial, Article 58-11 was perhaps most important to the prosecution of the British engineers since it made it easier to pursue a line of questioning which drew the periodic visits of C.S. Richards and other MVEEC personnel into a sinister international plot. This was particularly useful for Vyshinskii when he pressed Thornton on his confession of 13 March that had named Richards and 27 other British MVEEC engineers as active agents directed by British intelligence.[46] It was also the main hint during the trial that the Soviets had made the link themselves between the information gathered by the MVEEC's men in the field and its eventual transmission to the Industrial Intelligence Centre. For Vyshinskii's point to be made it was sufficient to remind the Court of Thornton's confession and then to minimize the engineer's attempts at repudiation. As we shall see, the Public Prosecutor was well armed with the necessary wit, sarcasm, and authority to succeed in the latter task once Thornton had provided the makings of a case against himself.

---

fellow-traveller for a short time and not an employee of the MVEEC. It appears that all 27 of the individuals named by Thornton were employed by the MVEEC at some time.

44 Cummings, *The Moscow Trial*, p. 181. Though the *News Chronicle* had a "Russophile" reputation, Cummings claimed that he had hitherto resisted the notion that saboteurs and wreckers were assaulting Soviet industrial enterprises and the State.

45 Solzhenitsyn, *The Gulag Archipelago*, vol. 1, p. 66.

46 *The Case*, p. 256-57.

5

The Metro-Vickers Show Trial

> The dictatorship of the proletariat is authority unlimited
> by any statutes whatever. But the dictatorship of the pro-
> letariat, creating its own laws, makes use of them, de-
> mands that they be observed, and punishes breaches of
> them. Dictatorship of the proletariat does not signify an-
> archy and disorder but, on the contrary, strict order and
> firm authority which operates upon strict principles.
> — Andrei Vyshinskii, *The Law of the Soviet State*

The trial which the British government had strained first to discourage, and then, to influence with the passage of embargo-enabling powers, took place 12-19 April as a special session of the Supreme Court of the USSR in the House of Trade Unions[1] in Moscow. As the drama of the trial unfolded under the able direction of the Public Prosecutor of the Russian Republic (RSFSR),[2] Andrei Vyshinskii, two dimensions of the Metro-Vickers affair became increasingly evident. At the level of inter-national politics the trial, amply covered by foreign reporters as well as the Soviet press, was an opportunity for the machinery of the Soviet Supreme Court to demonstrate to the world the measured and just re-sponse foreign spies and saboteurs would receive in the workers' state. In the end, the sentences would be light by standards of the day and Soviet justice could be portrayed, in this instance at least, as "gener-

---

1 Before the Revolution this building was known as the Hall of Columns or the Moscow Nobles' Club.
2 Vyshinskii would gain all-Union status in June 1933 as the Deputy Procurator under
Akulov and in 1935 would be promoted to the Procurator-General post himself.

ous." Explanations for Soviet behaviour in the trial varied, and the British government was quick to assert that the sentences rendered by the Soviet court were conditioned by the stern pressure exerted by the British diplomatic barrage and the threat of economic sanctions. While it would be wrong to ignore the force of this argument, the analysis offered below maintains that other factors firmly rooted in the politics of Stalin's Russia were at work as well.

In the realm of Soviet domestic politics the trial was significant for two reasons. In the short term, by summoning up renewed threats from saboteurs and wreckers the trial resurrected images from the earlier Shakhty and Industrial Party Trials and restated the need for continued vigilance against the remaining contaminants of the bourgeois order which still sought to undermine the achievements of the five-year plans. Unlike any of the trials that had come before or would follow in the Great Purges of 1936-38, the key defendants in the Metro-Vickers trial were foreigners[3] and thus the threat from foreign powers could be emphasized much more directly. In this sense the trial could be used by the Soviet leadership as a mechanism to deflect criticism over the recent hardships suffered by the populace away from the regime and onto British machinations.

More important for the development of Soviet society over the longer term, the trial also marked a decisive moment in the debates over what constituted "socialist legality" that had been raging during the cultural revolution of the late 1920s and early 1930s. On one side of this debate were those radical legal theorists such as Pashukanis, Stuchka, and the RSFSR Commissar of Justice, Krylenko,[4] who advocated the merits of "revolutionary justice." At the core of Pashukanis' radical analysis of law was a nihilist conviction that the socialist transition to communism could not be facilitated by new legal forms since the "law" was inherently a tool of bourgeios domination. Rather, the "law," like the state, would wither away (*otmiranie prava*) as the class

---

3 To be sure there were three Germans arrested at the time of the Shakhty trial of 1928, and one of them stood trial alongside the 50 Soviet mining engineers charged in the case. The central thrust of that case, however, was on the unreliable nature of "bourgeois specialists" generally in relation to the construction of socialism, and the main focus was on the Russian accused. See Bailes, *Technology and Society*, p. 82-84.

4 The most extensive discussion of the these debates is provided by Eugene Huskey in *Russian Lawyers*. Important contributions are made by Sharlet, "Stalinism and Soviet Legal Culture," p. 155-79; Sharlet and Beirne, "In Search of Vyshinsky," p. 153-77; Huskey, "Vyshinskii," p. 414-28; Solomon, "Local Political Power," p. 305-29; and P. Solomon, "Soviet Criminal Justice and the Great Terror," *Slavic Review*, 46, 3/4 (1987): 391-413.

conflict which the Bolsheviks had inherited from the old regime diminished with the gradual deepening of socialism's hold over Soviet society. The "law" would therefore be displaced in favour of criminal "policy." In the view of these advocates, any attempt to create "socialist law" was a contradiction in terms. Ironically, "bourgeois" observers of the Metro-Vickers trial might well agree with this statement.[5]

A major step towards this "simplification" of legal procedures occurred in 1927, when a new draft of the Code of Criminal Procedure was revised, largely under Krylenko's direction, to contain 32 articles instead of the previous 400 articles. The newly proposed system would create a two-tiered system of regionally based "extraordinary tribunals" that would handle cases involving "bourgeois crimes against the state" and would in inquisitorial fashion exclude advocates entirely, and "people's courts" that would hear normal criminal cases and retain a minimal measure of the adversarial system.[6] In essence, Krylenko's proposals would recreate the system of revolutionary justice that had operated during the Russian Civil War.

Resistance to Krylenko's suggestions, according to Huskey, came from somewhat surprising quarters and was inspired by both personal and institutional motives. Members of the Institute of Law of the Academy of Science, including Pashukanis himself, argued that the revised draft went too far in weakening the role of the defence advocate by making his appearance optional at the court's discretion. Moreover, with such a major reduction in the number of articles in the criminal procedure code, the role of Krylenko's Commissariat of Justice would be greatly increased, particularly in the cases involving the extraordinary tribunals. While radical legal theorists like Pashukanis thought that the increased "politicization" of legal procedure was desirable in theory, in the current context of transition from capitalism to socialism, the courts still needed professional defenders to insure the possibility of a defence.[7]

Opposition to Krylenko's draft produced a two-year debate over the criminal procedure code. In late 1929 another draft was submitted to the RSFSR Council of People's Commissars. This draft tried to strengthen the role of the advocates and "allowed the court to exclude the advocate only when the accused was caught red-handed or when

5 Sharlet and Beirne, "In Search of Vyshinsky," p. 162-63. See the revealing Foreword by John N. Hazard and the introduction in Beirne and Sharlet, eds., *Pashukanis: Selected Writings on Marxism and Law* (London: Academic Press, 1980).

6 Huskey, *Russian Lawyers*, p. 171.

7 Ibid., p. 172.

the case was not especially complex."[8] These deliberations produced a stalemate between the Commissariat of Justice and the Institute of Law of the Academy of Sciences which produced yet another draft code two years later. The new draft code, which now had 134 articles, rejected the formal division between "extraordinary" and "normal" criminal procedure — the arrangement that had been previously promoted by Krylenko and was seen by its critics as giving too much power to the Commissariat of Justice. Instead of this two-tiered system, the code would have "a unified procedural order that would be so flexible and elastic that it would enable the court to vary its approach to different criminal cases."[9]

In practice, the lack of clear direction from the Party and the inability to secure a new code during this period reinforced the desire of the Commissariat of Justice to engage in such radical experimentation and served to give Krylenko's bureaucracy an upper hand in the changes which occurred in criminal procedure.[10] This evolution in criminal procedures was given further impetus by the promotion to the judicial bench of the worker-*vydvizhentsy*, personnel who had no legal training, but were drawn from the proletariat and were moved rapidly into positions of responsibility. It was these judges who had the power to decide if an advocate, who was usually drawn from the pre-revolutionary intelligentsia, could participate in the criminal proceedings. Class hatred was not simply a part of criminal policy, then, but also a part of the procedures governing the legal profession.[11]

These simplified measures were useful to the Soviet government during the early years of the First Five-Year Plan, when the drive for collectivization, rapid industrialization, and proletarianization could be served by a very flexible, political, and often localized version of "proletarian justice."[12] Yet it was difficult to rely on such measures as the foundation for the Stalinist regime's desire to achieve more central-

---

8 Ibid., p. 169-73.

9 Ibid., p. 174.

10 Ibid., p. 175-76. For example the codes of the Uzbeck and Turkmen Republics of 1929 and 1932, respectively, closely resembled Krylenko's draft of 1927. Where simplified codes were not introduced, as in the RSFSR, Krylenko was able to undermine the existing Code by passing directives to the courts through the apparatus of the RSFSR Commissariat of Justice.

11 Ibid., p. 176-77. According to Huskey, in 1928 the percentage of worker-judges in the RSFSR was 34 percent. By 1932 that percentage had increased to just over 53 percent.

12 Solomon, "Soviet Criminal Justice and the Great Terror," p. 393-94; and "Local Political Power and Soviet Criminal Justice, 1922-1941," p. 314.

ized control and legitimacy.[13] By 1932, opposition to Krylenko's position came not only from radical advocates in the Soviet bar, but also
from Andrei Vyshinskii himself, who promoted a concept of a transi-
tional socialist legality based on a professionally trained and effectively
centralized legal apparatus. The key to Vyshinskii's approach was that
legal forms and institutions, if properly imbued with *partiinost* —
party-mindedness — could play an important role in the construction
of socialism in the USSR during this intermediate transitory phase of
development.[14] In Vyshinskii's view, the simplification of legal procedures which had typified the period 1928-31 had resulted in a lack of
central control over the administration of the legal decrees issued from
above. This meant that the law had been misinterpreted or ignored by
local authorities, which had resulted in both arbitrary and abusive
practices reminiscent of activities by a Party cadre that had been "dizzy
with success" in other sectors of socialist construction as well.[15] What
was needed was more educated lawyers, including defence lawyers,
and a legal-administrative structure that could and would respond effectively to the decisions of the Party leadership. In this type of socialist
legal order, even the bourgeois tool of law could become the weapon
of the proletariat.

It now appears that the appeal of an ordered, systematic, centrally
controlled legal apparatus advocated by Vyshinskii was increasingly
attractive to the Stalinist leadership. It was certainly the case that by
1933 Vyshinskii was moving into the forefront of legal reform from his
base in the Procuracy of the RSFSR and post of Deputy-Commissar of
Justice of the Russian Republic.[16] In the analysis of the Metro-Vickers
trial outlined below, this little-studied aspect of the victory of Vyshinskii's comparatively moderate conception of the rule of socialist law is
confirmed. This can be seen in the prominent role given to Vyshinskii
in the Metro-Vickers trial itself, as high-ranking radicals such as the
Commissar of Justice of the RSFSR, Krylenko, were excluded from the
proceedings. The moderate conduct of the professorial Vyshinskii, the
relatively light sentencing by the Court, and the promotion of Vyshinskii to the newly created Procuracy of the USSR immediately after the
resolution of the Metro-Vickers affair underscores the rise of the former
Menshevik who would soon become the *doyen* of the Soviet legal community.

---

13 Huskey, "Vyshinskii," p. 416.
14 Sharlet and Beirne, "In Search of Vyshinsky," p. 166.
15 Solomon, "Local Political Power," p. 314.
16 Huskey, "Vyshinskii," p. 417.

In contrast to the recent proposition by Amy Knight that the OGPU was, by 1932, in total control of the state's punitive apparatus,[17] the establishment of an All-Union Procuracy in June 1933, a body which was headed by a former moderate in the OGPU, I.A. Akulov, and seconded by Vyshinskii, makes it appear that the Party leadership wanted to create a rival legal apparatus to that of the OGPU. The little known Akulov[18] had been promoted to deputy-chief in the OGPU for a short time in 1931, apparently at the expense of G. Iagoda, who was also a deputy-chief in the secret police. The British diplomatic staff in Moscow associated his brief tenure with the curtailing of the more extreme activities of the OGPU after June 1931.[19] By December 1931, however, he was displaced by Iagoda, and it could not have been overlooked that Akulov's promotion within an enhanced Procuracy in 1933 was a deliberate attempt to position him in a parallel legal structure outside the apparatus of the OGPU.[20] Certainly, when the Central Executive Committee announced the creation of the USSR Procuracy in *Izvestiia* on 23 June, Strang relayed the view of the diplomatic community in Moscow, which saw the strengthening of the judiciary as an attempt to end the abuses of "revolutionary legality" that had resurfaced in OGPU actions throughout the first half of 1933.[21]

Such an interpretation is consistent with other "moderate" measures, such as the May 1933 directive signed by Stalin and Molotov which ordered an end to the mass deportations in the countryside—a move which added some substance to the peasant's right, recognized in 1932, to own private plots.[22] If doubts remain about the position of favour that would rapidly be bestowed upon figures such as Vyshinskii, it might be remembered that it was Vyshinskii and V.V. Ulrich, the

---

17 Knight, *The KGB*, p. 21.
18 According to the *Bol'shaia Sovetskaia Entsiklopedia* (Moskva, 1970), cols. 1068-69, Ivan Alekseevich Akulov held the post of Prokuror of the USSR until 1935 when he was sent to work for the Ukrainian Party in the Donbass region. Like his rival Iagoda, Akulov was eventually arrested, and put on trial. He was exiled, presumably to a labour camp, and died in 1939. It seems likely that it was this fate which kept him from receiving an entry in the 1950 edition of Stalin's "Big Encyclopedia."
19 Strang to Simon, 26 June 1933, FO 371/17251 N5119/113/38.
20 Jerry Hough and Merle Fainsod have argued that this tactic of avoiding a reliance on one individual or institution for advice or policy was a general feature of Stalin's rule. It not only avoided "group think," but also served as a tool to divide and control. See J. Hough and M. Fainsod *How the Soviet Union Is Governed* (Cambridge, MA: Harvard University Press, 1979), p. 167.
21 Strang to Simon, 26 June 1933, FO 371/17251 N5119/113/38.
22 See Jerry Hough's discussion of this "retreat" to "realism" in *How the Soviet Union Is Governed*, p. 164-65.

Prosecutor and Judge at the Metro-Vickers trial, who would preside over the Great Purge trials of 1936-38 which saw the decimation of the Old Bolsheviks and former rivals in the OGPU and Commissariat of Justice, including both Krylenko and Iagoda.

Given the appearance of these trends following the MVEEC trial, the decision to hold a "show" trial was undoubtedly a measure intended by the Soviet leadership to lay down the current legal policy in no uncertain terms. As was mentioned earlier, the Metro-Vickers arrests and trial had occurred on the heels of the OGPU's summary executions of 35 "enemies of the people."[23] In contrast to such manifestations of revolutionary terror, the carefully staged setting of the courtroom, the lack of red proletarian banners in the court, the demeanour of Vyshinskii, the enhanced role of the defence counsel particularly in the later stages of the trial, and the general tone of the well-rehearsed drama all served to emphasize that control from above, rather than proletarian justice from below, was now the order of the day. In the Metro-Vickers trial the wild outbursts that had typified Prosecutor Krylenko's behaviour at earlier show trials would be kept to a minimum, and it was likely for this reason that it was Vyshinskii and not Krylenko who played the prosecutor's role. On one occasion Vyshinskii did suggest that Thornton would best be used as "manure on a Soviet field," but on the whole he could never warm to the fever pitch he would attain in the later show trials which would find him recommending that Bukharin and others should be "shot like dirty dogs."[24] While the international pressure brought to bear on the Soviet Union by Britain was an important influence on the trial and its aftermath, these domestic factors combined with the international tension to give the Metro-Vickers trial its fundamental character.

At twelve o'clock noon, on 12 April 1933, the first session of the Metro-Vickers trial convened.[25] Ulrich, a member of the Supreme Court, presided as President of the Court and was flanked by A.F. Kostiushko as Secretary, and three members of the Court who had special

---

23 See Ovey's reaction to the arrests of the MVEEC's engineers and the OGPU executions cited above, p. 65-66.

24 See Stephen Cohen's account of Bukharin's confrontation with Vyshinskii, an account which contrasts markedly and convincingly with that of Arthur Koestler's depictions of Rubashov in *Darkness at Noon* (S. Cohen, *Bukharin and the Bolshevik Revolution: A Political Biography, 1888-1938* [New York: Alfred A. Knopf, 1973], p. 375-80).

25 The most detailed outline of the charges is found in the Soviet verbatim report of the subsequent trial, Supreme Court of the USSR, *The Case*.

expertise in electrical engineering.[26] The prosecution was handled in the main by the Public Prosecutor, Vyshinskii, who was assisted by G.K. Roginskii, the Assistant Prosecutor of the RSFSR. Consistent with the presence and background of the three additional technically trained members of the court was the inclusion of a special panel of five engineering experts.[27] These men would add detailed substantive technical grounds to the political grounds of the case that would be extracted from many of the defendants.

Both the British and Soviet defendants were represented by members[28] of the Collegium of Defence, who were generally docile, if not totally absent, from the course of the examination and testimony. Since Soviet trials of this type were meant to demonstrate, rather than to simply establish, the guilt of the defendants, the role of the defence counsel was largely relegated to attempts at minimizing the extent of the crime and pleading for a lenient sentence at the trial's conclusion. Related to this lack of a vigorous defence were the complaints raised by both Thornton and MacDonald, who maintained that their "confessions" during the pre-trial interrogation were partly encouraged by the "advice" they received from Braude and Smirnov, their respective counsels.[29]

The bulk of the first session was spent with the Secretary, Kostiushkov, reading an indictment which fills over 70 typed pages in the verbatim report. The document outlined in exhaustive detail the prosecution's view of the criminal actions, anti-Soviet motivations, and international organization of the "wreckers" at the Zlatoust, Cheliabinsk,

---

26 The three were L.K. Martens, Director of the Diesel Institute and Professor of the Chair of Internal Combustion Engines, G.A. Dmitriev, Manager of the Glavenergo Thermo-Electrical Planning Trust, and reserve member A.V. Zelikov, President of the Central Committee of the Trade Union of Workers, Engineers and Technicians in the Electro-Technical Industry and Electrical Power Stations.

27 The Commission included heating engineer G.P. Brailo, electrical engineer V.A. Golubtsov, turbine engineer M.F. Novikov, technological and electrical engineer B.N. Smirnov, turbine engineer A.N. Snedkov, and turbine engineer P.P. Ulatov. See The Case, p. 12-13. Allan Monkhouse knew three of these men and generally respected their technical training — he was at a loss to explain their testimony at the trial which ran counter to reason in his view. See Monkhouse, Moscow, p. 297-98.

28 The respective defence counsels and defendants were as follows: S.K. Kaznacheev defended Gussev, Sokolov, and Oleinik; L.G. Swartz defended Zorin, Krasheninnikov, and Sukhoruchkin; I.G. Pines defended Zivert, Lobanov, and Lebedev; A.A. Smirnov defended MacDonald; I.D. Braude defended Thornton; A.M. Dolmatovskii defended Gregory and Nordwall; P.P. Lidov defended Cushny; N.V. Kommodov defended Monkhouse; and I.N. Libson defended Kotliarevskii and Kutuzova.

29 Thornton, Foreign Office Deposition, 20 July 1933; and MacDonald, Foreign Office Deposition, 3 July 1933.

Zuevka, Ivanovo, MOSENERGO, and Baku power stations. It also made the fundamental character of the case clear by placing the Moscow office of the MVEEC and its British staff at the centre of this alleged "counter-revolutionary" cadre. The detail of the indictment and the inclusion of portions of the "confessions" that were extracted from MacDonald and Thornton and a number of their Soviet co-defendants combined with the careful crafting of the script to give the necessary coherence to the Prosecutor's case.

The charges against the British engineers were now stated in full for the first time. William MacDonald was charged under Articles 58-6, 58-7, and the wide-ranging powers of 58-11 of the Criminal Code of the RSFSR.[30] The prosecution alleged that, acting under the orders of Thornton, MacDonald had instructed Gussev, Sokolov, Vasiliev "and others" to commit acts of wrecking and diversion at a number of power stations where he had worked. The 29-year-old MacDonald was also active, according to the prosecution, in the collection and gathering of secret information "of State and military importance" and had paid his Soviet accomplices various bribes totalling "about 10 000 roubles" to conceal defects in MVEEC equipment and the effects of their anti-Soviet behaviour. The case that Vyshinskii would build around MacDonald was buttressed not only by the confessions of numerous Soviet "accomplices," but by MacDonald's own confession. It was here that the first sensation of the trial came when MacDonald, partly on the advice of his Soviet counsel, Smirnov, entered the first plea of a British defendant — he pleaded guilty.[31]

Leslie Thornton faced charges under Articles 58-6, 58-7, 58-9, and 58-11. Though he proved to be a more awkward defendant during the trial than MacDonald, as we have seen, he too had "confessed" to portions of the charges and, as the most senior of the MVEEC men who had buckled during interrogation, was portrayed as the chief operative in the counter-revolutionary group. Apart from this, attention was drawn to his place of birth, Leningrad (*sic*) and his socio-economic status — he was born, after all, the son of a "big manufacturer" in St. Petersburg. These "materialist" details made his leading role ever more plausible to a Soviet court. He, too, the indictment alleged, collected secret information and used his subordinates in the MVEEC as well as various other Soviet engineers to engage systematically in criminal activities meant to undermine the Soviet state. Like MacDonald,

---

30 For extracts from Article 58 of the Criminal Code, see Appendix F.
31 *The Case*, p. 79-80.

Thornton also allegedly paid Soviet citizens for their anti-Soviet services, although the prosecution had not been able to ascertain the total
amount of such "bribes."[32] Ulrich, as the President of the Court, was
taken aback when Thornton entered a plea of "not guilty." The Soviet
judge probed, "Not guilty on any count?" — Thornton: "No."[33] This
set the stage for a lengthy and instructive confrontation later in the trial
that would find Vyshinskii pressing Thornton on all fronts to account
for his "confession" and the confessions of others who substantiated
his "guilt."[34]

Allan Monkhouse faced charges along exactly the same lines as
Thornton but, despite the fact that he was the MVEEC manager, was
not assigned a major role by the prosecution during the trial. Unlike
Thornton, Monkhouse had been able to withdraw the most damaging
elements in his signed statements and throughout the trial he maintained a strong, combative disposition to the entire proceeding.

Of the remaining three British defendants, John Cushny and
Charles Nordwall faced a similar range of charges of engaging in
wrecking, espionage, and offering bribes to encourage criminal acts
under Articles 58-6, 58-7, 58-9, and 58-11. These two were clearly less
central to the case in that they had not confessed and were portrayed
more as pawns than instigators.[35]

Albert Gregory was the one British defendant who scarcely received any attention at all during the trial and was the only one of the
six to be cleared of all charges. He had been in the Soviet Union less
than a year and faced the single charge under Articles 58-6 and 58-11 of
collecting secret information.[36] The weakness of the case against Gregory was evident, since he had not confessed, and no successful attempt was made to connect him to the confessions of any other defendants. As Vyshinskii concluded at the end of the trial: "But when Thornton speaks about Gregory, I [Vyshinskii] must say that Thornton's bare
statement, unsupported by any other facts, is insufficient to support
the charge against Gregory. I think that a verdict of acquittal can be
passed on Gregory."[37] Gregory, Cushny, and Nordwall all pleaded not
guilty.

---

32 Ibid., p. 82-83.
33 Ibid., p. 85.
34 Ibid., p. 126-27.
35 Ibid., p. 78, 80-81, 85.
36 Ibid., p. 75.
37 Ibid., p. 671.

Of the Soviet defendants, the three who proved most vulnerable were V.A Gussev, L.A. Sukhoruchkin, and A.T. Lobanov. They were younger than the other Soviet defendants and had regular contact with MVEEC engineers in the field. Gussev and Sukhoruchkin served as chiefs of the Zlatoust and First Moscow Power stations respectively, and all three were accused of acting on the instructions of, and taking bribes from, the British engineers, MacDonald, Thornton, and Nordwall. The Soviet engineers were charged under Articles 58-7, 58-9, and 58-11. All three pleaded guilty to the charges and would, in the end, receive the most severe sentence from the court—10 years deprivation of liberty with loss of rights for five years and confiscation of all their property.[38]

V.A. Sokolov, M.L. Kotliarevskii, and M.D. Krasheninnikov were also junior men in the electrical engineering field who were charged with concealing defects in newly installed equipment. Sokolov, allegedly acting in concert with Gussev, was charged with wrecking a 1 400 horsepower engine at the Zlatoust station. Sokolov was also supposed to be involved in gathering secret information which was passed through Gussev to MacDonald. For their anti-Soviet efforts, Sokolov and Kotliarevskii had apparently received 1 000 roubles, while Krasheninnikov's "bribe" amounted to 500 roubles.[39] It was perhaps on this count that the former two ultimately received eight-year sentences, while the poorer-paid Krasheninnikov received a five-year term.[40]

In addition to this more junior cadre, which ranged in age from 29 to 39, and which was far and away the most severely dealt with, was a group of four older men ranging in age from 50 to 59. While the eldest, N.G. Zorin, received a stiff eight-year sentence, P.I. Oleinik, V.P. Lebedev, and I.I. Zivert received considerably lighter sentences, with Zivert receiving no punishment for his "crimes" at all. What this suggests is that, to the extent that the trial was an attack on specialists in the electrical industry, it was not a special attack on "old specialists" and, to the extent that generational factors played a role at all, the opposite seems true. With the singular exception of Zorin, who had a

---

38 Ibid., p. 74, 79, 81-82, 796-97.
39 According to Strang's calculations the official rate of exchange was 9.4 roubles = 1 pound sterling. As will be seen, however, the British engineers, like so many foreigners in the USSR then and since, availed themselves of the black market rates which were substantially more favourable to foreign currency. See Strang, Home and Abroad, p. 85, n. 1.
40 Ibid., p. 76-77, 83-84, 796-97. Sokolov was charged under Articles 58-6, 58-7, 58-9, 58-11 of the Criminal Code. Krasheninnikov and Kotliarevskii were charged under Articles 58-7 and 58-11.

great deal of responsibility for investigating the cause of breakdowns that occurred with foreign equipment as chief turbine engineer at MOSENERGO and had allegedly failed to be sufficiently vigilant in this work, it was the senior men who were dealt with most leniently. It must be borne in mind, however, that the OGPU did not bring to trial all those who were under suspicion — the numerous "confrontations" between MVEEC engineers and "old specialists" who were not brought to trial but were obviously a compromised and targeted cadre is the clearest evidence of this. Neither does the trial appear to be an attack against "red specialists,"[41] those rapidly promoted party members whose political views were often held to be more important than their technical expertise. None of the Soviet defendants was a Party member, a fact that made it easier to portray some of them as remnants of "White" forces who had revealed their true colours by collaborating with British engineers in their wrecking activities. Vyshinskii did not fail to make the link between the former Whites and the fact that Monkhouse and Thornton had served with the British interventionist forces during the Russian Civil War. The key to the prosecution's case against Soviet defendants appears to have been the relationship of the Soviet accused to the British accused. Those Soviets closest to Mac-Donald, and in positions of greater responsibility at their respective works, were dealt with most severely.

The lone woman in the trial was the MVEEC secretary, Anna Kutuzova. Her role, according to the indictment, had been limited to "systematically" making money payments to Gussev and "other Russian engineers and technicians" on the orders of Thornton and other British engineers. Though it did not form part of the indictment, the fact that she lived with Thornton and Monkhouse had evidently been used as a lever during her interrogation, and as has been pointed out above, she had confessed to engaging in "disgustful" acts with Thornton and Monkhouse which could at any moment have become part of the public record. Charged under Articles 58-6, 58-7, 58-9, and 58-11, Kutuzova received a sentence of 18 months' deprivation of liberty without loss of

---

41 Kendall Bailes made this point in his unpublished dissertation, which contains a short chapter on the MVEEC trial. This chapter was not included in his *Technology and Society under Lenin and Stalin*, perhaps because Bailes realized the major differences that underlay the show trial of 1933 and contrasted it with the earlier trials that formed the basis of his study. See K. Bailes, "Stalin and Revolution from Above: The Formation of the Soviet Technical Intelligentsia, 1928-1934" (Ph.D. dissertation, Columbia University, 1971), p. 192.

property.[42] As will become clear below, her close relationship to the MVEEC's British personnel made her a very valuable "hostage" in the case, and the pliability of Thornton, in particular, can partially be explained by his desire to avoid contradicting a terrorized Kutuzova.[43]

The case against this "counter-revolutionary" group was given additional coherence by the physical arrangements of the courtroom. The six British engineers sat with the 11 Soviet defendants in the "dock" which was flanked by guards with bayonets at the ready.[44] Thornton and MacDonald sat in the first row, but were separated by Zorin and Kutuzova. The other four British defendants were seated together in the last of the three rows and undoubtedly drew some solidarity from their close proximity to one another. It seems doubtful that presenting the defendants in this way was merely a matter of convenience. Taken individually, the defendants would not appear to be nearly the threat to the power of the Soviet state as they were when presented as a collection of 17 persons of varied ages, skills, and nationalities. This was something far more convincing to the audience of about 400 who responded with appropriate concern throughout the trial as Vyshinskii played the confessions and testimony out to develop a portrait of collective anti-Soviet behaviour and collective guilt.

One Soviet defendant, N.P. Vitvitskii, though included in the indictment, was not present during the trial apparently because of an illness which was certified by a doctor of the Butyrskaia Prison.[45] It is possible that his illness was the result of rough handling during his interrogation, but if such were the case, it would contrast with the treatment of the other prisoners who appeared in the courtroom neatly dressed and groomed and, while the psychological pressure of extended interrogation had produced visible strain, there was little physical evidence of "third-degree" methods. When asked by Vyshinskii about his treatment, Thornton confirmed that "third-degree" methods were not applied to secure his confession.[46] It was just such revelations which aggravated the mood of some British officials at home who found it difficult to understand why these men had collapsed so easily.[47]

---

42 *The Case*, p. 77, 796-97.
43 This was certainly the explanation given by Thornton in his deposition to the Foreign Office, 20 July 1933.
44 Cummings, *The Moscow Trial*; see plate following p. 32.
45 *The Case*, p. 5.
46 Ibid., p. 128.
47 See Vansittart's bitter remarks about the cowardice of MacDonald and Thornton in his minute to a Foreign Office Memo by Collier, 9 July 1933, FO 371/17273 N5329/1610/38.

Five of the six accused Metro-Vickers engineers, l-r: Thornton, Nordwall, Monkhouse, Gregory, Cushny.

V. V. Ulrich: the presiding Judge.

Anna Kutuzova, Secretary at Metro-Vickers and co-accused.

Thornton in the dock.

The Public Prosecutor: Andrei Vyshinskii.

Allan Monkhouse giving testimony.

Assistant Prosecutor G.K. Roginskii.

1 мая 1933г. в Москве.
т.т. Сталин и Каганович направляются на Красную Площадь.

Kaganovich and Josef Stalin.

MacDonald and Thornton.

All of the accused, both Soviet and British, in the dock at the Metro-Vickers trial.

Insight into the relationship between the prosecution, the court, and the defence was provided at the end of the first afternoon session. It was Prosecutor Vyshinskii, not the President of the Court, Judge Ulrich, who provided an outline of the procedures to be followed during the remainder of the trial. The defence had no objection to Vyshinskii's proposal for examination, and the Court adopted the prosecution's procedure as its own. All of this clearly suggests that this was Vyshinskii's show, and he would be given his lead over the next week. That he did so with an intense professorial authority, to be very much distinguished from the behaviour exhibited in the periodic interventions by his "excitable" and "pugnacious"[48] assistant Roginskii, served to enhance the prosecution's case by presenting the complexities of the indictment with assurance and calm.

The evening session of the opening day set the tone for the remainder of the trial. The President of the Court called the 35-year-old Gussev to testify about his activities in the Kolchak army during the Civil War of 1918-21, and Vyshinskii had little difficulty demonstrating the long history of anti-Soviet sentiment which Gussev himself claimed had never wavered. After establishing this "motive," Vyshinskii led Gussev through his initial contact with MacDonald and the origins of his wrecking and espionage activities. At each juncture Gussev was precise about the dates and circumstances of his involvement with the British engineer. He also introduced MacDonald's apparent motive for wanting information about the industrial capabilities of the USSR. According to Gussev, both he and MacDonald believed that the Soviet Union did not need to develop its own machine-building capability, but should rely on foreign suppliers for their needs. Moreover, Gussev also claimed that MacDonald was particularly interested in the Zlatoust Mechanical Works, where Gussev was employed, since part of the works was engaged in producing munitions. In short order, then, Gussev's testimony introduced the theme that the MVEEC had an interest in keeping the USSR dependent on foreign machinery and that, at the root of the espionage activities of the group, was an interest in assessing the military production of the country.

When Vyshinskii turned to query MacDonald about the veracity of Gussev's testimony the MVEEC engineer complied:

Vyshinskii: Accused MacDonald. You hear the testimony of Gussev? Do you corroborate what he said regarding your acquaintance in 1929?

---

48 See the portrait of Roginskii in Cummings, *The Moscow Trial*, p. 109-10.

MacDonald: Regarding our acquaintance, yes.

Vyshinskii: You corroborate that during this time, from 1929 and on, your relations with Gussev were of friendship, of intimacy?

MacDonald: From 1930 on.

Vyshinskii: You did indeed ask Gussev to furnish you the information of which he spoke?

MacDonald: Yes in my personal interests.

Vyshinskii: Perhaps you will explain more exactly what you mean by your own interests? Did you ask Gussev for information on the power supply?

MacDonald: I did.

Vyshinskii: Military information?

MacDonald: I did.

Vyshinskii: This is all I wanted.[49]

From this point on Gussev's testimony provided an account of how he and Sokolov, inspired by MacDonald's instructions and encouraged by the "bribes" he offered the Russians of about 2 500 roubles, proceeded to sabotage engines, conveyors, and boilers at Zlatoust, with an eye to inhibiting the production of military goods. In this way Gussev provided ready answers for the numerous breakdowns that had occurred with machinery under his charge and, in the instance of the coal conveyor which fed the power plant, he insisted the capacity of the station was undermined for a period of almost two years.[50]

MacDonald was asked to confirm Gussev's account once again. While he disputed the story that he had helped plan the wrecking activities, adding only that he had been told of them after the fact,[51] MacDonald did admit that he had given Gussev about 2 500 roubles. When pressed about where he came up with such a sum, MacDonald claimed that Thornton had arranged the payment through the Moscow office of the MVEEC.[52] According to Monkhouse, MacDonald and Thornton had traded on the black market in order to clear a number of MacDonald's debts, and this was the real source of the funds. MacDonald had exaggerated the amount under the pressure of interrogation, Monkhouse maintained.[53]

---

49 *The Case*, p. 98.
50 Ibid., p. 104-105.
51 Ibid., p. 108.
52 Ibid., p. 104.
53 Bush House Interviews, 9 May 1933.

The remainder of Gussev's examination was handled by Roginskii. He led Gussev through the organizational features of the wrecking operation and in the process drew MacDonald's housekeeper, Riabova, and her sons, into the case. This seemed to make an impression on the attitude of MacDonald, who had been told during his interrogation[54] that his confession would make things easier for Riabova. Now her name was part of the public record of the trial and for the remainder of the session MacDonald was a much less manageable defendant. After he denied further aspects of Gussev's testimony, the session was abruptly adjourned. Strang's account of this, the first of two such adjournments, suggests that the prosecution was rattled by the change in attitude and that this had created a "stir" in the courtroom.[55] As will become clear below, the adjournment which occurred the following day after similar resistance from MacDonald and Thornton had a definitely threatening tone.

Upon resumption of the session, Roginskii asked Thornton to confirm a few trivial points in Gussev's testimony as to the time and place of their various meetings. Once again there were no quibbles from the British accused, and it seems very likely that part of the prosecution's strategy was to get the MVEEC engineers to agree to small points early on, and thereby build momentum for the more serious dimensions of the case that were to follow.

After these small triumphs, Roginskii turned the examination of Thornton over to Vyshinskii. It was here that Thornton's plea of "not guilty," which he had entered earlier that day, was challenged by the Public Prosecutor. Vyshinskii asked Thornton to account for the portions of his confession that admitted guilt on grounds of spying. Vyshinskii was at his best when attacking with a mixture of sarcasm and exaggerated politeness:

Vyshinskii: Do you confirm this?
Thornton: No.
Vyshinskii: Why did you say it then?
Thornton: I did not say that I was forced to say it.
Vyshinskii: Then permit me to ask — did you say it?
Thornton: Yes, I did.
Vyshinskii: That is to say, what is written in the records is actually what you said?

---

54 MacDonald, Foreign Office Deposition, 3 July 1933.
55 Strang, *Home and Abroad*, p. 100.

Thornton: Yes, that is what I said.
Vyshinskii: Did you speak the truth or an untruth?
Thornton: In this case it was an untruth.
Vyshinskii: Do you usually speak the truth or not?
Thornton: In this case I did not speak the truth, I was excited.
Vyshinskii: That is to say, when you are excited you don't speak the truth.
Thornton: Yes.
Vyshinskii: You are not excited now?
Thornton: No, I am not excited.
Vyshinskii: That is to say, you are now speaking the truth?
Thornton: Now I am speaking the truth.
Vyshinskii: Why then did you write this and not something else? You said: "I think, it is right." You did not affirm, but you thought. I ask why, when you were excited, you thought precisely this and not something else? Were you forced to do it?
Thornton: No.
Vyshinskii: You said this voluntarily?
Thornton: Voluntarily.
Vyshinskii: Perhaps some special methods were applied to you?
Thornton: No.
Vyshinskii: Were you tortured?
Thornton: No.
Vyshinskii: Third degree?
Thornton: No.
Vyshinskii: I have no more questions.[56]

In Strang's account of this confrontation he noted that Thornton found it easier to handle Vyshinskii when operating in English and making use of the court interpreter. It may also have been the case that the use of the interpreter not only added precision to the statements, but also gave Thornton more time for his response.[57] At one point during Vyshinskii's questioning the interpreter disappeared, and Thornton,

---

56 *The Case*, p. 127-28.
57 The defendants were supposed to be free to use English or Russian in their testimony, but there was, from time to time, some confusion over the exact meaning of words which did not have precise equivalents. In the case of engineers such as Gregory, for example, he spoke virtually no Russian and had to rely on the interpreter throughout.

despite his facility in Russian,[58] appeared to lose confidence in his ability to offer a rebuttal to Vyshinskii.

Despite this barrage by Vyshinskii, Thornton's nerve held up throughout the first day, the remainder of which was spent with the various defence counsels offering cautious rebuttals to specific details of the testimony of Gussev. Thornton's counsel, Braude, cast doubt on whether Thornton had ever actually talked to one of the alleged wrecking group, Vitvitskii, and this in turn hampered the prosecution's claim, which was based on Gussev's testimony, that Vitvitskii was Thornton's main agent in the Cheliabinsk region. This was a particularly important point to make, since Vitvitskii was not present during the trial and yet was a central figure among the Russians in the alleged organization. If the prosecution was able to use the testimony of someone who could not be cross-examined in person, such as Vitvitskii, the defence had to show some weakness in the written testimony itself. Braude also encouraged Thornton to specify the type of information that he had required from MacDonald, and here Thornton insisted that it was limited to information necessary "so that, should there be a breakdown with a machine, we should have every opportunity of finding the cause."[59]

Similarly, MacDonald's counsel, Smirnov, managed to provoke some awkwardness in Gussev's account when the Soviet counsel noted that all the breakdowns at Zlatoust came a year after MacDonald had left the area.[60] Gussev also had difficulty remembering how many installments and in what sums MacDonald had paid his alleged accomplices.[61] Thus, after the damage caused by Gussev and Vyshinskii, the defence counsels managed to retake some ground on behalf of the British accused.

The second day of the trial found the pattern outlined in the first sessions repeated. Ulrich called another Soviet defendant, this time Sokolov, and he dutifully recalled his participation in Kolchak's army, noting that he had served in the very same regiment, the 22nd Zlatoust training company, as had Gussev. It was scarcely a surprise, then, that

---

58 Strang's depiction of Thornton as someone who struggled with Russian in the courtroom should be contrasted with the portrait offered earlier in this study which was based on Thornton and Monkhouse's own claims that they managed to communicate easily in the language. Perhaps speaking Russian when in the "dock" was a different matter from speaking the language in the field. See Strang, *Home and Abroad*, p. 100.

59 Ibid., p. 142.

60 Ibid., p. 132.

61 Ibid., p. 134.

Sokolov should end up as Gussev's assistant in the Zlatoust electrical department some 10 years later, fully equipped with the anti-Soviet attitudes that a defeated "White" would have. With this testimony acting as a foundation it was easy for Vyshinskii to make the link to MacDonald via Gussev.[62] A portrait of the wrecking team gradually developed.

Sokolov was then asked to recount the relationship that developed between Gussev, MacDonald, and himself, and he provided a picture of hard-drinking parties full of anti-Soviet toasts that were often enjoyed by the trio. Vyshinskii made sure to direct the Court's attention to Sokolov's written confession:

> The conversation was of an open anti-Soviet nature. Do you confirm this? Then: "Gussev gave a toast for the Five-Year Plan in Four. . . . MacDonald corrected him: "For the Five-Year Plan in Ten Years." Moreover, he said again that the Soviet Union would not be able to free itself from foreign dependence anyhow . . . would not be able to manage the production of machines, etc."[63]

Sokolov testified that MacDonald did not simply provide variations on Soviet toasts to the Russian pair of engineers. He also advised them on how they could proceed to undermine the Zlatoust works in readiness for a possible foreign intervention. A necessary component of these criminal activities was intelligence gathering which, Sokolov claimed, went from him to Gussev to MacDonald.[64]

As he had done the previous day, Vyshinskii now turned to MacDonald to confirm the testimony of the Russian defendant. Vyshinskii began by reading MacDonald's statement of 2 April which read: "I [MacDonald] confirm that in my conversation with Sokolov at the end of 1930 I have not given him definite instructions on wrecking of equipment but I told him that he and Gussev had to undertake the taking out of service of plant and that he (Sokolov) had to come to an understanding directly with Gussev."[65] MacDonald immediately disputed the prosecution's claim that he had told Sokolov to carry out wrecking activities, and this resistance prompted Vyshinskii to ask MacDonald to account for his confession. MacDonald recalled that the initial statement had been written in Russian by the interrogator and that after much badgering he had been compelled to translate the state-

---

62 *The Case*, p. 150-61.
63 Ibid., p. 162.
64 Ibid., p. 163-64.
65 Ibid., p. 166.

ment into English and sign it. When pressed by Vyshinskii to account for why he signed the document, MacDonald asserted that the interrogator "did not allow me to do otherwise."[66] He also claimed that he thought it better to challenge the legitimacy of his confession in an open court than to resist the pressure of his interrogators.[67] One might also add that it was easier to confess earlier and hope to defend oneself later when under the psychological strain of interrogation.

It was at this point that Vyshinskii found MacDonald's resolve to resist the claims of the prosecution at its height. MacDonald told the Court that he wanted to change his plea to "not guilty" at this time. He also challenged the claim by Gussev that the money MacDonald had paid him was for wrecking activities. Instead, the British engineer now insisted that money was for the overtime wages of workmen employed in the erection of MVEEC equipment.[68]

Vyshinskii, meeting with continued obstinacy from MacDonald, directed his questioning to Thornton. Various passages in Thornton's deposition had implied that MacDonald and 27 other MVEEC employees were engaged in various types of intelligence gathering. When Vyshinskii asked Thornton to account for his testimony, the Public Prosecutor met with opposition from Thornton as well:

Thornton: I gave a plainly false deposition.
Vyshinskii: We shall examine later whether it was false or not.
Thornton: I say that it was false. You can say what you like.[69]

This was clearly not Vyshinskii's finest hour, and after a few more approaches to MacDonald and Thornton, the President of the Court decided that a recess of 20 minutes was needed.[70]

At this juncture the decisive blow was struck at MacDonald. MacDonald's subsequent deposition alleges that during this adjournment, he was taken aside and told that Riabova would be shot if he did not stick to his confession. From that point on, MacDonald offered no resistance to the prosecution's case.[71] Strang noted the contrast in MacDonald's behaviour: "before the break, he had spoken firmly and confidently. After it, he spoke in a low, toneless voice, meekly confirming

---

66 Ibid., p. 167.
67 Ibid.
68 Ibid., p. 170.
69 Ibid., p. 176.
70 Ibid., p. 178.
71 MacDonald, Foreign Office Deposition, 3 July 1933.

his original testimony."[72] MacDonald might well have been a weak, naive, and nervous individual,[73] but here he did summon up the courage to face an unknown fate at the hands of a Soviet court in the hopes that his compliance might spare Riabova and her family. There was not a hint of bitterness towards his Russian associates in MacDonald's deposition concerning his fate and, following his release from prison, he asked the Foreign Office to seek permission for Riabova to come to stay with him in England.[74]

The main attention of Vyshinskii now shifted from MacDonald to Thornton. After watching his British associate give way to Vyshinskii's questions, Thornton apparently decided that he had to attack the testimony of MacDonald directly. At one juncture he not only denied MacDonald's testimony about alleged espionage activity, but claimed that the whole idea "was an absolute lie."[75] Thornton also was able to resist Vyshinskii's tendency to pursue a line of questioning and then change course just when Thornton was ready to clarify a point that had been left intentionally ambiguous by the Prosecutor. One such example occurred when Vyshinskii asked about Thornton's interest in the general and local affairs at the Zlatoust works:

Vyshinskii: Perhaps you were interested in the weak spots of the power station, from the point of view of breakdowns?
Thornton: I was very much interested in this, but allow me to say why.
Vyshinskii: We will clear that up later on.
Thornton: That won't do. I want to finish what I have to say.
Vyshinskii: Very well.
Thornton: I had to know the weak spots so as to judge, if there should be a breakdown on the generator, what kind of switchboards there were, the transformer lines and in general, what was the state of the internal wiring.[76]

Of course Vyshinskii was unwilling to leave matters rest on this technical level and he brought in the testimony of one mechanic, Marin, yet

---

72 Strang, *Home and Abroad*, p. 102.
73 These were the unflattering judgements rendered by the four British engineers who were not imprisoned after the trial. They were very disappointed in MacDonald's behaviour and did not shy away from accounting for his plight as that which befalls weak men. See Bush House Interviews, 9 May 1933.
74 Richards to Foreign Office, 20 July 1933, FO 371/17274 N5682/1610/38. There is no indication in the existing documents that an exit visa for Riabova was ever a serious possibility.
75 *The Case*, p. 186.
76 Ibid., p. 190.

another witness who could not be cross-examined during the trial. Marin apparently had told the OGPU that he was paid by the MVEEC to fix small defects without advising the management at Zlatoust. Here Thornton did not dispute the payment of some 300 to 400 roubles for these repairs, "possibly without the knowledge of the management," but he insisted that this was not meant for diversion or wrecking. When asked to explain why he had given a written statement during his interrogation that the sum paid to Marin was in the order of 4 000 roubles, Thornton responded that he had hoped, just as MacDonald had hoped, to clear this matter up in court rather than resist during his interrogation.[77]

The bulk of the remainder of the morning session was spent with questions posed to Thornton by both the prosecution and defence counsel on the subject of the various "loans" that had been arranged for MacDonald. Evidently, Thornton handled the MVEEC accounts in Moscow with the black market currency rate firmly in mind, since he explained that he allowed the repayment of roubles exchanged at the official rate to be written off with black market roubles. In effect this meant that instead of a loan to MacDonald from the MVEEC coffers of 2 000 roubles costing MacDonald 200 pounds of his salary to repay, he could get the black market rate which reduced his cost to 66 pounds to repay the 2 000 roubles as long as he handled the transaction through Thornton. While Thornton readily admitted this was "illegal," he claimed that it was simply a personal matter and had no relationship to MVEEC policy.[78] Given the earlier statements of Richards, the MVEEC director, that the MVEEC often advanced money to its employees, it seems likely that here Thornton was stretching matters a bit himself.

The prosecution continued in the evening session of 13 April to develop a portrait of a wrecking organization inspired and funded through the offices of the MVEEC. Strang noted in his account of this session that the testimony which recounted the activities of Richards, Monkhouse, and Thornton during the Russian Civil War, and the brief tenure of these future MVEEC men as Russian experts in British Army intelligence, drew noticeable murmurs from the audience.[79] Cummings also recalled the strong impression this line of questioning produced and concluded that Russians found it impossible to make the distinction between Army intelligence during war and peace-time

---

77 Ibid., p. 191.
78 Ibid., p. 218-22.
79 Strang, *Home and Abroad*, p. 102.

intelligence gathering.[80] Given the apparent involvement of the MVEEC with the IIC, however, it may simply be easier to make the distinction if your side benefits from such a distinction. In any case, the shape of the prosecution's case was now assuming its full dimensions.

At the heart of the intelligence charges against the MVEEC was Thornton's handwritten confession from the second day of his confinement, 13 March 1933. The Soviet verbatim report provided a facsimile of the document that was read to the Court:

> All our spying operations on U.S.S.R. territory are directed by the British Intelligence Service, through their agent, C.S. Richards, who occupies the position of Managing Director of the Metropolitan-Vickers Electrical Export Company, Ltd.
>
> Spying operations on U.S.S.R. territory were directed by myself [Thornton] and Monkhouse, representatives of the above-mentioned British firm, who are contractors, by official agreements, to the Soviet Government, for the supply of turbines and electrical equipment and the furnishing of technical aid agreements. On the instructions of C.S. Richards given to me to this end, British personnel were gradually drawn into the spying organization after their arrival on U.S.S.R. territory and instructed as to the information required. During the whole period of our presence on U.S.S.R. territory, from the total of British staff employed, 27 men were engaged in spying operations. Of the above 15 men which included

Monkhouse	Clark	MacDonald
Waters	Tearle	Annis, A.
Cox	Shutters	Annis, H.
Nordwall	Burke	Shipley
Thornton	Riddle	Pollitt

> were engaged in Economic and Political spying, also in the investigation of the defence and offence possibilities of the Soviet Union.
>
> The remaining 12 men who included the following

Jule	Cornell	Richards, C.G.
Gregory	Fallows	Charnock
Jolley	MacCracken	Cushny
Smith, A.	Noel	Whatmough

> were engaged in political and economic spying.
>
> On March 11, 1933 the following men were engaged in spying operations:
>
> Nordwall — economic, political, defence and offence investigation
> Gregory — economic and political
> Pollitt — economic, political, defence and offence investigation
> Whatmough — economic and political

---

80 Cummings, *The Moscow Trial*, p. 164.

Riddle — economic, political, defence and offence investigation
Thornton — economic, political, defence and offence investiga-
tion
Monkhouse — economic, political, defence and offence investi-
gation
Cushny — economic and political
Facts above [about?] the spying activities of the above mentioned
men who were under my direction, I shall give in a further protocol.[81]

To his credit Thornton parried the queries of Vyshinskii concerning this very damaging document with constant denials that it truly reflected the nature of MVEEC's interests and activities in the Soviet Union. Vyshinskii mocked Thornton's claim that what the engineer wrote was opposite to what he now said, and the Prosecutor tried to cast doubt on Thornton's character by underscoring the disservice he did to the MVEEC and to the reputations of his colleagues by his confession.[82] At best Vyshinskii was able to show that certain details in the written statement were very accurate while other, less convenient facts that pertained to criminal motive were now contested by Thornton.[83] All in all, Thornton managed to fend off the pressure well, but given the detail and intrinsic importance of his confession, his belated resistance could not entirely undo the damage that had been done to the MVEEC engineers he had named.

After a short intermission, the defence counsel for Thornton, Braude, led the British accused through a series of questions which helped establish the climate of "moral pressure" that was exerted on Thornton to obtain his signature. Braude also attacked the prosecution's claim that Thornton came from a wealthy industrial St. Petersburg family and pointed out that Thornton's father owned only a small part of the family business. When the October Revolution came Thornton himself lost about 20 000 Kerensky roubles — a trifling sum which the defence maintained scarcely constituted a motive sufficient for the charges Thornton faced.[84]

Two remaining issues of importance were explored in the remainder of the evening session. The first involved the defence counsel for Anna Kutuzova, Libson, asking Thornton about the sort of information that she was privy to in her post as Secretary and as a house-mate of Thornton and Monkhouse. It was important for Libson to cast doubt

---

81 *The Case*, p. 256-58 and facsimile enclosed following p. 256.
82 Ibid., p. 258.
83 Ibid., p. 260-64.
84 Ibid., p. 266-67.

on Kutuzova's confession by having Thornton explain that she simply could not have known about the financial and organizational details that she had claimed to know about. The most grand of these was her statement that the MVEEC office had received some 50 000 roubles from the British Embassy in Moscow.[85] Vyshinskii could not let matters rest at that and tried to develop an argument that was based on Kutuzova's confession about her "intimate" living arrangement with Thornton. Kutuzova, apparently mortified at Vyshinskii's request to state publicly the details of this part of her confession, refused to answer the Prosecutor, and only barely managed to confirm her written statement.[86] This was sufficient for Vyshinskii to imply that Kutuzova was more than a secretary living in the MVEEC compound at Perlovka, and that as an intimate confidante of the MVEEC engineers, she was trusted with "pillow-talk" information that formed the basis of her confession.

The last major detail of the case to be raised before the close of testimony on 13 April was the issue of the "loan" to Dolgov, the manager of the Control Department at Electro-Import. When queried by Vyshinskii on this matter, Thornton proceeded to explain that the 3 000 roubles was a loan, but it was not meant to be repaid. It was subsequently written off as an expense with the approval of Monkhouse and Richards. Naturally Vyshinskii wanted to know why a loan that was not meant to be repaid could possibly be given. When he turned to Monkhouse, the story changed slightly from that of a loan, to the 3 000 roubles now being offered as a "present." Vyshinskii then directed the Court's attention to Monkhouse's pre-trial statement:[87]

> I presume that Thornton, when he gave Dolgov the money, allegedly as a loan, wanted in this way to secure Dolgov's favourable disposition to the firm in those cases when Dolgov, as the manager of the installation department, would be called upon to decide on disputes which occurred in connection with compensation claims for defects in the equipment which we are supplying.[88]

As was admitted by Richards back in London, this transaction was written off by the MVEEC as a business expense incurred because Dolgov had hitherto worked very closely with the British company — one

85 Ibid., p. 272-73. The British had known about this element of Kutuzova's confession since her return from the Lubianka prison late in January.
86 Ibid., p. 281-82.
87 Monkhouse claimed that Vyshinskii had actually written the statement in Russian and that Monkhouse had only signed it.
88 Ibid., p. 288. The statement was signed on 26 March.

might add, no wonder.[89] At best the "present" offered to Dolgov, apparently for the purpose of his purchasing a new flat, was intended as a "bribe" for general goodwill on Dolgov's part, if not a payment for specific information or specific actions on his part. From the point of view of the MVEEC the amount was inconsequential. Kutuzova explained that the deficit was easily recovered by selling 250 Torgsin roubles for 3 000 regular roubles at black market rates.[90] The Court then adjourned, but not before noting that Dolgov would be summoned as a witness the following day. He would be the only person physically to testify during the trial who was not one of the accused and it was for this reason that British officials considered him an agent provocateur.

Dolgov's testimony on 14 April (ironically, it was Good Friday) did further damage to Thornton, Monkhouse, and the MVEEC management. The Soviet manager alleged that Thornton had first suggested that the MVEEC regularly helped out its employees with advances of salary and that Dolgov's own troubles might be alleviated in a similar manner. While Thornton challenged this statement, he could not get away from Dolgov's claim that Thornton had told him the 3 000 roubles would be kept to himself and Monkhouse and that there was no need to specify any time limit for the "loan."[91] Very damaging testimony was then drawn out of Monkhouse who confirmed that, in the British manager's view, Dolgov regarded the sum as a bribe and that the MVEEC came to regard it as a "present" to the Soviet manager.[92] Monkhouse admitted that when the sum, which was given to Dolgov in July 1932, went unpaid for six months the whole transaction came to "smack of bribery."[93]

The prosecution's case here was made easier by the fact that they had recovered some of Thornton's account books in their raid at the MVEEC compound, and records of the Dolgov "loan" were included in one of these books. It showed the sum being charged to Thornton in early July and then shifted to a "suspense account" towards the end of the month. It was only in December that Richards made the decision to use 250 Torgsin roubles to balance the ledger.[94] Another surprise awaited the British defendants when Dolgov and the prosecution alleged that on the same day that Dolgov received the funds from Thorn-

89 Richards to Collier, 21 March 1933, FO 371/17265 N1802/1610/38.
90 Ibid., p. 290.
91 *The Case*, p. 298-300.
92 Ibid., p. 303-304.
93 Ibid.
94 Ibid., p. 306.

ton, he turned the sum over to the OGPU and made a report of the transaction. Thus, one of the men whom the MVEEC relied upon for day-to-day information and cooperation and had indulged in the Company's usual policy of friendly "indiscretion" was, from July 1932 until their arrests, part of a network of informants who were aiding the OGPU in their investigation of the MVEEC. The lead editorial on the trial carried the same day by the Commissariat of Heavy Industry's newspaper, *Za Industrializatsiiu*, seemed to capture the impact of the damage done to the MVEEC thus far—it was entitled, "Facts Are Stubborn Things."[95]

After the sensations of the Dolgov testimony, the remainder of the morning session saw Lobanov, Lebedev, and Kotliarevskii outline the scope of their wrecking activities and the role of various British engineers in their anti-Soviet machinations. When MacDonald's counsel, Smirnov, attacked the testimony of Kotliarevskii on the grounds that the British engineer was in England when the problems at Zuevka power station occurred, the President of the Court pointed out that "a whole group of people were arrested in connection with this and are under preliminary investigation."[96] This was the first sign during the trial that those defendants in the show trial were only a small portion of those caught up in the sweep of the electrical industry—a fact that was given additional substance when purges occurred in the Moscow power station system later in the summer of 1933.[97]

The evening session of 14 April continued to develop the portrait of Soviet engineers being bribed and instructed by Thornton, Mac-Donald, Nordwall, and others not even named in the indictment. Nordwall resisted the charges made against him, but it was evident that most of the fight had gone out of Thornton, and MacDonald continued to respond as one who had been defeated. The most forthright challenge to the prosecution's case came from an indignant Albert Gregory, who insisted that he be allowed to read a prepared statement. He began by complaining that Zivert was "fouling" his reputation and went on to challenge the panel of engineering experts to find anything objectionable in his work record at the Dzerzhinka or Dneiprostroi

---

95 *Za Industrializatsiiu* carried a fairly full account of the trial throughout the week, often featuring the testimony and photographs from the proceedings as one of its leading stories.

96 Ibid., p. 327.

97 Strang to Simon, 17 June 1933, FO 371/17251 N4720/1610/38 discussed the significance of the purge of personnel at MOGES I power station reported in *Rabochnaia Moskva*, "Lessons Have Not Been Learned," 9 June 1933.

projects where he supervised the erectors of three of the world's largest electrical switches in 48 days. Upon completion of his statement he thanked Ulrich for allowing him the floor.[98] According to Cummings, the fiery Welshman stormed back to his seat "looking very much like he would like to hit something or someone very hard indeed."[99] After Gregory's strong showing Ulrich decided to adjourn for 20 minutes!

The final defendant called upon resumption was, according to Cummings, perhaps the most convincing "wrecker," Sukhoruchkin.[100] His testimony was littered with connections to engineers tried in the famous Industrial Party Trial[101] and, in this way, linked the current OGPU action against the electrical industry to past crimes and criminals. Sukhoruchkin also managed to take credit for very major breakdowns, such as the Moscow blackout of 22 November 1932, as well as claiming numerous more petty wrecking projects as his own. Thornton gathered himself together enough to dispute Sukhoruchkin's allegation that the British engineer had paid him for and instructed him in the wrecking activities he had carried out. The follow-up questions from the defence counsel, Braude, served to confirm the tenuousness of Thornton's relationship to the Soviet engineer.[102]

The final full day of testimony began with a sharp exchange between Monkhouse and Ulrich. According to Strang, Monkhouse had decided to spring a prepared statement denouncing the whole trial as a frame-up and had gained the assent of his colleagues on the matter.[103] Ulrich tried to restrain him three times at the outset of the session, but Monkhouse managed to blurt out that "after the showing which Sukhoruchkin made last night, it is perfectly clear to me that this case is a frame-up against the Metro-Vickers, based on the evidence of terrorized prisoners."[104] Ulrich assured Monkhouse that he would get a chance to make a closing statement later in the trial and only with great difficulty did he succeed in proceeding with the testimony of Krasheninnikov, Oleinik, and Zorin.

---

98 Ibid., p. 399.
99 Cummings, *The Moscow Trial*, p. 193.
100 Ibid., p. 181, 193. The MVEEC and William Strang had strong reservations concerning Sukhoruchkin's "guilt" and found the excessive detail of his confession one of the clear indications of its fabrication. See Strang's commentary on Cummings's portrait in Strang to Bullard, 10 August 1933, Strang MSS 4/5.
101 *The Case*, p. 414.
102 Ibid., p. 423-24.
103 Strang, *Home and Abroad*, p. 104.
104 *The Case*, p. 427.

During the testimony that followed, Cushny, and to a lesser extent, Thornton, disputed allegations of bribing and wrecking that were attributed to them by the Soviet accused in much the same manner that had occurred before. Cushny managed to prove that the breakdowns that had occurred at the Baku station where he and Oleinik worked together had not occurred with MVEEC equipment. Moreover he pointed out that the boilers that did break down were brand new and of an innovative design — suggesting to him that the Soviet engineers charged with the operation of the new technology did not really understand the latest developments.[105]

The featured event of the evening session of 15 April was the examination of Monkhouse. After providing a biographical sketch which included references to his activities at Archangel during the Russian Civil War, Monkhouse was asked to detail the types of problems MVEEC equipment had incurred in the Soviet Union. Monkhouse did not deny that defects, sometimes serious defects, had been present in MVEEC equipment at various sites around the country. One source of the problem with MVEEC turbines was that they were to be run at 2 000 work hours per annum for peak efficiency, but Soviet practice paid little attention to such requirements.[106] For the most part Monkhouse fended off Vyshinskii's attempts to "interpret" the British manager's replies as the prosecutor wanted to, and Monkhouse took great exception to Vyshinskii's introduction of portions of his written statement which he had retracted prior to the trial's beginning.[107] Vyshinskii claimed that he had allowed no such retraction and that he was not even present at such a meeting. Monkhouse was placated somewhat when it became clear that the testimony Vyshinskii wanted to recall was not that which Monkhouse feared most. Even so, Monkhouse's written statement asserted that he would not have bought the latest MVEEC machinery to fulfill the tasks intended by the Commissariat of Heavy Industry because of known defects in the systems.[108] Monkhouse did not try to deny his or MVEEC's knowledge of the defects, but excused this as something practised by businessmen everywhere. He added, the MVEEC "did everything to satisfy the demands of our clients. We sent machines which we guaranteed and these machines we shall rebuild."[109]

---

105 Ibid., p. 477.
106 Ibid., p. 527.
107 Ibid., p. 534-35.
108 Ibid., p. 535-37.
109 Ibid., p. 536.

At the end of the session Vyshinskii took care to demonstrate that Monkhouse's outburst in the morning, which claimed that he had been interrogated for 18 hours straight, was false. Monkhouse accepted the revision to a 12-hour total which he now agreed had been endured in two separate sessions.[110] As to *The Times* (London) editorial after the trial that to "most people the distinction between 19, 18, or even 12 hours of continuous examination will appear a distinction with hardly a difference," Monkhouse's own concern about the matter would appear to falsify such a view.[111] In any event, this incident went some way to bolstering the legitimacy of the methods used in the pre-trial examination and undermined the impact of Monkhouse's indignant protest in the eyes of some observers.[112] When views of the foreign diplomatic corps in Moscow turned to the negative impression made by the MVEEC engineers, Monkhouse's admission was often cited as a particularly damaging one. Such behaviour was "disgraceful and unworthy of Englishmen."[113]

The final submission of evidence took place on 16 April in the form of 10 questions submitted by Monkhouse to the Commission of Experts charged with assessing the technical aspects of the case. It is hard to know what Monkhouse hoped to achieve with these questions, since he scarcely opposed the adverse answers each question was treated with by the Commission. In general, the Commission emphasized the possibility, if not certainty, that the breakdowns occurred along the lines of the Soviet testimony rendered in the case. In short, these breakdowns were not "accidental," but were politically motivated.[114] Monkhouse chose only to point out that a lengthy technical dispute could be justified on a number of the Commission's conclusions but that he did not want to pursue it at this juncture. Most probably Monkhouse thought there was little to lose by having the Commission pass judgement and if they came down against the MVEEC he could attack them, along with the whole orchestration of the trial, during his final statement.

This left the floor open for the concluding remarks of the Public Prosecutor, Vyshinskii. His comments fill almost 100 pages of the verbatim report as he brought the drama of this trial of "social scum" to its

---

110 Ibid., p. 564-65.
111 "The Moscow Trial: A New Survey," *The Times* (London), 22 May 1933, p. 16.
112 See Cummings' discussion of the uses and abuses of the interrogation methods in *The Moscow Trial*, p. 212-15.
113 Strang to Simon, 18 July 1933, FO 371/17273 N5521/1610/38.
114 Ibid., p. 577-83.

final climax. He heaped ridicule on most of the accused and once again demonstrated the prosecution's conviction that these wreckers were agents of both the MVEEC and the British Secret Service. The Prosecutor defended Soviet judicial methods by quoting from a speech by Sir Stafford Cripps in the House of Commons who had recently complained about British justice holding prisoners without the benefit of knowing what the charges were to be, as in the Scottish Silks case.[115] Here Vyshinskii understood that attack was the best defence, and he brought out statements by the British accused and gave them a severe and sarcastic reworking. He portrayed the confessions of Thornton and Monkhouse as evidence which demonstrated that they knew that while living in the Soviet Union they were subject to Soviet law, and that they also knew they had transgressed the bounds of that law by being overzealous in the gathering of information.[116] Vyshinskii asserted:

> This is exactly what Thornton says: in admitting that he was guilty of espionage, he says, he thought that in this country spying information meant, not information having military State significance, as it is in actual fact, but all information including such information [gossip] as I have just spoken about. Why did he argue like that? Perhaps because he wanted to take advantage of the really fairly wide definition in this sphere of law of capitalist countries.[117]

By arguing in this way, Vyshinskii was responding to Thornton's attempt to discredit the charge of espionage by likening it to a charge of collecting common gossip. The Prosecutor instead maintained that Soviet law was very specific, and since MVEEC engineers had admitted they were subject to the law, this meant they knew its specifics and therefore had confessed to the specifics — not to any broad interpretation of its meaning.

Vyshinskii also attacked the complaints made by Monkhouse about long interrogations by drawing attention to the written requests submitted by Litvinov in March which asked that the MVEEC case be expedited as quickly as possible.[118] Thus, it was out of courtesy, not out of vindictiveness, that the interrogators had worked long and hard to get to the heart of the case, Vyshinskii contended.

In winding up his performance, Vyshinskii did not neglect to pay tribute to his leader:

---

115 Ibid., p. 590. See H.D. Deb. 5 s., # 276, cols. 1795-1795, 1802-05, 5 April 1933.
116 Ibid., p. 609-10.
117 Ibid., p. 611.
118 Ibid., p. 664.

> And from the lofty height of this scaffolding of our socialist construc-
> tion, crowning with new and new [sic] victories the efforts, the cre-
> ative labour and the enthusiasm of the proletariat of our Party under
> the leadership of the Central Committee, and of the leader of our
> Party, Comrade Stalin, of the proletariat which is marching along the
> heroic path of victory, the despicable crimes by which these insignifi-
> cant, venal, corrupt, and treacherous people, who betrayed the social-
> ist fatherland, and tried to hold up the victorious march of the social-
> ist revolution, will appear still more insignificant, more shameful and
> more repulsive.[119]

The former Menshevik, Vyshinskii, had definitely found his calling as
Prosecutor in Stalin's court.

The responses of the various defence counsels and final statements
by the accused were all that remained in the trial before sentencing.
Even Strang had to admit that the Soviet lawyers, "within their limits,
did their best for their clients."[120] Arkady Vaksberg, the author of the
first *glasnost* study of Vyshinskii,[121] has noted the importance of the efforts of some of the defence counsel — notably Dolmatovskii and Pines
(counsels for Gregory and Nordwall and Lobanov and Lebedev) —
who did not appear in subsequent trials and were themselves purged
later on because of their efforts on behalf of the accused. Vaksberg is no
doubt correct on this count, but it appears that the efforts of these men
proved somewhat infectious as it must be said that some kind of defence — though by no means as robust as would be provided in a Western court — was offered for all the accused. One of the chief difficulties
that arose for the defence, aside from the obvious political considerations that enveloped the case, was that in a trial with multiple accused, most of whom had incriminated one or another of their associates in the dock, it was impossible to argue that one defendant was innocent without further incriminating another defendant or group of
defendants. This feature played an important role when defence counsel defended Soviet accused by trying to demonstrate the transformation of character that had occurred once the Russian met the foreigner.
At one juncture there was even some bickering between the defence
counsels about this tactic since some had to defend Russians and others the British accused. Libson took up this problem in response to
Braude:

---

119 Ibid., p. 673.
120 Strang, *Home and Abroad*, p. 108-109.
121 A. Vaksberg, *Stalin's Prosecutor: The Life of Andrei Vyshinsky* (New York: Grove
     Weidenfeld, 1990), p. 66-67.

> For instance, we heard it said from the mouth of Braude that in de-
> fending the Russians my associates went to extremes, that we made it
> appear that these Englishmen had in some potent, mystical manner
> brought pressure to bear upon the Russians, in consequence of which
> they committed crimes. . . . It is incorrect to term us Counsel for the
> defence for the Russians. We Soviet Counsel are quite aware that
> Richards is not Mephistopheles, that Thornton is not Faust and that
> the Russian engineers are not Marguerites.[122]

Despite this disavowal by an advocate for a Russian accused, each set
of defenders responsible for either the British or the Russian accused
had to "prosecute" the other group of defendants.[123]

Kaznacheev defended Gussev, for example, by underscoring the
humble background of Gussev, who was the son of an engineer, and
stressing that "the decisive role in transforming Gussev's anti-Soviet
sentiments into active counter-revolutionary activity was played by
these gentlemen [Thornton and MacDonald]."[124] Kaznacheev could
not get around Gussev's own confession that claimed the Russian engineer had volunteered for Kolchak's army, but at least Gussev had
honestly confessed this counter-revolutionary behaviour and, in any
case, the son of an engineer could not be a class enemy. Apparently
Kaznacheev thought the sons of the technical intelligentsia were necessarily allies of the proletariat.[125] What is more, the defence argued, in
cases of wreckers such as Gussev, and Sokolov too, they were second-
rate wreckers at best, and therefore did not warrant the "supreme
measure" — death by shooting.[126]

Of course if the defence argued that some of the Russian wreckers
were only second rate, it had to acknowledge that there were individuals on trial who were first-rate criminals. For Kaznacheev, the most
likely candidate for this dubious accolade was Oleinik. Oleinik had
had a long involvement with foreign firms dating back to before the
Revolution and had travelled to Manchester for training with the
MVEEC. Vyshinskii had painted him in "repulsive colours," Kaznacheev admitted, and Oleinik himself had characterized his own crimes
"pointedly and quite correctly." The only point Kaznacheev could
raise in his defence was that Oleinik had become so much a part of the
foreign firm that he could no longer distinguish the borderline "be-

---

122 Ibid., p. 765-66.
123 See Libson's rebuttal to Braude on this point, *The Case*, p. 764-65.
124 Ibid., p. 678.
125 Ibid., p. 677-78.
126 Ibid., p. 680-81.

tween the legal and permissible and the illegal and impermissible." He was, "without knowing it himself," an obedient "tool" of Thornton, his employer.[127] As a defence, this was not much, but Kaznacheev hoped the Court could see fit to allow such men to be rehabilitated after the lapse of some term in order that they could "join in that great work of constructing socialist society."[128]

For the most part, then, the strategy of defending the Russian accused amounted to an attempt to show that "active" anti-Soviet behaviour, as opposed to a general anti-Soviet predisposition, only took over once contact with the British employees of the MVEEC had taken place. Anna Kutuzova's defence, presented by Libson, attacked the notion that this capable secretary, who was recommended to the MVEEC by the "untouchable" Professor Graftio, could scarcely avoid contact with the British staff and could in no way be connected to any particular act of wrecking.[129] Libson maintained that it was the MVEEC that had proposed that Kutuzova should live at the company compound once living arrangements became hard to procure in Moscow. Finally, the Court was asked to consider the psychological strain that Kutuzova was under, and here Libson made sure to direct attention to what he called the "psychological condition peculiar to her as a woman" (whatever that means) as employee and friend of Thornton and Monkhouse.[130] Her only crime, Libson argued, was that she failed to inform promptly on people to whom she was professionally and psychologically attached.[131]

Undertaking the defence of the British accused was, as Braude noted, a "far from simple task."[132] Still, the strategy used by the defence counsel for the British was, in general, more aggressively contentious of the nature of the "evidence" rendered in the testimony given during the trial and openly hostile to the notion that the Russian accused were simply pawns in the hands of conspiratorial foreigners. In his turn, Braude mocked the strategy of those advocates who defended the Russians.

> Comrade Judges, we in this country are living in an epoch of the sound materialist conception of human relationships. Idealist ravings about a powerful, all absorbing personality who subjects all who sur-

---

127 Ibid., p. 681.
128 Ibid., p. 682.
129 Ibid., p. 771.
130 Ibid., p. 772-73.
131 Ibid., p. 774.
132 Ibid., p. 708.

round him to his own will, who forces all around him to carry out his desires, do not suit us; the mystical images of demons, of evil geniuses who seduce and tempt others, that were depicted in the speeches of the defence, do not suit us. . . . [W]e know only sound, normal, human mutual relationships and it is on this plane of mutual relationships that I will try to define my assumptions concerning the charges against Thornton.[133]

Thornton's defence was made more demanding than most of the other British defendants because of his confession and the corroborating testimony of a number of the other accused. Braude attacked the case against Thornton by arguing that quantity is not the same as quality and boldly asserting that "such a combination of testimony by accomplices may be strong legal proof only if it is impossible to presuppose the presence of a common motive for giving such testimony, of a common psychological reason which, without a preliminary agreement on their part, would dictate their line of behaviour."[134] This struck at the heart of the whole series of "confessions" rendered in the trial and was one of the startling examples of the latitude allowed in the defence of the MVEEC accused.

As to Thornton's signed statements, Braude asserted that Thornton's denial of almost all of his pre-trial confessions meant that he was only guilty of collecting "economic information." On this charge, Braude could see no way out for Thornton, but there was the mitigating circumstance that the legal boundaries in the USSR and elsewhere on such a charge varied markedly and, in contrast to Vyshinskii's depiction of Thornton, Braude maintained the British engineer simply had failed to pay close enough attention to the local norms.[135] Finally, the charge of bribing could be understood in the same way — in capitalist countries such payments were common. The "whole trouble is that the accused transferred these methods of capitalist economy to our country."[136] This showed, in Braude's view, the "light-minded" approach of the MVEEC to their affairs in the Soviet Union. Such action constituted a crime, but a crime that could be understood more as a mistake than as an act designed to aid in the wrecking of the USSR.[137]

---

133 Ibid., p. 709-10. It was this speech by Braude which provoked Libson's response on behalf of the "Counsel for the Russians" cited above.
134 Ibid., p. 712.
135 Ibid., p. 717-19.
136 Ibid., p. 718-19.
137 Ibid.

Of those foreigners accused of the most serious involvement in the anti-Soviet "organization," William MacDonald received perhaps the most moving defence. Smirnov took the Court through the engineer's biographical profile, recalling the childhood accident that left the 10-year-old MacDonald lame and emphasizing that while MacDonald came from a society dominated by the bourgeoisie, he, himself, was from the working class. This tactic, of course, pointed to the weakness of any argument against MacDonald based on his "class origins" and was built into a defence for MacDonald which stressed that, unlike Thornton or Monkhouse, he had little political knowledge or managerial abilities to utilize as instruments for any anti-Soviet behaviour whatsoever. Rather, the young, lame, politically naive engineer came to the Soviet Union only to encounter "the terrible and ghastly image of Vassily Alexeyevitch Gussev."[138] Thus, the roles were to be reversed in the defence of the British. How could these engineers teach anti-Soviet spirits such as Gussev, Sokolov, or Sukhoruchkin anything about "White-guardist" sentiment?[139]

This argument was used in the defence of all the British defendants except Gregory, who was to be cleared of all charges, but in these other cases more attention was paid to debunking the actual testimony raised against the British engineers. The testimony of Kutuzova was alleged to be inconsistent throughout and lacking in specifics.[140] Testimony against Nordwall and Cushny reduced itself to the prosecution relying on the word of a "confessed" Russian wrecker against the word of a British engineer who had consistently claimed to be innocent.[141]

In the defence of Monkhouse, Kommodov had to deal with the issue of Monkhouse's participation in the Russian Civil War. This, he said, was a point that counted against the British engineer, though even here it was necessary to note that Monkhouse had refused to serve under Denikin.[142] Despite this, Kommodov thought that in the years since 1918, Monkhouse "may have changed his attitude."[143] He observed that Monkhouse was,

---

138 Ibid., p. 700.
139 Ibid., p. 713.
140 Ibid., p. 715-16, 751, and 758.
141 Ibid., p. 724-25.
142 Ibid., p. 762.
143 Ibid., p. 761.

an intelligent man, a man with a broad outlook, [who] cannot have failed to see how the face of our land has changed during these years. ... He has seen that where the muzhiks used to till the soil with wooden ploughs, tractors and mechanical ploughs are now in operation. Where formerly dugouts in which all those who produced all the wealth once lived like moles, palaces of labour and clubs now rise.[144]

The British manager of the MVEEC was, in Kommodov's view, one of a group of foreign specialists who were "working with no less enthusiasm than the whole country is working; they are sincere friends of the Soviet Union."[145] Like Thornton, Monkhouse could not escape some responsibility for minor issues such as the Dolgov "bribe," but he was not an anti-Soviet wrecker bent on undermining the Soviet state.[146]

After the members of the Collegium of Defence finished with their final statements, each of the accused was given the opportunity for a final personal plea. All of the Russian accused quietly restated their guilt, and from the British defendants only Monkhouse thought it necessary to add to the final drama of the trial. He began by making a veiled comment that implied Vyshinskii was lying if he continued to insist that he had taken no part in Monkhouse's interrogation. Monkhouse asserted that the evidence from testimony such as Thornton's confession was not given "voluntarily" and the countervailing testimony of the other four British accused had such weight that such "confessions" as Thornton gave would not be accepted as real evidence in any "Court of Law."[147] Monkhouse went on to insist that the MVEEC itself had a great interest in continued work in the USSR and had no interest whatsoever in "cutting our own throats" by engaging in "wrecking activities."[148] Moreover, as engineers, the staff of the MVEEC could not bring themselves to destroy their own creations. He argued that "engineers, when they build works of this kind, they look upon them as their own children. And I know of no parents who would put a dag-

---

144 Ibid., p. 762.
145 Ibid., p. 750.
146 Ibid., p. 751-52.
147 Ibid., p. 780.
148 Ibid. Monkhouse also alleged that the Soviets still owed the MVEEC about 15 million roubles (about 1.4 million pounds), an odd error, since Richards had told the Foreign Office in March that the outstanding balance was in the order of 30 thousand pounds. It may be that Monkhouse's figure was an estimate of the amount of business the MVEEC was hoping to gain by continued access to the Soviet market. See Foreign Office Minute by Collier, 17 March 1933, FO 371/17265 N1827/1610/38.

ger into the heart of their own child."[149] It was a fitting summation by a man who had spent 20 years working in Russia and the Soviet Union.

The final session of the trial of the Metropolitan-Vickers engineers began in the twilight hours of 18-19 April. A long statement of the findings of the Court was read which recounted the key points of the prosecution's case and made it clear that the "aforesaid State employees of power stations were connected with the criminal activity of certain employees of the private British firm of Metropolitan-Vickers."[150] Thornton was assigned the leading criminal role in the indictment against the British engineers. The Court also cited a decree by the Central Executive Committee of the USSR of 14 March 1933, which stipulated that "State employees guilty of wrecking are regarded as traitors to their fatherland and must be held more strictly responsible than employees of private enterprises."[151] This was the first real sign that the British would receive lighter sentences than the Russians in the dock.

At this point the sentences were read out and it became clear that no one would receive the "supreme measure of social defence" — death by shooting. The explanation given for this act of generosity was that "the Court was guided by the fact that the criminal wrecking activities of the aforesaid convicted persons bore a local character and did not cause serious damage to the industrial power of the U.S.S.R."[152] With this proviso the sentences were:

1. Gussev, Sukhoruchkin, and Lobanov — 10 years
2. Sokolov, Zorin, and Kotliarevskii — 8 years
3. Krasheninnikov — 5 years
4. Lebedev — 2 years, "in view of the fact that he was merely a tool of Lobanov"[153]
5. Thornton — 3 years
6. MacDonald — 2 years, "in so far as he acted under the direct instigation of his immediate superior, Thornton, on the one hand, and in view of his frank confession"
7. Monkhouse and Nordwall — expulsion from the USSR for five years, "in so far as they did not take part in causing breakdowns"
8. Cushny — expulsion from the USSR for five years, "in view of the lapse of time since the crime . . . (1928)"

---

149 Ibid., p. 781.
150 Ibid., p. 794.
151 Ibid., p. 796.
152 Ibid.
153 Ibid.

9. Oleinik — 3 years, "taking into consideration the fact that he was subordinate to Thornton and that he was an employee of a private firm"

10. Kutuzova — 18 months, "for the same reasons as above [Oleinik]"[154]

11. Zivert — no punishment, "taking into consideration that by the work he has done since 1931 he has proved that he has sincerely broken off all connections with the wreckers"

12. Gregory — acquitted, "in view of the inadequacy of the evidence"[155]

The Court asked that Monkhouse, Nordwall, and Cushny leave the USSR within three days time.

Though the sentences were light, it had already been decided in London that if any prison terms were handed down the embargo that had been provided for before the trial would go into effect immediately. Since the Anglo-Soviet trade agreement of 1930 had officially been terminated on 17 April, there were no legal impediments to the enactment of the embargo, and it was duly authorized by the Privy Council on 19 April 1933.[156] The stage was thus set for the final confrontation of the Metro-Vickers affair.

---

154 Ibid., p. 797.
155 Ibid., p. 798.
156 See Strang's account of this decision in *Home and Abroad*, p. 110.

6

Crisis Contained

On the whole intelligent opinion here holds: that (1) the sentences are lighter than expected; (2) there was some foundation for the Bolshevist case; and (3) that we mishandled the case from the beginning.
— Sir Robert Bruce Lockhart, Diary entry, 19 April 1933

Soviet authorities seem to have fallen between two stools in fixing sentences on Russians and on English. On the one hand they have failed to satisfy His Majesty's Government. On the other they have disappointed their own partisans by leniency displayed. Audience at the trial was obviously disappointed that there were no death sentences and I gather that communist circles are mortified to lose golden opportunity to strike home at enemies of State.   — William Strang, Moscow, 20 April 1933

Recall, say, the pressure that was brought to bear upon us by Britain; the embargo on our exports, the attempt to interfere in our internal affairs and to use this as a probe — to test our power of resistance. . . . It is well known that a certain section of the British Conservatives cannot live without such sallies. And precisely because they are not accidental we must reckon that in the future, too, sallies will be made against the U.S.S.R., all sorts of menaces will be created, attempts will be undertaken to damage the U.S.S.R.   — I.V. Stalin, Report to the Seventeenth
Party Congress, 26 January 1934

153

The completion of the show trial did not signify an end to the Metro-Vickers crisis, but instead clarified many of the issues at stake. For formal Anglo-Soviet relations, the verdict of the trial presented a challenge to the British government to act on its threat of economic sanctions by swiftly bringing the pressures of a trade embargo to bear on the Soviet Union. For the MVEEC it meant trying to maintain a significant and profitable business relationship, while at the same time assisting the efforts of His Majesty's Government to secure the release of the imprisoned engineers.

On the Soviet side, as the crisis dragged on from April to July, it became increasingly clear that Litvinov and the Narkomindel would be busily engaged trying to minimize and defuse a difficult situation against the international backdrop of the Disarmament Conference in Geneva, the World Economic Conference in London,[1] heightened American concerns about the recognition of the USSR, and a Soviet domestic scene replete with continuing purges and Party *chistki*.

During the course of the trial, the British Cabinet had debated the merits of various schemes pending the trial's outcome. Early on in the deliberations, Runciman suggested that a measure targeting the Russian Petroleum Products Co. (ROP) in Britain, a subsidiary of the Soviet oil agency, Neftsindikat, would "appear to inflict maximum disadvantage on Soviet Russia with a minimum disadvantage to ourselves."[2] Vansittart argued that if the Soviet court acquitted all the British defendants, H.M.G. could not be justified in taking any punitive action whatsoever. While the Permanent Under-Secretary agreed that the passing of light sentences would merit the type of measure indicated by Runciman in Cabinet, he maintained that heavy sentencing would warrant substantially more punishment than simply closing up ROP, which ran at a loss and was "basically a propaganda enterprise," anyway. In a memo the following day, Vansittart cautioned Simon that, "we should be an object of some derision not only in Russia but throughout the world if, out of all our labours, so ridiculous a mouse were born."[3]

The decisive steps were taken on 18 April, just prior to the final sentencing in Moscow, and were based on the accurate assessment of the Foreign Office that all of the British defendants but Gregory would be found guilty. While there was some sentiment voiced in the Cabinet meeting that day that, even if all the defendants were acquitted, a

---

1 The Conference met from 12 June to 27 July 1933.

2 CAB 23/75 27(33)1, C.P. 101(33), 12 April 1933.

3 Vansittart to Simon, 13 April 1933, FO 371/17268 N2782/1610/38.

strong embargo should be put into effect, the actual Import Prohibition Act that was approved could not be empowered if all six British defendants were simply expelled from the USSR.[4]

The main targets of the embargo were oil and timber. Flax was not on the list for fear of encouraging the development of a native Soviet linen industry, and it was hoped the Russians would continue to export the raw material that was so essential for industry in Scotland and Northern Ireland. Taken as a whole, the embargo against Soviet exports to Britain covered roughly 80 percent of goods from the USSR.[5]

Consistent with the optimistic premise that had originally informed the British decision to seek embargo-enabling powers was the conviction that the USSR was decidedly vulnerable to economic sanctions. Simon told the Cabinet that "Russian balances here are rapidly drawn on by Soviet Government to pay for purchases from other countries, especially Germany, and it is the view of my advisers that if the proclamation is sufficiently wide, it is very improbable that Soviet Russia could stand the strain for more than month."[6] Moreover, British estimates of the balance of trade with the USSR made the Soviet market less and less valuable to British producers.[7] The supplies that would be lost from refusing imports of Soviet goods could easily be made up by increasing imports from Scandinavia, the Empire, and British-owned oil companies.[8] As events would show, even this hope was not easily realized. Britain found its supply of timber seriously disrupted, and businessmen who normally traded with the USSR found that they suffered from the embargo as well.[9]

The signals coming from Moscow offered the British some initial confirmation of their assessment of the trade situation. Indications from the Soviet diplomatic corps pointed to a continuing rift between the Narkomindel and other branches of the Soviet government. Strang related the view of one source:

> The wife of one of the People's Commissars told one of my colleagues two days ago that her husband had remarked to her "I really cannot understand why the authorities have held this trial." She said that

---

4 CAB 23/76 29(33)1, 18 April 1933.

5 Ibid.

6 Ibid.

7 Simon to Lord Hailsham, 25 April 1933, FO 800/288; and Strang to Simon, 22 April 1933, FO 371/17270 N2987/1610/38.

8 Ibid.

9 See the discussion in the Cabinet meeting and Runciman's complaints in CAB 23/76 43(33), 29 June 1933.

other people in the same circles were saying the same thing. Her own view was that if the Soviet Government had wanted to "Kick the British" they should have waited until they had substantial cause. . . . Strength of our reaction has apparently surprised the authorities.[10]

Given the position taken, and the intimacy of the source, it is almost certain that the opinions expressed in this instance stemmed from Ivy Litvinov, the British-born wife of Maxim Litvinov. It was probably for this reason that Strang kept his source anonymous, since he transmitted the message by telegram.

Strang had also received word from Boris Steiger, a shadowy figure employed in the Commissariat of Education and attached to the Narkomindel, that he did not think the trial had produced the necessary evidence to warrant action against Britain.[11] Steiger was used by many foreign missions in the 1930s, including the British, French,[12] and the American embassies, as a liaison with the Narkomindel and as an "independent channel of communication" with the Soviet leadership.[13]

While these sources indicate that those associated with the Soviet diplomatic corps were unhappy with the current state of Anglo-Soviet relations and were concerned about the added strain imposed by the British embargo, there are reasons to question the British assumption that they were bargaining for the release of Thornton and MacDonald from a position of strength. In the first instance, the Soviets immediately imposed their own counter-embargo on the remaining trade items which were left out of the British Act. The Soviet decree was to remain in effect only as long as the British embargo was in force.[14] This was not merely a token gesture, as Owen has argued,[15] since the export of items that the British had deliberately left out of their own restrictions, such as flax, dropped markedly from the levels of 1932. It was

---

10 Strang to Simon, 23 April 1933, FO 371/17270 N2984/1610/38.

11 Ibid.

12 According to French Chargé d' Affaires Payart, Steiger disappeared, along with so many Soviet diplomats, in the Great Purge of 1937. He wryly observed, "M. Staline reste maître de la situation" (Payart to Delbos [Foreign Secretary], *Documents diplomatiques français*, 2nd series, Vol. V, #301, 17 April 1937, and #331, 24 April 1937). Also see the discussion by Jiri Hochman in *The Soviet Union and the Failure of Collective Security, 1934-1938* (Ithaca: Cornell University Press, 1984), p. 128-29; and T. Uldricks, "The Impact of the Great Purges on the People's Commissariat of Foreign Affairs," *Slavic Review*, 36, 2 (1977): 187-203.

13 This according to George Kennan as he indicated to the political scientist, Jerry Hough. See Hough and Fainsod, *How the Soviet Union Is Governed*, p. 167, n. 61.

14 *Izvestiia*, 22 April 1933, p. 1, carried the text of the Commissariat of Foreign Trade's Decree on Trade with Great Britain of 21 April 1933.

15 Owen, "The Metro-Vickers Crisis," p. 101.

only after another Anglo-Soviet trade agreement was negotiated in 1934 that export of such raw materials regained their earlier levels.[16]

More important for an assessment of the leverage available to the British in this apparent test of economic strength is an evaluation of the broader trends in Soviet trade. The British correctly assumed that Soviet exports normally helped the USSR pay for German goods, and this trend increased in 1933.[17] Trade figures show, however, that Soviet imports were declining sharply across the board,[18] and in absolute terms Britain, the United States, France, and Germany were all hit hard from 1930 to 1935. While the British were undoubtedly correct in reasoning that the British market was much more important to the USSR than the Soviet market was to Britain,[19] it is hard to sustain the notion that the Soviets were critically reliant on the foreign exchange they generated from sales in the United Kingdom. Soviet exports were generally declining in this period, though not at nearly as fast a rate as imports,[20] and they were shifting from a heavy reliance on the British market, which normally bought about 25 percent of Soviet goods, to other countries.[21] Ironically, just when Britain sought to squeeze the USSR, the Soviet economy began to enjoy the first year of a four-year run of a surplus in its balance of trade.[22] Even if the USSR had lost the entire British market this would still have been the case. Alexander Baykov has argued that after the massive purchases of the First Five-Year Plan,

---

16 Based on data from *Vneshniaia Torgovlia SSSR za 1918-1940 gg.*, p. 460.

17 Note the disparities between the balance of trade figures for the major trading partners of the USSR in Appendix G.

18 See Appendix B, in particular the change from 1931 to 1934. Similar trends appear in Appendix G as the amount of trade with all three major trading partners declined sharply. The discrepancy between the two sets of rouble totals from Appendix B to Appendix G occurs because the former uses 1950 rouble values and the latter uses 1936 values.

19 It should be noted that certain British industries were heavily reliant on the Soviet market for exports. In 1932 the USSR bought 84 percent of British machine tools sold abroad and 25 percent of British electrical equipment exported. See Strang to Simon, 30 April 1933, FO 371/17239 N3247/5/38.

20 See Appendix B, "Soviet Foreign Trade, 1913-1940." The Soviets also tried, not too successfully, to interest Italy and Poland in more extensive trade arrangements. See Strang to Vansittart, 22 May 1933, *DBFP*, #496, n. 3, especially the minute by Shone of 1 June 1933.

21 See Appendix G. While Soviet sales to its largest markets, Britain and Germany showed some decline in 1932-34, countries such as Belgium, the Netherlands, and Sweden showed short-term increases. The Mongolian Republic's purchases of Soviet imports increased from 4.6 percent of the Soviet total in 1931 to 10.7 percent in 1934. See A. Baykov, *Soviet Foreign Trade: International Finance Section* (Princeton: Princeton University Press, 1946), Table 7.

22 Ibid.

the Soviets were suffering from a shortage of foreign exchange by 1932, but has also pointed out that the Soviet economy could do without the level of imports it had required in the early years of the First Five-Year Plan.[23] What this suggests is that by 1933, at a time when the world economy was suffering from the effects of the Great Depression more generally, the Soviet economy had gained a sufficient level of development, flexibility, and self-reliance to withstand the pressures of a British embargo. This does not mean that the economic pressure exerted by the British embargo was not a factor in the Anglo-Soviet conflict, but it does make it necessary to look beyond economics for an explanation of the conflict's resolution.

At the same time as the British Cabinet deliberated over its strategy in this confrontation, the MVEEC was reassessing its business ventures in the Soviet Union and trying to help extricate Thornton and MacDonald from their Soviet jail. It had evidently become apparent to the directors of the MVEEC that it was no longer possible to participate in Soviet industrial enterprises without the active support of the British government. Sir Felix Pole directed the MVEEC lawyer in Moscow, Robert Turner, to use the services of Strang to begin negotiations for the release of the engineers. He told Turner to emphasize that the MVEEC had a strong interest in continuing to work in the USSR and that it would be very difficult to encourage engineers to work in that country if two of their colleagues remained in prison.[24]

The issue of how to continue work in the USSR was taken up at the Foreign Office on the strength of a lengthy memo by Strang which reviewed the history of the MVEEC's practices in the Soviet context. Collier made the memo available to Pole and Richards, but the MVEEC Directors showed little interest in adopting its main points. Strang had warned that

> The Metro-Vickers trial points [to] the pitiless moral which is important to all foreigners working in Russia and to the company in particular. This is that any foreigner working in Russia whose business brings him in contact with enterprises of national importance runs a grave risk of arrest, trial and sentence for espionage, bribery or wrecking if he establishes other than the barest business or professional relations with the Russians. . . .
>
> The company may well think it desirable to replace all these men with fresh men from England to serve in Russia for a short time only

---

23 Baykov, *Soviet Foreign Trade*, p. 55-56, 59-60.
24 Pole to Turner, 19 April 1933, FO 371/17270 N2886/1610/38.

and with strict instructions to be most circumspect in his relations with Russians. Perhaps this is not practicable.[25]

While the MVEEC indicated an initial willingness to replace those engineers named in Thornton's confession, men such as Buckell, Burke, and especially Tearle,[26] were now, after the loss of the services of Monkhouse and Thornton, among the most experienced MVEEC employees in the Soviet Union.[27] For the time being, Richards ordered Buckell to continue to fulfill the minimum obligations of the technical assistance contract and noted that new "volunteers" would be sent to the USSR to assist in the work.[28] Richards also asked the Foreign Office to consider pressuring Maisky for a guarantee of safe passage for the MVEEC personnel. As a sign of the new relationship that was developing between the MVEEC and the Foreign Office, Richards requested that all these communications be sent to the Moscow Embassy using a Foreign Office code.[29]

While the MVEEC dealt with these personnel problems it also sought to facilitate the release of Thornton and MacDonald. The Company sent to Turner the text of an appeal to the Presidium of the Central Executive Committee of the USSR it had drafted on behalf of Thornton which admitted "serious mistakes" and conceded that he had engaged in the "collection of economic information."[30] The appeal requested either the granting of a pardon, or the substitution of expulsion from the country for the sentence of three years deprivation of liberty which was now being served.[31] At the Foreign Office, Collier was unhappy about the MVEEC decision to admit any guilt whatsoever, but agreed with Strang that this was an "unofficial" matter to be handled between the prisoners and their counsels.[32] In its final form Thornton's appeal petitioned that he had "unwittingly committed a number of actions which were regarded by the Court in its verdict as

25 Strang to Simon, 20 April 1933, FO 371/17270 N2944/1610/38.
26 Foreign Office minute by Vyvyan, 9 August 1934, FO 371/18330 N4719/3114/38, which characterized Tearle as a "key" man. J. Vyvyan had been posted to the Moscow Embassy as Third Secretary when the arrests and trial had occurred in 1933. As a consequence of his involvement at that time he was often relied upon at the Foreign Office for his view of MVEEC affairs in the USSR.
27 Richards to Collier, 27 April 1933, FO 371/17270 N3191/1610/38.
28 Richards to Buckell via Collier, 4 May 1933, FO 371/17270 N3390/1610/38.
29 Ibid.
30 Strang to Simon, 20 April 1933, FO 371/17270 N2842/1610/38.
31 Ibid.
32 Ibid.

serious transgressions of Soviet laws."[33] Evidently the MVEEC had decided that an obsequious approach would expedite matters more surely than a continuance of their previous Company policy which denied all wrongdoing.

Initially it did not appear that the Soviet authorities were interested in actively pursuing more measures against the MVEEC following the trial despite the fact that Thornton had named virtually all the remaining British MVEEC employees still resident in the USSR in his "confession." The most convincing surmise on this count, which will receive more thorough treatment below, is that the British embargo had the paradoxical effect of strengthening Litvinov's hand by demonstrating that the ineptly orchestrated OGPU foray into Anglo-Soviet relations had now proved to have a serious international cost.

Still, the trial did have a damaging effect on the ability of MVEEC employees to interact with their Soviet associates. One British erector, Ball, was under consideration for an "Order of Lenin" prior to the trial, but the local authorities who were to nominate him had now thought such a move unwise.[34] The treatment of Ball differed markedly from that of Leon Swazian, an American engineer who was awarded an Order of Lenin for his work at the Kharkov tractor plant. Swazian, when receiving his honour from the Presidium of the Central Committee on 19 April 1933 (revealingly, the last day of the Metro-Vickers trial), did not fail to provide a gracious interpretation for his host's action: "Whoever works well with the Soviet Union receives awards. Whoever obstructs the work, receives a trial."[35]

In contrast, the circumspect approach of local authorities to British electrical engineers was validated a month later when the major purge of the Moscow electrical development (MOGES) took place. The Soviet press explained that such action was necessary since the "lessons had not been learned."[36] The attention of the Soviet authorities was apparently now to be directed towards "cleansing" the electrical industry of "enemies of the state."

The main difficulty the MVEEC faced in carrying out its work on the ground was a lingering suspicion, particularly in more provincial areas, that the MVEEC engineers were nothing but a source of trouble.

---

33 Ibid., 22 April 1933, FO 371/17270 N2980/1610/38.
34 Ibid., 12 May 1933, FO 371/17272 N3801/1610/38.
35 "Russian-American Gets Order of Lenin for Work," *New York Herald Tribune*, 19 April 1933, p. 9.
36 See *Rabochaia Moskva*, 9 June 1933, which was summarized in Strang to Simon, 17 June 1933, FO 371/17251 N4720/113/38.

Reports from engineers working in Novo-Sibirsk, Sudenko, and Kuznetsk all found the local populace hostile to the MVEEC's presence months after the Metro-Vickers affair had been defused.[37] One engineer, Embleton, reported an unsettling tendency on the part of the local Russians to blame any problem on MVEEC personnel or equipment.[38]

There is evidence that the trial did convince some Russians of the guilt of the British engineers. Bullard reported from the Leningrad Consulate on a conversation he had had with a foreign student on the impact of the trial on public opinion:

> some of those that have least cause to accept OGPU evidence as valid nevertheless believe that the British accused were guilty, on the curious ground that if only Russians had been accused the case would have at once been dismissed as a put-up job.... [E]veryone also knows that foreign countries are all the time planning "intervention" in the affairs of the Soviet Union.[39]

Official Soviet propaganda about the fear of foreign invasion had obviously met with some success, even among groups of people who had suffered at the hands of the OGPU, Bullard concluded.[40]

An echo of this theme can also be found in the memoir account of A. Ciliga, a Yugoslav Comintern official imprisoned in the USSR in the early 1930s because of his involvement with the Left-opposition underground in Moscow. While in internal exile he met a technical student who was also imprisoned in the Ikurtsk region of Siberia following the Metro-Vickers trial. The student claimed that the charges against the MVEEC were even more serious than the trial testimony had revealed. Ciliga observed that the student, who came from the new technical intelligentsia and was the "embodiment of 'Our Soviet Students' of the post-revolutionary era," insisted that the charges of wrecking were true. According to the student,

> The government, he thought, did not want too many revelations, and deliberately conducted it as a wreckers' case, whereas it was in fact a real conspiracy.... The conspiracy had apparently been exposed quite accidentally. One of the chief engineers of the "Electric Combinat" in Moscow, a leader of the plot, while taking some papers from the safe in his office, had inadvertently dropped a map of Mos-

37 Coote (Moscow) to Collier, 30 November 1933, FO 371/17274 N8784/1610/38.
38 Ibid. See report by Rapp (Leningrad Consulate).
39 Memo by Bullard (Leningrad Consulate), 29 September 1933, FO 371/17260 N7159/639/38.
40 Ibid. Bullard did not explain exactly which Russians had spoken to the foreign students.

cow with the points to be blown up marked on it in front of the nose of a communist who happened to be there.[41]

The student was apparently a close relative of one of the principal accused[42] and had tried to escape immediately after the first arrests had taken place. He was captured after six months of running from the authorities, having made his way to what he hoped would be a safe haven near Lake Baikal. Almost certainly his arrest was part of the purge in June 1933 of the MOGES works in Moscow noted above.

Throughout the period of the mutual trade embargoes there was a considerable battle in the British and Soviet press over the true character of the Metro-Vickers crisis. The Soviets came out with a full-length English translation of the verbatim report in April, described by Strang as a "workmanlike production," which supplemented the already extensive coverage British readers had received in the daily press. Soviet readers were also assured in an *Izvestiia* article by the eminent Leningrad academician Ioffe that Thornton was an agent of British military intelligence and that the working class of the USSR had to continue to guard against wreckers while seeking to improve their own technical skills.[43] The MVEEC staff who knew Ioffe thought the whole tone of his article was "suggested to him" since it was out of keeping with his "style and ideas." They noted that the article was also published in the English-language paper *Moscow News* in order to widen its international circulation and impact.[44] It was characteristic of Soviet articles on the trial that the main focus of Ioffe's piece was on the validity of evidence gained from the "confessions" of the defendants and it was heavily stressed that such "facts" were indeed facts. The Foreign

---

41 A. Ciliga, *The Russian Enigma* (London: Ink Links, 1979), p. 344.

42 Understandably but unfortunately, Ciliga did not reveal the student's name. The story had a "happy" ending for the young man. A few days after he had told Ciliga about his view of the Metro-Vickers affair, he picked up a job in the Political Education Department of the camp. When questioned about this apparent change in orientation, he told Ciliga, "Well, it can't be helped. One has to look out for oneself." Ciliga remarked somewhat bitterly that this fellow was, "in his innermost thoughts contemptuous of the people and a worshipper of technique." See the account in Ciliga, *The Russian Enigma*, p. 344-45.

The three principal Soviet defendants accused of wrecking activities at the Moscow power station of MOGES I were Sukhoruchkin, Krasheninnikov, and Zorin. While it is always possible that the student was an agent provocateur, if his story is accurate as far as his identity goes, he was likely related to one of these men.

43 *Izvestiia*, 21 April 1933, p. 2; and Richards to Collier, 12 June 1933, FO 371/17273 N4481/1610/38.

44 See comments by Richards and Bullard in Richards' letter to Collier of 12 June, cited immediately above.

Office took some solace from the Soviets need to base their continued assertions on the defendants' "confessions" since they thought evidence of this type was suspect in the eyes of much of the British public.[45]

For their part, the engineers who had been expelled from Soviet territory were finding ready press coverage in Britain as well. The press took a special interest recounting details of their deliverance from the USSR, and the course of their travels enroute to Britain was reported in major papers.[46] Allan Monkhouse received sums in the order of 500 pounds for his version of events from the *Daily Express* and *The Times*.[47] *The Times* thought the whole affair important enough to devote a four-day serial running 22-25 May, under the heading "The Moscow Trial: A New Survey." This special series gave the engineers, in particular Monkhouse and Cushny, a venue to rebut the Soviet version of events. The tone of the editorial lead to the series captures their general purpose. "History must wait patiently and may wait long for some truthful explanation from the Soviet itself why this trial was ever undertaken," *The Times* claimed. The arrests and trial were "groundless," and the paper hoped the testimony of Monkhouse and Cushny would make that clear.[48]

The Soviets were sufficiently concerned about the efforts of the liberated British engineers to chip away at the credibility of the trial to employ the propagandistic talents of the former oppositionist and Comintern official, Karl Radek. Radek summoned his considerable store of anti-British venom to attack the claims made in *The Times* and argued in an article in *Izvestiia* entitled, "Useless Attempts to Whitewash the Nigger," that he had found what he called "Monkhouse's law." According to Radek, Monkhouse's story became more and more courageous in direct proportion to the distance the British engineer was from the court. He also objected that *The Times* was seeking to inflame anti-Soviet opinion just as the World Economic Conference in London was about to convene. It was obvious, Radek observed, that the publication of the Soviet verbatim report of the trial in English, and the very openness of the Soviet judicial procedure, had "settled like stones in the stomach of English imperialism" and it was this discomfort which had motivated the anti-Soviet barrage in the British press.[49]

---

45 Ibid.; and Strang to Simon, 29 May 1933, FO 371/17273 N4274/1610/38.

46 See "Deported Britons in Poland," *Observer*, 23 April 1933.

47 Strang to Simon, 26 April 1933, FO 371/17270 N3123/1610/38; and Richards to Collier, 12 June 1933, FO 371/17273 N4481/1610/38.

48 "The Moscow Trial: A New Survey," *The Times* (London), 22 May 1933, p. 15-16.

49 *Izvestiia*, 29 May 1933, p. 2; and Strang to Simon, 29 May 1933, FO 371/17273 N4274/1610/38.

On the same day *Pravda* carried an article critical of *The Times* coverage which placed the British paper in the role of Gogol's character, the Non-Commissioned Officer's wife, who beat herself, but accused a government official of the crime. Picking up on the main theme of the other articles on the Metro-Vickers trial, *Pravda* claimed the confessions submitted to the court were "facts" and therefore evidence.[50]

As this war of words between the Soviet press and *The Times* continued throughout May and June, British officials were divided over the merits of the public propagandistic campaigns. In Moscow, Strang thought that continued attacks on the merits of the Soviet case against the engineers served the interests of both the MVEEC and His Majesty's Government. Senior officials at the Foreign Office, more distant from the hue and cry of the Soviet press, and perhaps more interested in guiding Anglo-Soviet relations into quieter waters, were decidedly less convinced of the usefulness of continued public debate. Vansittart and Lancelot Oliphant (Assistant Under-Secretary of State), both opposed the release of a third White Paper on the crisis even after the engineers had been released.[51] Oliphant had opined earlier that he wished *The Times* serial "had never been written"[52] and he now hoped that tensions would ease enough for trade negotiations to resume.

While there were few hopeful signs to be found in the shrill discourse of the press, tentative steps were being taken by Litvinov to defuse the impasse through diplomacy. On 23 May the Soviet Commissar approached the British government through an "unofficial channel" and let it be known that his government wanted an end to the dispute and a cessation of trade hostilities.[53] The Riga correspondent for *The Times* had also caught wind of a leak by Narkomindel officials in Moscow, which appeared to confirm that the Soviets were interested in a deal.[54] Periodically throughout May and June, Strang had received further hints from Steiger that "matters were developing smoothly" behind the scenes.[55] It was hoped, Steiger said, that the "incident should be cleared up some time in June or early July."[56] This timetable coincided with Litvinov's visit to the World Economic Conference in London and, in the end, would facilitate the release of Thornton and MacDonald.

---

50 *Pravda*, 29 May 1933, p. 4; and Strang to Simon, 29 May 1933, FO 371/17273 N4274/1610/38.
51 See minutes by Collier, Vansittart, and Oliphant, 9 July 1933, FO 371/17273, N5329/1610/38.
52 Minute by Oliphant, 12 June 1933, FO 371/17273 N4481/1610/38.
53 See note to minute by Collier, 22 June 1933, *DBFP*, # 503.
54 "Soviet and British Prisoners," *The Times* (London), 25 May 1933, p. 18.
55 Strang to Simon, 4 June 1933, *DBFP*, # 500.
56 Ibid.

A number of factors, both international and domestic, appear to have been at work in the Soviet decision to approach the British. On the international front, the Soviets were concerned about the negative impact the Metro-Vickers affair was having on the possibilities of American recognition. The British themselves had taken some delight in reports from Ambassador Ronald Lindsay in Washington, who noted that the flow of events in favour of recognition had been checked by the Metro-Vickers affair which, in the view of officials at the State Department, had greatly strengthened the position of those who opposed recognition.[57]

Despite this difficulty and the continuing problem in the Far East with Japanese threats in Manchuria, there were signs that Soviet diplomacy was having some success. While the British may have overestimated the significance of the renewal of the Berlin Treaty with Germany,[58] it was true that relations with Italy, France, and Poland had improved over the past year.[59] The Soviet press echoed these moves towards wider participation in the international order. Early in May, *Izvestiia* carried an article by Radek that somewhat awkwardly defended aspects of the Versailles Treaty settlement which could serve to enhance stability in Europe. Strang thought that this was yet another indication of the new trend in Soviet thinking. The most troublesome power for the USSR, in Strang's estimation, was Japan and it was to counter this Eastern threat that Soviet diplomacy had moved in the direction of closer contact with the West.[60] With these currents running through Soviet foreign policy in the summer of 1933, it made good sense to resolve the Anglo-Soviet dispute as part of the basic shift towards more cooperation in the international arena which was to become a hallmark of Litvinov's tenure as Commissar for Foreign Affairs.

There were also signs that Soviet concerns about Germany were growing despite the renewal of the Berlin Treaty. German Ambassador

---

57 Lindsay to Simon, 25 April 1933, *DBFP*, # 453. This theme also appears in the articles written by Duranty in the *New York Times* during this period.

58 The renewal of the Berlin Treaty of 1926 meant a continuation of the Rapallo collaboration "at least on paper," between the two outcasts of the Versailles system — Germany and the USSR. Adam Ulam suggests that the Soviets were not deceived by such reassurances from Hitler, but were hoping to delay his anti-Soviet agenda as long a possible. See A. Ulam, *Expansion and Coexistence: Soviet Foreign Policy, 1917-1967* (New York: Holt, Rinehart & Winston, 1974), p. 194-95.

59 Strang noted these "credits" in a report to Simon, 20 May 1933, *DBFP*, # 495. In 1932, the Soviets signed non-aggression treaties with Finland, Latvia, Estonia, Poland, and France.

60 "On the Revision of the Versailles Treaty," *Pravda*, 10 May 1933, p. 2; Strang to Simon, 23 May 1933, *DBFP*, # 497; and ibid., 4 June 1933, *DBFP*, # 500.

Dirksen had made his objections about Radek's article on the Versailles settlement known to Narkomindel officials and was particularly critical of the Soviet Union's apparent about-face on the merits of that treaty.[61] Dirksen also complained about the recent treatment of "Reich citizens living in Russia," and pointed out to the Soviet Deputy-Commissar, Krestinskii, that such policies did nothing to assist those in Germany who did not wish to pursue an anti-Soviet line.[62]

Similar statements made at the World Economic Conference by the German Reich Minister of Economics, Food and Agriculture, Dr. Hugenberg, stressed the coexistence of "independent national economies," flatly stated that Germany had no money for continued credits to debtor nations, and most seriously pointed to the need for German colonies and additional *Lebensraum*.[63] These pronouncements apparently made a strong impression in Moscow. *Izvestiia* carried the text of the Soviet objection to Hugenberg's most disquieting remarks which underscored the contradiction between the renewal of the Berlin Treaty in May and more recent German statements.[64] The Narkomindel intermediary Steiger, who claimed to have knowledge of the instructions Litvinov had taken to London, told Strang that it was after this sounding from the Germans that a "definite impulse in favour of a settlement" of the Anglo-Soviet quarrel had taken hold in Moscow. The Soviets had also been impressed by Simon's continuing public assurances[65] that the embargo was to be used only as a device to aid in the release of Thornton and MacDonald, Steiger added.[66]

It was against this international backdrop, then, that the negotiations for the release of Thornton and MacDonald took place in London during the last two weeks of June. Acting on his own initiative, the MVEEC Director, Sir Felix Pole, met with Litvinov at the Soviet Embassy before the Foreign Office had made any similar arrangements.[67] Undoubtedly recognizing that news of Pole's interview would find its

---

61 Dirksen to Foreign Ministry, 14 May 1933, *Documents on German Foreign Policy*, Series C, Vol. 1 (hereinafter cited as *DGFP*) #232.

62 Ibid.

63 Hugenberg released a statement to the press in London on 16 June 1933 (*DGFP*, #312, n. 2, 14 June 1933).

64 *Izvestiia*, 24 June 1933, p. 1. See J. Degras, ed., *Documents on Soviet Foreign Policy* (London: Oxford University Press, 1951-53), p. 22-23.

65 See Simon's response to Parliamentary questions, 27 April 1933 in *H.C. Deb. 5 s.*, 277, col. 264.

66 Strang to Simon, 18 July 1933, FO 371/17273 N5526/1610/38.

67 Minute by Collier, 15 June 1933, FO 371/17273 N4591/1610/38. Sir Felix Pole met with Litvinov on 15 June.

way to the Foreign Office, Litvinov warned the MVEEC Director of the damaging consequences to British trade caused by the 1927 Anglo-Soviet rupture. That disagreement had only strengthened Germany's hand in the Soviet market at Britain's expense.[68] The private discussions proved very unsatisfactory from the perspective of the Foreign Office, who thought Pole a poor negotiator, and the British officials soon decided that only direct official conversations could carry any weight with the Soviets.

When Simon, accompanied by Colonel Colville, the Parliamentary Secretary to the Department of Overseas Trade, finally met with Litvinov in London the impasse that had afflicted Anglo-Soviet relations for the past three months was rapidly resolved. An initial exchange of views on 26 June served to emphasize that both men preferred a quick solution to the affair. The main point of discussion in the first meeting between them revolved around Litvinov's suggestion that the prisoners might be released a few days after the expiration of the British embargo. The Soviet Commissar erroneously thought that this would come in mid-July, but due to the vagaries of the Parliamentary schedule,[69] Simon insisted the bill would continue to have effect until October. Both men agreed that this was an unacceptable duration and agreed to meet in the next few days to seek another solution.[70]

The interval between meetings was sufficient time for Litvinov to come up with another measure to deal with the problem at hand. When the two met again on 28 June, Litvinov opened the discussion with a request that the British embargo be lifted; only then the Soviets would release the prisoners. As this offer was quickly refused by Simon, Litvinov abruptly changed course and suggested the plan of a "simultaneous" announcement of the end to embargoes to be immediately followed by the release of the prisoners. Litvinov, who was apparently armed with the authority to pursue variations on such a scheme, told Simon that President Kalinin and the Presidium of the Central Executive Committee were prepared to issue a pardon for Thornton and MacDonald just as soon as Britain could take the steps necessary to end the economic sanctions. Litvinov also made it clear that the Soviets hoped the resumption of trade negotiations could be part of the renewal of friendly relations. Both men agreed that they

---

68 Ibid.

69 The three-month limit of the British embargo meant three months of Parliamentary working days. Given the Easter recess and other holidays, the three-month limit would extend into the summer recess and push the embargo into the autumn months.

70 See Simon to Strang, 26 June 1933, *DBFP*, # 504.

should continue to keep news of their talks from reaching the press, and Simon assured Litvinov that he would say nothing of their proposed arrangement in the Commons.[71]

Simon did seek and obtain Cabinet approval for the scheme the following day. He emphasized that continued silence was important for the plan to work and told the Cabinet that on the weekend[72] there would be a joint statement ending the British and Soviet embargoes. Simon stressed that the repeal of the British embargo did not necessarily influence any future decision about the resumption of trade talks. Runciman noted that a number of British traders had been hurt by the embargo and that timber purchases had been hampered as well.[73]

That same evening Litvinov telephoned Simon to confirm the acceptance of their plan.[74] In order to protect himself, Litvinov also asked Simon for a written assurance from the Foreign Secretary that the Import Prohibition Act would not be used for anything other than the release of the two prisoners.[75] This request serves to confirm that Litvinov had some latitude in the negotiations, but nonetheless thought it wise to have confirmation of points in the agreement where he may have had less precise authorization. Along similar lines the Commissar also asked that the negotiations between him and Simon not be seen as "constituting an agreement for record, but rather as interviews, in the course of which our respective Governments were prepared on certain conditions to take."[76] It was always wise to remember who was boss in Moscow, especially when the *vozhd'* was Stalin! Litvinov and Simon managed to agree that a "free pardon" was not necessary for the release of the engineers and that if the sentences were simply commuted to expulsion, the deal would go through.[77]

The two engineers were finally released at about 11 p.m. on 1 July 1933. The events surrounding their liberation were not without a touch of "Soviet perversity"[78] when the prison authorities held up the release

---

71 Ibid., 28 June 1933, *DBFP*, #505.
72 The Cabinet meeting fell on Thursday.
73 CAB 23/76 43(33), 29 June 1933.
74 Simon to Strang, 30 June 1933, *DBFP*, #510.
75 Ibid.
76 Ibid.
77 Ibid. Saturday morning, 1 July, King George V met with the Privy Council to take the powers necessary to raise the trade ban. A short time later a brief communiqué to the press was issued by Simon which revealed the subject of the recent Anglo-Soviet talks but did not disclose the final solution. See "Release from Russia," *The Times* (London), 3 July 1933, p. 14.
78 See Lammers, "The Engineers' Trial," p. 266.

because they lacked an apparently vital document. Strang, who was
sent to secure the engineers, dealt with this obstruction by energetically
trying to contact a number of Narkomindel officials and the Foreign
Office. He stubbornly refused to leave and waited at the prison until
the stir he had created worked to its desired effect. Some two hours after the scheduled time of release (9 p.m.), the shadowy Sheinin,[79] of the
Procurator's Department, hurriedly informed Strang and the engineers
that everything was in order — the mysterious missing document
never did materialize.[80]

The decision to end the Anglo-Soviet dispute was explained to Soviet readers in *Izvestiia*. The commutation of Thornton's and Mac-
Donald's sentence to expulsion for five years continued to protect the
USSR against the harmful damage the pair might inflict, the Soviet paper claimed. The struggle forced on the USSR did not do serious injury
to the Soviet Union, and *Izvestiia* "graciously" noted that His Majesty's
Government "acted very reasonably in deciding to end a struggle
which could cause material damage to both countries but could never
have ended in a victory for England."[81]

Of course the Soviets who had been imprisoned as a result of the
Metro-Vickers trial did not fare as well as Thornton and MacDonald.
Beyond the actual defendants in the trial, there were a number of Russians employed by the MVEEC who suffered badly as a result of their
close relationship to the foreign firm. The Company's typists in the
Moscow office, Bosovakaia and Kononchuk, were arrested and exiled
to the Archangel region for three years. Zharov, the MVEEC chauffeur,
received a similar sentence. Other office staff in Leningrad and Moscow were arrested and then released. Several had returned to work at
the MVEEC, since it was difficult for them to get employment anywhere else.[82]

---

79 Lev Sheinin was, according to Arkady Vaksberg, the man behind all the investiga-
    tions that Vyshinskii so carefully constructed and prosecuted in the public show tri-
    als of the 1930s. He was one of the only investigators ever mentioned in speeches by
    Vyshinskii, and their careers worked in tandem until 1948, when Sheinin was
    purged for failing to blame the mysterious death of producer and actor Solomon
    Mikhoels on a "zionist" conspiracy. Sheinin survived Stalin, however, and though
    Vyshinskii did nothing to protect him in his hour of need, the investigator who had
    aided Vyshinskii's career remained loyal until his death in 1967. See Vaksberg, *Sta-
    lin's Prosecutor*, p. 66, 335-36 n. 7.
80 Strang to Simon, 3 July 1933, *DBFP*, # 519.
81 Ibid., FO 371/17273 N4898/1610/38.
82 Ibid., 29 May 1933, FO 371/17273 N4211/1610/38, and Chancery (Moscow) to
    Northern Department, 18 July 1933, FO 371/17273 N5446/1610/38; and Strang to
    Northern Department, 2 June 1933, FO 371/17273 N4298/1610/38.

Of the other Soviet citizens who were actually sentenced in the trial, only Anna Kutuzova's fate received any attention from the MVEEC or the British diplomatic corps. Such attention was scarcely avoidable since, after serving 14 months of her 18-month sentence she went directly to the MVEEC compound at Perlovskaia.[83] Prior to this the former MVEEC secretary had been seen twice by MVEEC accountants[84] at the Butyrskaia prison and there was some speculation among company employees that she was now actually working in the prison.[85] When Kutuzova was released she sought the assistance of Buckell and told him that she wanted to contact Thornton privately. This did not impress Collier at the Foreign Office, who commented that, "I do not suppose that Thornton would be very pleased to have Madame Kutuzova in England." He chose not to elaborate on the nature of the complications which might ensue if such an eventuality did come to pass.[86] In the event, the proposed reunion never took place since the OGPU ordered Kutuzova to return to Leningrad and warned her that she should not seek employment from the MVEEC again.[87] Beyond this rather sad tale of Kutuzova's "liberation," nothing else is known about her ultimate fate, or the fate of the other Soviet defendants who received lengthier sentences in the trauma that followed in subsequent purges of the 1930s.

It has been noted throughout this study that assessing the relationship between the Soviet leadership, in particular Stalin's role, and the interests of the OGPU, Litvinov and the Narkomindel, and the Procuracy during the Metro-Vickers crisis remains problematic. At best, it is possible to give a "kremlinological" reading of the resolution of the crisis which provides some useful indications about the relative play of forces at work in the Soviet actions. The British diplomats in Moscow, who had a good deal of access to officials of the Narkomindel, were continuously being told that the entire Metro-Vickers trial had been a blunder by the OGPU and that Stalin had been misinformed by the secret police who had acted without the advice of the Narkomindel.[88] It has already been suggested[89] that the subsequent promotion of Akulov and Vyshinskii to posts in a new All-Union Procuracy represented a defeat for

---

83 Charles (Moscow) to Collier, 21 May 1934, FO 371/18330 N3114/3114/38.
84 The accountants were sent to pay for the cost of Kutuzova's defence counsel.
85 Strang to Simon, 29 May 1933, FO 371/17273 N4211/1610/38.
86 Charles to Collier, 2 May 1934, FO 371/18330 N3114/3114/38.
87 Ibid.
88 Strang to Simon, 20 June 1933, DBFP, # 502.
89 See the discussion in chapter 5.

Iagoda and the OGPU and this was certainly the interpretation that many in the foreign diplomatic community placed on the decision.[90] Such administrative changes suggested that the Soviet leadership wanted to create another judicial apparatus to curb the recent excesses of the OGPU.[91] Though it might well be a mistake to presume too much rationality in the events that afflicted Soviet society during the Great Purges, it should be noted that of the four men most closely associated with the rivalry within, and between, the judiciary and the OGPU at this time, Krylenko, Akulov, and Iagoda would themselves be victims in the trials where Vyshinskii, the sole survivor of the four, acted as Public Prosecutor.

There is also the question of why the MVEEC was allowed to continue operating in the USSR after the arrests and trial if, as has been argued above, it seems likely that the Soviet authorities knew of the role the Company played in the supply of general information for the IIC. Apart from Vyshinskii's own closing statement at the trial, which oddly claimed the Company was not the real target of the OGPU investigation,[92] there remains the possibility that the OGPU was told to monitor the MVEEC's operations without disclosing the Soviet Union's own set of informants in British intelligence circles. The subsequent treatment of the MVEEC's personnel in the USSR outlined below offers support for the latter interpretation. While there is a regrettable lack of material available on the business activities of the MVEEC in the years after the trial, the new relationship established between the Company and His Majesty's Government makes it possible to trace some of the difficulties the foreign company faced when doing business in the USSR. The MVEEC sought the advice of the Foreign Office in the summer of 1934, when the Central Executive Committee refused to extend the work visa of the engineer Pollitt. Pollitt had been named by Thornton in his "confession" and had worked in the Kuznetsk region from March 1932 to 1933. Like Nordwall, Pollitt had a wide circle of Soviet friends and had married a Soviet citizen. Recently he had taken surprisingly successful steps to get an exit visa for her. The Com-

---

90 This was also the view of the Lithuanian Minister, a man who was said to have special contacts with persons in authority (Strang to Simon, 3 July 1933, FO 371/17251 N5127/113/38).

91 Ibid., 10 July 1933, FO 371/17251 N5119/113/38; Minute by Walton, 8 May 1934, FO 371/18327 N2828/1189/38; and Strang to Collier, 16 July 1933, FO 371/17277 N5478/5478/38.

92 This caught the attention of the foreign press as well. See articles by Ralph Barnes, "Soviet Mercy for 6 Britons is Implied by Prosecutor," *New York Herald Tribune*, 17 April 1933, p. 1; and Will Duranty, "Britons' Expulsion after Trial Held to Be Likely," *New York Times*, 17 April 1933, p. 9.

pany was distressed at how "ominously prompt" arrangements were made to provide a visa for Pollitt's wife and was very concerned that Pollitt would not be allowed to return to the USSR once the couple had left the country. On the basis of advice from Britain's First Secretary in Moscow, E. Coote, Terence Shone at the Foreign Office recommended that if Pollitt returned at all, he should leave his wife in Britain.[93]

Early in June 1934, Pollitt and his wife left the USSR, but the Russian woman's Soviet citizenship had not as yet been revoked. The view held by Coote was that Pollitt was suffering from the aftermath of the trial, but it did not seem that anything major was underway against the MVEEC itself.[94] From the standpoint of the Company, Pollitt was not a key man in the Soviet operations, but when both he and Tearle were refused work visas a month later, Richards and Buckell sought Foreign Office support for Tearle's visa. It will be remembered that Tearle, too, had been named by Thornton during the trial, and the refusal of both men made it awkward for the MVEEC properly to staff its projects. One additional factor that needed to be taken into account, which Vyvyan noted, was that the region of Kuznetsk was a particularly sensitive military area along the Volga and that this might account for the vigilance Soviet authorities now exhibited.[95]

In consultation with Foreign Office officials, Richards and Buckell decided to test the temper of the Soviet authorities by arguing that Tearle was an essential part of the MVEEC personnel in the USSR and was needed to aid in the work of Hoseson, a new man. Hoseson, who could not speak Russian, was about to be sent to the Soviet Union, and the MVEEC argued that he could not be expected to manage his affairs in such a foreign venue without Tearle's assistance. This gambit was refused by Soviet authorities on the grounds that Hoseson was being sent to work on a electrical problem and Tearle was a mechanical, not electrical, engineer. There was no real technical reason, therefore, why Tearle was "essential."[96] Meeting with this rebuff, the MVEEC pursued an alternate and apparently successful course, which was to have Burke, already resident in Moscow, accompany Hoseson to Kuznetsk. Vyvyan's view from the Foreign Office was that this was a "good ex-

---

93 Minutes by Coote (Moscow), Vyvyan, and Shone, 9 June 1934, FO 371/18330 N3451/3114/38.

94 Coote to Shone, 19 June 1933, FO 371/18330 N3725/3114/38.

95 Minute by Vyvyan, 9 July 1934, FO 371/18330 N4719/3114/38.

96 Ibid.

periment" since continued Soviet obstinacy would be more evidence that the MVEEC was to be perpetually harassed by Soviet authorities.[97]

Consistent with these aggravations was the decline in Soviet orders for the MVEEC's equipment or technical expertise during this period. By February 1935, the Company was asked by Mashino-Import[98] to close its Moscow bureau and sign all subsequent agreements in London.[99] This blow to the MVEEC operations prompted Sir Felix Pole to request that Anthony Eden raise the issue during his upcoming visit to Moscow, and the Foreign Office was provided with an extensive dossier on the MVEEC's affairs in the USSR to facilitate such an intervention.[100] Oliphant was not very optimistic about Eden's role in the venture and rightly observed that the Soviets would be "very sore" about his recent Berlin sojourn in any case. At best Eden's visit helped to allay Stalin's concerns over the recent Anglo-German conversations.[101] There is no evidence at all that Eden found time to make representations on behalf of the beleaguered British company even though the Foreign Office was increasingly concerned that another crisis might be pending.[102]

The information Pole delivered to British officials revealed important material about the state of the MVEEC's Soviet operations. The Leningrad office had already been closed down after the 1933 trial, and Buckell had just been informed by Mashino-Import that the MVEEC contract of February 1932, which ran through 1937, was to be cancelled as of May 1935.[103] All these setbacks came at a time when the Company continued to train about 20 Soviet engineers at their Trafford Park works and employed as many as 1 000 men in Manchester.[104]

As discussions about the MVEEC's future in the USSR proceeded in London, Collier and Oliphant came to believe that the Company's Directors were understating the possible dangers that were threatening MVEEC personnel. The combination of unending hassles over visas,

---

97 Ibid.

98 Electro-Import was subsumed into Mashino-Import after 1932.

99 Chilston to Simon, 23 February 1933, FO 371/19468 N1024/1024/38.

100 Ibid. See the enclosed letter by Sir Felix Pole to Vansittart, 20 March 1933.

101 This is the view expressed in A. Peters, *Anthony Eden at the Foreign Office, 1931-1938* (New York: St. Martin's Press, 1986), p. 91-94. For a similarly dismissive view of the importance of the Lord Privy Seal's diplomatic tour, see D. Carlton, *Anthony Eden: A Biography* (London: Allen Lane, 1981), p. 62-63.

102 Ibid. Eden arrived in the Soviet Union 28 March 1935. For his own version of a largely uneventful trip see Earl of Avon (Anthony Eden), *Facing the Dictators* (Boston: Houghton, Mifflin, 1962), p. 160-82.

103 Ibid. See Buckell to Richards, 16 February 1933.

104 Ibid.; Pole to Vansittart, 20 March 1933. See "The Moscow Trial: A New Survey," p. 16.

the rough handling of Kutuzova upon her release, the closing down of the Moscow office, and the cancellation of the Leningrad technical agreement, taken together, suggested to Collier that a serious "vendetta" was being directed at the MVEEC which emanated from the highest quarters in the USSR.[105] After consulting with Vansittart, it was decided that Oliphant should take up the MVEEC's cause with Soviet Ambassador Maisky after Vansittart had had a chance to "wade in at him" on the issue of Comintern propaganda. When Oliphant finally did meet with Maisky, the Soviet Ambassador assured the British Assistant Under-Secretary that he would make inquiries in Moscow. Maisky noted in passing that Tearle's name was not "unfamiliar" to him and he now remembered that local authorities around Leningrad were particularly suspicious of the British engineer.[106]

These Soviet suspicions of engineers who were named by Thornton's "confession" did not run sufficiently deep to prevent Maisky from offering the British a deal for a visa exchange two weeks later. The Soviet Ambassador suggested that Tearle could receive permission to work in the USSR if Boris Kraievskii, the Chairman of Export-Les (Timber Export), would receive similar consideration in Britain.[107] For years the British had refused a visa for this Soviet gentleman, but a month later Simon received clearance from the Home Office to make such a deal. He authorized Passport Control to make the visa good for six months, noting that no purpose would be served by requesting the proviso that "subversive activities" were forbidden. Vansittart tried to quiet Ambassador Chilston's concerns over setting this type of precedent by insisting that the Soviets would "behave" in view of the "German danger."[108]

When Tearle finally did get permission to work in the USSR there was disagreement between the MVEEC and British officials in Moscow over the success of his ventures. Moscow Consul T. Rapp interviewed Tearle just prior to his return to the UK after two months of travel in the USSR. Tearle related that local officials in the provinces did not receive him very well, an observation which the Foreign Office saw as confirmation that policies in Moscow often had limited application outside the capital.[109] The fact that Soviet authorities were still ob-

---

105 Collier to Vansittart, 23 May 1935, FO 371/19468 N2716/1024/38.
106 Memo by Oliphant, 30 May 1935, FO 371/19468 N2785/1024/38.
107 Ibid., 15 June 1935, FO 371/19468 N3016/1024/38.
108 Memo by Simon and minute by Vansittart forwarded to Chilston, 19 July 1935, FO 371/19468 N3704/1024/38.
109 Moscow Chancery to Foreign Office, 21 October 1935, FO 371/18468 N5536/1024/38.

structing MVEEC personnel also prompted Collier to consult with Richards over the merits of threatening Kraievskii's visa status in retaliation for the treatment of Tearle. This did not appeal to Richards who put more stock in a recent visit from Soviet trade officials in the UK which reassured the MVEEC of Soviet intentions to pursue the negotiations of new contracts.[110] Thus, despite the concerns of the Foreign Office and its willingness to offer punitive measures in defence of MVEEC personnel, the Company decided to forgo any further confrontation at this juncture in the hopes that better times were ahead.

The MVEEC's determination to remain in the USSR was rewarded in 1936 with a sizable contract to build 14 marine turbines valued at some 620 000 pounds.[111] By the fall of 1937, however, a series of problems had arisen as a result of the dismissal of the Soviet engineers who had initially negotiated the deal with the MVEEC. Richards complained to Collier that after repeated attempts to convince the new Soviet inspectors at Trafford Park and Soviet engineers in Moscow of the soundness of the original design, the MVEEC was close to its wits' end. "Not one of the Engineers who agreed with original specifications has now anything to do with the Contract and the new Engineers appear to consider that they have to justify the dismissal of their predecessors by upsetting most of the decisions made by the latter."[112] It is almost certain that the abrupt changes in the Soviet engineering corps were directly related to the politics of the Great Terror which shook Soviet society during these years. Men who were more politically "reliable," if possibly less skilled, were now employed on the MVEEC project.

The new demands made by Soviet authorities in September 1938 were, in the view of the MVEEC, "technically wrong," and no steel company in the UK was even willing to quote on the material needed. At that time Soviet trade representative D. Bogomolov instructed the MVEEC to build four turbines on the basis of the new specifications and to stop work on the other 12. The MVEEC had already worked for over a year on the basis of the initial specifications and the minimum expense to alter the design at this juncture would cost an additional 130 000 pounds.[113] Richards told Collier that the Soviets had agreed to

---

110 Richards to Collier, 1 November 1935; and Collier to Charles (Moscow), 28 November 1935, FO 371/19468 N5700/1024/38.

111 These were negotiated with Mashino-Import in December 1936 and January 1937. Edwards (Department of Overseas Trade) to Halford (Northern Department), 31 March 1939, FO 371/23681 N1740/92/38.

112 Richards to Collier, 5 January 1939, FO 371/23680 N92/92/38.

113 Edwards to Halford, 31 March 1939, FO 371/23681 N1740/92/38.

entertain an MVEEC mission to Moscow in January 1939 to discuss these specifications. The Company was now approaching the Foreign Office in the hopes that something might be worked out in league with Department of Overseas Trade officials who were currently in Moscow for the negotiation of a new Anglo-Soviet trade agreement, which was now underway.[114]

With the help of British officials, visas were hurriedly obtained for the MVEEC delegation,[115] which had a short but successful preliminary discussion with Soviet Foreign Trade (Vneshtorg) officials in February.[116] The MVEEC also sought and gained the intervention of Department of Overseas Trade representative Hudson, who secured Mashino-Import assent to continue discussions in the near future. According to the new British Ambassador, William Seeds, the Politburo member and Commissar for Foreign Trade, Anastas Mikoyan, had agreed quickly to arrange for more visas for MVEEC representatives to come to Moscow. Though Richards was more interested in having a fully authorized Soviet representative come to London, the Company recognized that this was a helpful step towards the resolution of the impasse.[117]

This final episode in MVEEC-Soviet relations demonstrates once again that the British company had learned in the aftermath of the 1933 affair that it was best served, when dealing with the trade monopoly of the USSR and the vagaries of Soviet domestic politics, by relying on the influence of government officials to facilitate its business. It proved impossible for the MVEEC to escape the stigma of the 1933 trial, and while Soviet authorities sometimes encouraged business with the MVEEC, they constantly harassed those remaining men[118] who formed the basis of the MVEEC's Russian cadre. Given this situation, it was much safer to make clear the MVEEC's close relationship with the Foreign Office and Board of Trade than to pretend that such connections did not exist.

---

114 Richards to Collier, 5 January 1939, FO 371/23680 N92/92/38.
115 The members were I.R. Cox (MVEEC Director), H.L. Guy (MVEEC Director, Chief Turbine Engineer and Fellow of Royal Society), R.W. Bailey (Head of Metallurgy at Trafford Park), and N. Elce (Assistant to H.L. Guy).
116 Cox to Collier, 13 February 1939, FO 371/23681 N793/92/38.
117 Seeds to Foreign Office and minute by Halford, 27 March 1939, FO 371/23681 N1627/92/38.
118 Aside from the Directors Richards, Pole, and Cox who all took a strong interest in Metro-Vickers Soviet contracts, Burke, Tearle, and Pollitt seem to have succeeded Monkhouse and Thornton as the MVEEC's "Russia hands."

7

Conclusions

Few events in Anglo-Soviet relations of the interwar period demonstrate the problems and challenges posed by the Stalin revolution as clearly as does the Metro-Vickers crisis of 1933. The "confrontation" between the British government and its subjects and the emerging Stalinist state and its subjects was not simply a test of will and power, though both these factors were involved, but was also the product of the perceptions and misperceptions caused by the clash between two cultures in all their political, economic, social, legal, and even moral aspects. As a revolutionary state refashioning an old and battered country into a socialist variant of a modern "totalitarian" society, the USSR openly celebrated, through both Soviet foreign and domestic policy, its challenge to the "bourgeois-capitalist" order that Britain represented. Viewed in this context, the Metro-Vickers crisis, though substantially a product of the domestic tensions that racked the Soviet Union during the late 1920s and early 1930s, must also be considered part of the challenge Stalinism posed to the international order which Britain sought to protect. In an effort to respond to this new challenge, British diplomats in Moscow offered portraits of the regime and society that captured some, if not all, of its essence, and the British government created new institutions such as the IIC to analyze Soviet capabilities and help to define new policies for use against Stalin's Russia. The task for this first generation of "kremlinologists" was difficult indeed, and at times it is surprising to see how well they managed under the circumstances.

This study has also maintained that the MVEEC's interaction with the Soviet trade and electrical authorities and the general populace was transformed over the years 1922-33 from a relationship of stimulating and profitable collaboration to one characterized by guarded ex-

177

changes and ultimate disaster. One of the clear lessons that emerges in this case was the difficulty which British engineering corps faced when trying to work safely in a culture that was not only foreign, but was, as the Stalin Revolution took hold, increasingly alien.

Here, too, without an appreciation of the interplay between international relations and Soviet domestic politics it is impossible to comprehend the evolution of the relationship between the Metropolitan-Vickers Electrical Export Company, the Soviet authorities with whom the British company had to deal, and the Soviet citizens closely attached to the MVEEC. There is good reason to believe that the main reason the MVEEC was targeted by the Soviet authorities for a full judicial assault was, in addition to its reputation as one of the best-informed foreign firms operating in the USSR, its apparent cooperation with the Industrial Intelligence Centre in Britain. That the IIC turned its attention away from the USSR towards Nazi Germany after 1933 may help explain why continued MVEEC involvement in the Soviet Union, while never easy after the trial, was even permitted.

Though mutual concerns about espionage were never far from the surface in Anglo-Soviet relations of this period, the extensive contact with Soviet citizens enjoyed by the British personnel of MVEEC stationed in the USSR involved them, however unwillingly, in the changing politics of the technical-intelligentsia in Stalin's Russia. While it remains doubtful that any of the British defendants were actually engaged in acts of wrecking or sabotage, the number of personal indiscretions with Soviet associates, the use of business practices applicable in Western-capitalist societies, but decidedly suspect in the "worker's paradise," and the unfortunate, if understandable, reaction of Thornton and MacDonald to Soviet interrogation and trial techniques combined to make the initial and absolute claims of innocence by the British government premature and misleading.

Having said this, it is hard to see that the shrill reaction of Ovey, or Vansittart's more moderate policy of confrontation, which also failed in its attempt to prevent the trial, could have been better served by an alternative course. Given the Soviet domestic agenda of 1933, which saw further purges of the Party and the electrical industry in that year, it is virtually certain that a trial would have been held involving MVEEC operations in any case. The trial, cleverly stage-managed by the Public Prosecutor, Vyshinskii, and the presiding Judge, Ulrich, reflected a keen Soviet awareness of the international import of the event, and this most likely worked to the British defendants' benefit.

The trial was also a very important step in the advancement of the career of Andrei Vyshinskii and, hence, in the development of Soviet judicial policy in the 1930s. In its size, structure, courtroom tactics, and through the use of Vyshinskii and Ulrich in tandem, the formula that would be used to grim effect in the subsequent Great Purge trials of 1936-38 was in full view for the first time. This case is also one of the rare occasions where documentation into the process of interrogation and cross-examination which Vyshinskii perfected as Stalin's Prosecutor is available in sufficient quantity. Perhaps the one unusual aspect of the trial proceedings was the role of the defence counsel, relatively passive by Western standards, but by no means absent or useless.

For students of Maxim Litvinov's career, his imprint on Soviet policy after the initial arrests were made appears clear. While he was probably kept out of the decision to proceed against the MVEEC, once the international aspect emerged, his efforts to minimize the damage and repair the open rift with Britain are evident. It seems likely that the tone and verdict of the trial made Litvinov's task somewhat easier when he came to London in June, and the outcome was undoubtedly orchestrated, in part, to facilitate that end. Despite the serious nature of the conflict in 1933, which was heightened by the imposition of mutual trade embargoes, there would be no suspension of diplomatic relations between the world's two largest empires. In the midst of the Great Depression, with the challenges that Hitler and Japan now posed, the debacle of May 1927 would not be repeated.

Appendices

Appendix A
Electrical Capacity and Production of the USSR

Year	Generating Capacity		Total Electrical Output	
	kWh (000)	% 1913	kWh (000 000)	% of 1913
1913	1 098	100.0	1 945	100.0
1917	1 192	108.6	2 575	132.5
1921	1 228	112.0	520	26.7
1922	1 247	113.6	775	39.8
1923	1 279	116.5	1 146	59.0
1924	1 308	119.3	1 562	80.4
1925	1 397	127.3	2 925	150.3
1926	1 586	144.6	3 608	185.4
1927	1 698	155.0	4 205	216.0
1928	1 905	173.6	5 000	258.0
1929	2 296	209.0	6 224	320.0
1930	2 876	262.1	8 368	430.0
1931	3 972	362.0	10 687	555.0
1932	4 677	425.9	13 540	696.1
1933	5 583	508.5	16 360	842.0
1934	6 287	572.6	21 010	1 080.0

Production of Power Equipment in the USSR
(measured by capacity)

	1928	1935
Boilers (heating surface 000 m^2)	87.9	228.2
Steam turbines (000 kW)	35.7	672.1
Hydraulic turbines (000 kW)	12.0	74.6

Appendix A *(continued)*

	1928	1935
Generators (000 kW)	92.6	651.4
Transformers (000 kVA)	403.2	3 454.0
A.C. motors (000 kW)	258.6	1 590.0

Sources: B. Weitz, ed. *Electric Power Development in the U.S.S.R.* (Moscow: INRA Publishing Society, 1936), p. 24 and 101.

Appendix B
Soviet Foreign Trade, 1913-40
(000 000 roubles; constant 1950 rate and annual rouble rate)

Year	Exports		Imports		Balance	
	1950	Annual	1950	Annual	1950	Annual
1913	5 298	1 520	4 792	1 375	+506	+145
1918	28	8	367	105	−339	−97
1921	70	20	734	211	−664	−191
1921-22	221	63	945	271	−724	−208
1922-23	467	134	518	149	−51	−15
1923-24	1 300	373	814	234	+486	+139
1924-25	2 014	578	2 521	723	−507	−145
1925-26	2 451	703	2 636	756	−185	−53
1926-27	2 812	807	2 487	714	+325	+93
1927-28	2 759	792	3 295	946	−536	−154
1928*	754	216	708	203	+46	+13
1929	3 219	924	3 069	881	+150	+43
1930	3 612	1 036	3 690	1 059	−78	−23
1931	2 827	811	3 851	1 105	−1 024	−294
1932	2 004	575	2 454	704	−450	−129
1933	1 727	496	1 214	348	+513	+148
1934	1 458	418	810	232	+648	+186
1935	1 281	367	841	241	+440	+126
1936	1 082	1 359	1 077	1 353	+5	+6
1937	1 312	1 738	1 016	1 346	+296	+392
1938	1 012	1 353	1 090	1 444	−69	−91
1939	462	612	745	986	−283	−374
1940	1 066	1 412	1 091	1 446	−25	−34

Source: *Vneshniaia Torgovlia SSSR za 1918-1940 gg.: Statisticheskii obzor* (Moscow: Vneshtorgizdat, 1960), p. 13. Note that up until 1929 economic years ran from 1 October. The year 1928* signifies the trade figures from October to December 1928.

Appendix C
Soviet Trade with Great Britain, 1913-39
(000 000 roubles at constant 1950 rate)

Year	Exports to		Imports from		Balance	Ratio
	UK	% of USSR	UK	% of USSR		
1913	933	17.6	603	12.6	+330	1.5:1
1918	7	25.0	42	11.4	−35	.17:1
1921	33	47.0	215	29.3	−182	.15:1
1921-22	63	28.5	185	19.6	−122	.34:1
1922-23	101	21.6	130	25.1	−29	.78:1
1923-24	291	22.4	171	21.0	+120	1.7:1
1924-25	674	33.5	386	15.3	+288	1.8:1
1925-26	769	31.4	451	17.1	+318	1.7:1
1926-27	769	27.3	352	14.1	+417	2.2:1
1927-28	543	19.7	166	5.0	+377	3.3:1
1928*	163	21.6	23	3.2	+140	7.1:1
1929	705	21.9	191	6.2	+514	3.7:1
1930	976	27.0	279	7.5	+697	3.5:1
1931	927	32.8	256	6.6	+671	3.6:1
1932	482	24.1	320	13.0	+162	1.5:1
1933	303	17.5	107	8.8	+196	1.8:1
1934	241	16.5	109	13.5	+132	2.2:1
1935	301	23.5	78	9.3	+223	3.8:1
1936	288	26.7	76	7.1	+212	3.8:1
1937	422	32.2	48	4.7	+374	8.8:1
1938	283	28.0	132	12.1	+151	2.1:1
1939	101	21.9	85	11.4	+16	1.2:1

Source: Based on *Vneshniaia Torgovlia SSSR za 1918-1940 gg.*, p. 21. Note that up until 1929 the economic years ran from October 1. The year 1928* signifies the trade figures from October to December.

Appendix D
Soviet Foreign Trade: Commodities, 1913-40

	Exports			Imports	
Year	Grain (000 000 tons)	Timber (000 tons)	Oil (000 tons)	Machinery (000 000 roubles)	Meat (000 tons)
1913	9.182	7 353.6	952.5	796.8	14.7
1921-22	.001	594.1	52.3	203.4	42.3
1922-23	.728	919.0	84.3	110.9	21.5
1923-24	2.576	2 009.1	711.6	108.1	25.9
1924-25	.569	2 086.6	1 372.5	344.3	227.8
1925-26	2.016	1 872.5	1 473.5	542.1	38.1
1926-27	2.099	2 429.1	2 086.1	547.2	4.27
1927-28	0.289	2 912.9	2 782.8	788.0	3.66
1928*	.001	1 098.1	795.9	172.1	.001
1929	.178	5 376.6	3 858.6	923.3	.283
1930	4.764	7 229.8	3 713.0	1 726.6	1.35
1931	5.056	5 914.6	5 224.5	2 076.2	1.97
1932	1.727	5 546.1	6 117.7	1 366.9	9.34
1933	1.684	6 115.7	4 930.1	521.9	6.09
1934	.769	6 323.5	4 315.2	202.9	9.59
1935	1.517	6 605.8	3 368.6	198.1	5.99
1936	.321	5 888.4	2 665.6	419.4	2.86
1937	1.277	4 994.3	1 929.3	278.5	2.87
1938	2.054	3 151.7	1 388.4	376.4	2.69
1939	.277	1 715.6	474.2	288.3	2.47
1940	1.155	1 006.9	874.3	353.6	5.57

Source: R. Clarke and D. Matko, *Soviet Economic Facts, 1917-1981* (London: Macmillan, 1983), p. 74, 77. Note that up until 1929 the economic years ran from 1 October. The year 1928* signifies the trade figures from October to December.

Appendix E
Soviet Gross Production, 1913-40

	Industrial		Agricultural	
Year	Index	% increase	Index	% increase
1913	100	–	100	–
1917	71	–29.0	88	–12.0
1921	31	–56.3	60	–22.8
1924	45	45.1	90	50.0
1925	73	62.2	112	24.4
1926	98	34.2	118	5.5
1927	111	13.3	121	2.5
1928	132	18.9	124	2.5
1929	158	19.7	121	–2.4
1930	193	22.2	117	–3.3
1931	233	20.7	114	–2.6
1932	267	14.6	107	–6.1
1933	281	5.2	101	–5.6
1934	335	19.2	106	5.0
1935	411	22.7	119	12.3
1936	529	28.7	109	–8.4
1937	588	11.2	134	22.9
1938	657	11.7	120	–10.5
1939	763	16.1	121	0.8
1940	852	11.7	141	16.5

Source: Clarke and Matko, *Soviet Economic Facts, 1917-1967*,
    p. 8-11.

Appendix F:
Article 58 of the Criminal Code of the RSFSR

Special Section

Counter-Revolutionary Crimes

Art. 58 (vi).

Espionage, i.e., the transmission, theft or collection, with a view to transmission to foreign States, counter-revolutionary organizations or private persons, of information accounted by reason of its contents an especially guarded State secret is punishable by:

> deprivation of liberty for a period of not less than three years, with the confiscation of all or part of property; in cases when espionage has caused, or might have caused, especially grievous consequences to the interests of the USSR, the supreme measure of social defence — death by

shooting, or the declaration to be an enemy of the labouring masses and the deprivation of citizenship of the Union Republic and thereby of the USSR and banishment beyond the frontiers of the USSR forever, and confiscation of property.

The transmission, theft or collection with a view to transmission of economic information not constituting by virtue of its contents an especially guarded State secret but not intended for divulgence to the organizations or persons enumerated above, as the result of direct prohibition by law or by order of the heads of departments, establishments, or enterprises, either for recompense or gratis is punishable by:

deprivation of liberty for a period not exceeding three years.

Art.58 (vii)

The undermining of State industry, transport, trade, monetary exchange or the credit system and also of the co-operative network, committed for counter-revolutionary purposes by means of making use to such ends of State establishments and enterprises, or by means of impeding their normal functioning, and also the utilization of State establishments and enterprises, or the impeding of their functioning in the interests of their former owners or of capitalist organizations interested in them is punishable by:

the measures of social defence, indicated in Article 58 (ii) of the present code:

the supreme measure of social defence — death by shooting, or declaration as an enemy of the labouring masses, and the confiscation of property and deprivation of citizenship of the Union Republic and thereby of the USSR, and banishment beyond the frontiers of the USSR forever; in extenuating circumstances a reduction of sentence is permitted to deprivation of liberty for a period of not less than three years and the confiscation of all or part of the property.

Art. 58 (ix)

The destruction or damage, for counter-revolutionary purposes, by explosive, arson or other means, of railways or other means of transportation, of the means of public communication, of water conduits, or public stores and other constructions or of State or public property, is punishable by:

the measures of social defence, indicated in Article 58 (ii) of the present code.

Art. 58 (xi)

Any type of organizational activity, directed towards the preparation or the commission of crimes provided for in the present chapter, and also participation in an organization formed for the preparation or the commission of one of the crimes provided for in this chapter, is punishable by:

the measures of social defence, indicated in Article 58 (ii) of the present code.

Art. 58 (xiv)

Counter-revolutionary sabotage, i.e. deliberate nonfulfilment by anyone of duties laid down or the wilfully careless execution of those duties with a view to weakening the authority of the Government, the functioning of the State apparatus, entails:

deprivation of liberty for period of not less than one year, with confiscation of all or part of his property; to be increased in especially grave circumstances, to the supreme measure of social defence — death by shooting with confiscation of property.

Source: Juridical Publishing House, Moscow, 1949. Translation by R. Conquest, *The Great Terror*, appendix G.

Appendix G
Major Soviet Trading Partners, 1929-34

Year		Percentage of Soviet				Balance/ USSR (000 000 roubles)
		Exports		Imports		
1929	Britain	21.9	[887.2]	6.2	[239.8]	+647.4
	Germany	23.3	[942.2]	22.1	[852.6]	+89.6
	U.S.A.	4.6	[187.1]	20.1	[776.2]	−589.1
1930	Britain	27.0	[1 226.0]	7.6	[351.0]	+875.0
	Germany	19.8	[901.0]	23.7	[1 098.6]	−197.6
	U.S.A.	3.9	[179.3]	25.0	[1 158.0]	−978.7
1931	Britain	32.8	[1 165.4]	6.6	[321.4]	+844.0
	Germany	15.9	[566.5]	37.2	[1 798.6]	−1 234.1
	U.S.A.	2.8	[99.4]	20.8	[1 007.0]	−907.6
1932	Britain	24.1	[606.6]	13.1	[402.6]	+204.0
	Germany	17.5	[440.2]	46.5	[1 435.3]	−995.1
	U.S.A.	3.0	[75.3]	4.5	[138.7]	−76.4
1933	Britain	17.6	[381.0]	8.8	[134.0]	+247.0
	Germany	17.3	[375.6]	42.5	[648.5]	−272.9
	U.S.A.	2.8	[61.2]	4.8	[72.6]	−11.4
1934	Britain	16.5	[303.0]	19.9	[202.6]	+100.4
	Germany	23.5	[431.1]	12.0	[125.0]	+305.1
	U.S.A.	3.4	[62.5]	7.7	[78.3]	−15.8

Source: Based on A. Baykov, *Soviet Foreign Trade: International Finance Section* (Princeton: Princeton University Press, 1946), Table 7. Figures in [ ] are based on 1936 rouble rate in millions of rubles as are the figures for the balance of trade.

Bibliography

Primary Sources

Great Britain

Government Documents (Public Record Office unless otherwise specified)
Board of Trade
Cabinet Minutes, 1929-33. CAB 23.
Cabinet Memoranda, 1929-33. CAB 24.
Committee of Imperial Defence, Subcommittee on Industrial Intelligence in Foreign Countries. CAB 48
Department of Overseas Trade
Foreign Office. *Documents on British Foreign Policy*, 2nd Series, VII, 1929-34. London: Her Majesty's Stationery Office, 1957.
_____ . General Political Correspondence: Russia, 1924-33. FO 371.
Parliamentary Debates: Commons, 5th Series, 1929-1933.
War Office

Private Documents
Baldwin, Stanley. Cambridge University Library.
Chamberlain, Sir Austen. Birmingham University Library and PRO, FO 800/256-63.
Chamberlain, Neville. Birmingham University Library.
Caillard, Sir Vincent (Vickers Ltd.). Cambridge University Library. R.215.
Churchill, Winston S. Volume 5 Companion Part 2: *Documents: The Wilderness Years, 1929-1935*. Edited by Martin Gilbert. London: Heinemann, 1981.
Hankey, Sir Maurice. PRO, CAB 63.
Henderson, Sir Arthur. PRO, FO 800/280-84.
Noel-Baker, Sir Philip. Churchill College Archives.
Oliphant, Sir Lancelot. PRO, FO 800/252-54.
Sargent, Sir Orme. PRO, FO 800/272-79.
Simon, Sir John (Viscount Simon). PRO, FO 800/284-91.
Strang, Sir William (Lord Strang). Churchill College Archives.
Vansittart, Sir Robert (Lord Vansittart). Churchill College Archives.

Vickers Ltd., Cambridge University Library.

The Diaries of Sir Robert Bruce Lockhart, 1915-1938. Edited by Kenneth Young. London: Macmillan, 1973.

USSR

The Communist International, 1929-1953. Edited by Jane Degras. London: Oxford University Press, 1971.

Poletaev, V., ed. *Istoriia Industrializatsii SSSR, 1929-1932: Dokumenty i Materialy*. Moscow: Izdatel'stvo Nauka, 1970.

Ministerstvo Inostrannykh del SSSR. *Dokumenty Vneshnei Politiki SSSR*, Vol. 16. Moscow: Izdatel'stvo Politicheskoi Literatury, 1970.

Ordzhonikidze, G. *Stat'i i Rechi*. Vol 2. Moscow: Gosydarstvennoe Izdatel'stvo Politicheskoi Literatury, 1957.

Resolutions and Decisions of the Communist Party of the Soviet Union, 1929-1953. Edited by R. McNeal. Toronto: University of Toronto Press, 1974.

Soviet Documents on Foreign Policy. Edited by J. Degras. London: Oxford University Press, 1951-53.

Soviet Foreign Policy, 1928-1934: Documents and Materials. Edited by X. Eudin and R. Slusser. University Park: Pennsylvania State University Press, 1967.

Soviet Trade Series: A Collection of Bilateral Treaties Between the Soviet Union and Foreign Powers. Edited by L. Shapiro. Washington: Georgetown University Press, 1955.

Stalin, I. *Works*. Moscow: Foreign Languages Publishing House, 1955.

Supreme Court of the USSR. *The Case of N.P. Vitvitsky, V.A. Gussev, A.W. Gregory, Y.I. Zivert, N.G. Zorin, M.D. Khrasheninnikov, M.L. Kotlyarevsky, A.S. Kutusova, J. Cushny, V.P. Lebedev, A.T. Lobanov, W.L. MacDonald, A. Monkhouse, C. Nordwall, P.Y. Oleinik, L.A. Sukhoruchkin, L.C. Thornton, V.A. Sokolov: Charged with Wrecking Activities at Power Stations in the Soviet Union, in Moscow, April 12-19, 1933*. Moscow: State Law Publishing House, 1933.

Vneshniaia Torgovlia SSSR v Gody Dovoennykh Pyatilok (1929-1940): Statisticheskii Sbornik. Moscow: Izdatel'stvo Mezhdunarodnye Otnosheniya, 1968.

Vneshniaia Torgovlia SSSR za 1918-1940 gg.: Statisticheskii Obzor. Moscow: Vneshtorgizdat, 1960.

Weitz, B. *Electric Power Development in the U.S.S.R.*. Moscow: INRA Publishing Society, 1936.

France

Documents diplomatiques francais, 1932-1939, Commission de publication de documents relatifs aux origines de la guerre 1939-45, 2nd series. Paris: Imprimérie nationale, 1972-79.

Germany

Documents on German Foreign Policy, 1918-1945: Series C (1933-1937) The Third Reich: First Phase, Vol. 1: January 30-October 14, 1933. Washington, DC: United States Government Printing Office, 1953-59.

United States

Foreign Relations of the United States Diplomatic Papers: The Soviet Union, 1933-1939. Washington, DC: United States Government Printing Office, 1952.

Newspapers and Journals

Great Britain

The Economist
The Journal of the Institution of Electrical Engineers (London)
Manchester Guardian
Observer
The Times (London)

USSR

Izvestiia
Pravda
Za Industrializatsiiu

United States

The New York Times
The New York Herald Tribune

Memoirs

Barmine, A. *Memoirs of a Soviet Diplomat*. London: Lovat Dickson, 1938.
Bohlen, C. *Witness to History, 1929-1969*. New York: W.W. Norton, 1973.
Braude, I. *Zapiski Advocata*. Moscow: Izdatel'stvo Sovetskaya Rossiya, 1974.
Ciliga, A. *The Russian Enigma*. London: Ink Links, 1979. Originally published as *Au Pays du Grand Mensonge*, France, 1938.
Cummings, A.J. *The Moscow Trial*. London: Victor Gollancz, 1933.
Dalton, H. *Memoirs: Call Back Yesterday, 1887-1931*. London: F. Mueller, 1953.
Duranty, W. *I Write as I Please*. New York: Simon and Schuster, 1935.
Eden, A. (Earl of Avon). *Facing the Dictators*. Boston: Houghton Mifflin, 1957.
Fischer, L. *Men and Politics: An Autobiography*. New York: Duell, Sloan, & Pearce, 1941.
Hilger, G., and A. Meyer. *The Incompatible Allies: A Memoir History of German-Soviet Relations, 1918-1941*. New York: Macmillan, 1953.
Lyons, E. *Assignment in Utopia*. New York: Harcourt, Brace, 1937.

Maclean, F. *Eastern Approaches*. London: J. Cape, 1949.

Maisky, I. *Memoirs of a Soviet Ambassador*. New York: Charles Scribner's Sons, 1968.

Monkhouse, A. *Moscow, 1911-1933*. Boston: Little, Brown, 1934.

Rukeseyer, W. "Do Our Engineers in Russia Damage America?" *Scribners Magazine*, 90 (November 1931): 521-24.

_____. *Working for the Soviets: An American Engineer in Russia*. New York: Covici-Freide Publishers, 1932.

Scott, J. *Behind the Urals*. Bloomington: Indiana University Press, 1973 (1942).

Smith, A. *I Was a Soviet Worker*. London: Robert Hale, 1937.

Strang, W. (Lord). *Home and Abroad*. London: Andre Deutsch, 1956.

_____. *The Diplomatic Career*. London: Andre Deutsch, 1962.

Vansittart, R. (Lord). *The Mist Procession*. London: Hutchinson, 1958.

Von Dirksen, H. *Moscow, Tokyo, London: Twenty Years of German Foreign Policy*. Norman: University of Oklahoma Press, 1952.

Von Herwarth, H. *Against Two Evils*. With S.F. Starr. New York: Rawson Wade, 1981.

Secondary Sources

Andrew, C. "The British Secret Service and Anglo-Soviet Relations in the 1920s. Part 1: From the Trade Negotiations to the Zinoviev Letter." *Historical Journal*, 20, 3 (1977): 673-706.

_____. *Secret Service: The Making of the British Intelligence Community*. London: W.H. Heinemann, 1985.

_____, and D. Dilks, eds. *The Missing Dimension: Government and Intelligence Communities in the Twentieth Century*. London: Macmillan, 1984.

Arch Getty, J. *Origins of the Great Purges: The Soviet Communist Party Reconsidered, 1933-1938*. Cambridge: Cambridge University Press, 1985.

_____, G. Rittersporn, and V. Zemskov. "Victims of the Soviet Penal System in the Pre-War Years: A First Approach on the Basis of Archival Evidence." *The American Historical Review*, 98, 4 (1993): 1017-49.

_____, and R. Manning, eds. *Stalinist Terror: New Perspectives*. New York: Cambridge University Press, 1993.

Bailes, K. *Technology and Society under Lenin and Stalin: Origins of the Technical Intelligentsia, 1917-1941*. Princeton, NJ: Princeton University Press, 1978.

_____. "Stalin and the Revolution from Above: The Formation of the Soviet Technical Intelligentsia, 1928-1934." Ph.D dissertation, Columbia University, 1971.

Baransky, N. *Economic Geography of the U.S.S.R.* Moscow: Foreign Languages Publishing House, 1956.

Baykov, A. *Soviet Foreign Trade: International Finance Section*. Princeton: Princeton University Press, 1946.

Beirne, P., and R. Sharlet, eds. *Pashukanis: Selected Writings on Marxism and Law*. London: Academic Press, 1980.

Berman, H. *Soviet Criminal Law and Procedure: The RSFSR Codes*. Cambridge, MA: Harvard University Press, 1972.

Biliankin, G. *Maisky: Ten Years Ambassador*. London: Allen & Unwin, 1944.

Bishop, D. *The Administration of British Foreign Relations*. Syracuse: Syracuse University Press, 1961.

Boadle, D. "The Formation of the Foreign Office Economic Relations Section, 1930-1937." *Historical Journal*, 20, 4 (1977): 919-36.

Cannadine, David. *The Decline and Fall of the British Aristocracy*. New York: Anchor Books, 1990.

Carlton, D. *MacDonald versus Henderson: The Foreign Policy of the Second Labour Government*. New York: Humanities Press, 1970.

Carr, E. *What Is History*. New York: St. Martin's Press, 1961.

_____. *Anthony Eden: A Biography*. London: Allen Lane, 1981.

_____, and R. Davies. *Foundations of a Planned Economy, 1926-1929*. Vol. 1. London: Macmillan, 1969.

Carswell, J. *The Exile: A Life of Ivy Litvinov*. Boston: Faber and Faber, 1983.

Carynnyk, Marco, Lubomyr Luciuk, and Bohdan Kordan, eds. *The Foreign Office and the Famine*. Kingston, ON: Limestone Press, 1988.

Clarke, R. *Soviet Economic Facts, 1917-1967*. London: Macmillan, 1972.

_____, and D. Matko. *Soviet Economic Facts, 1917-1981*. London: Macmillan, 1983.

Coates, W.P., and Z. Coates. *A History of Anglo-Soviet Relations*. London: Lawrence & Wishart and Pilot Press, 1945.

Cohen, S. *Bukharin and the Bolshevik Revolution: A Political Biography, 1888-1938*. New York: Alfred A. Knopf, 1973.

Conquest, R. *The Great Terror: Stalin's Purge of the Thirties*. New York: Macmillan, 1968.

_____. *Inside Stalin's Secret Police: NKVD Politics 1936-1939*. Stanford: Hoover Institution Press, 1985.

_____. *The Harvest of Sorrow: Collectivization and the Terror-Famine*. New York: Oxford University Press, 1986.

Coopersmith, J. *The Electrification of Russia, 1880-1926*. Ithaca: Cornell University Press, 1992.

Craig, G., and F. Gilbert, eds. *The Diplomats, 1919-1939*. Princeton, NJ: Princeton University Press, 1953.

Daniels, R. *The Conscience of the Revolution: Communist Opposition in Soviet Russia*. Cambridge: Cambridge University Press, 1960.

Davies, R. *The Socialist Offensive: The Collectivization of Soviet Agriculture, 1929-1930*. London: Macmillan, 1980.

Degras, J., ed. *Documents on Soviet Foreign Policy*. London: Oxford University Press, 1951-53.

Deutscher, I. *Stalin: A Political Biography*. London: Oxford University Press, 1967.

Dohan, M. "The Economic Origins of Soviet Autarky, 1927/28-1934." *Slavic Review*, 35, 4 (1976): 603-35.

Drummond, I. "Empire Trade and Russian Trade: Economic Diplomacy in the Nineteen-Thirties." *Canadian Journal of Economics/Revue canadienne d'Économique*, 5, 1 (1972): 35-47.

Dummelow, J. *1899-1949*. Metropolitan-Vickers Electrical Company, 1949.

Dyck, H. *Weimar Germany & Soviet Russia: A Study in Diplomatic Instability*. London: Chatto & Windus, 1966.

Fainsod, M. *Smolensk under Soviet Rule*. London: Macmillan, 1958.

Fischer, L. *Machines and Men in Russia*. New York: Jonathan Cape & Robert Ballou, 1932.

_____. *Russia's Road from Peace to War*. New York: Vintage Books, 1960.

_____. *The Soviets in World Affairs*. New York: Harper & Row, 1969.

Fitzpatrick, S. "The Foreign Threat during the First Five Year Plan." *Soviet Union/Union Soviétique*, 5, 1 (1978): 26-35.

_____. *The Russian Revolution, 1917-1932*. Oxford: Oxford University Press, 1984.

_____. "Ordzhonikidze's Takeover of Vesenkha: A Case Study in Soviet Bureaucratic Politics." *Soviet Studies*, 37, 2 (1985): 153-72.

_____, ed. *Cultural Revolution in Russia, 1928-1931*. Bloomington: Indiana University Press, 1978.

Flory, H. "The Arcos Raid and the Rupture of Anglo-Soviet Relations, 1927." *Journal of Contemporary History*, 12, 4 (1977): 707-23.

Gladkov, T., and M. Smirnov. *Menzhinskii*. Moscow: Izdatel'stvo Molodaya Gvardiya, 1969.

Gorodetsky, G. *The Precarious Truce: Anglo-Soviet Relations, 1924-1927*. Cambridge: Cambridge University Press, 1977.

Gorokhov, A. "Leninist Diplomacy: Principles and Traditions." *International Affairs* (Moscow), 5 (1968): 38-44.

Graham, L. *The Soviet Academy of Sciences and the Communist Party, 1927-1932*. Princeton, NJ: Princeton University Press, 1967.

_____. *The Ghost of the Executed Engineer*. Cambridge, MA: Harvard University Press, 1993.

Gruber, H. *Soviet Russia Masters the Comintern: International Communism in the Era of Stalin's Ascendancy*. New York: Anchor Press, 1974.

Haslam, J. *Soviet Foreign Policy, 1930-1933: The Impact of the Depression*. London: Macmillan, 1983.

_____. *The Soviet Union and the Struggle for Collective Security in Europe, 1933-1939*. London: Macmillan, 1984.

Hinsley, F. *British Intelligence in the Second World War: Its Influence on Strategy and Operations*. Vol. 1. London: Her Majesty's Stationery Office, 1979.

Hochman, Jiri. *The Soviet Union and the Failure of Collective Security, 1934-1938*. Ithaca: Cornell University Press, 1984.

Hollander, P. *Political Pilgrims: Travels of Western Intellectuals to the Soviet Union*. New York: Oxford University Press, 1981.

Hough, J., and M. Fainsod. *How the Soviet Union Is Governed*. Cambridge, MA: Harvard University Press, 1979.

Huskey, E. "Vyshinskii, Krylenko, and the Shaping of the Soviet Legal Order." *Slavic Review*, 46, 3/4 (1987): 414-28.

_____. *Russian Lawyers and the Soviet State: The Origins and Development of the Soviet Bar, 1917-1939*. Princeton, NJ: Princeton University Press, 1986.

Jansen, M. *A Show Trial under Lenin: The Trial of the Socialist Revolutionaries, Moscow 1922*. Translated by Jean Sanders. Boston: Martinus Nijhoff, 1982.

Jones, B. *The Russian Complex: The British Labour Party and the Soviet Union*. Manchester: Manchester University Press, 1977.

Jones, Raymond A. *The British Diplomatic Service, 1815-1914*. Waterloo: Wilfrid Laurier University Press, 1983.

Kahan, V. "The Communist International, 1919-1943: The Personnel of Its Highest Bodies." *International Review of Social History*, 21, 2 (1976): 151-85.

Knight, A. *The KGB: Police and Politics in the Soviet Union*. Boston: Unwin Hyman, 1990.

Kuromiya, H. *Stalin's Industrial Revolution: Politics and Workers, 1928-1932*. Cambridge: Cambridge University Press, 1988.

_____. "Edinonachalie and the Soviet Industrial Manager, 1928-1937." *Soviet Studies*, 36, 2 (1984): 195-204.

Kuzmin, V. *V Bor'be Za Sotsialisticheskuiu Rekonstruktsiiu, 1926-1937*. Moscow: Izdatel'stvo Mysl', 1976.

Lacquer, W. *The Fate of the Revolution: Interpretations of Soviet History From 1917 to the Present*. New York: Charles Scribner's Sons, 1987.

Lammers, D. "The Engineers' Trial (Moscow 1933) and Anglo-Soviet Relations." *South Atlantic Quarterly*, 62, (1963): 256-67.

_____. "Fascism, Communism and the Foreign Office, 1937-1939." *Journal of Contemporary History*, 6, 3 (1971): 66-86.

_____. "The Second Labour Government and the Restoration of Relations with Soviet Russia (1929)." *Bulletin of the Institute of Historical Research*, 37 (May 1964): 60-72.

Langhourne, R. *Diplomacy and Intelligence during the Second World War: Essays in Honour of F.H. Hinsley*. Cambridge: Cambridge University Press, 1985.

Lel'chuk, V. *Sotsialisticheskaia Industrializatsiia SSSR i ee Osveshchenie b Sovetskoi Istoriografii*. Moscow: Izdatel'stvo Nauka, 1975.

Levyetsky, B. *The Uses of Terror: The Soviet Secret Police 1917-1970*. New York: Coward, McCann & Geoghegan, 1972.

Lewin, M. *Russian Peasants and Soviet Power: A Study of Collectivization*. Evanston: Northwestern University Press, 1968.

_____. *Political Undercurrents in Soviet Economic Debates*. Princeton, NJ: Princeton University Press, 1974.

_____. *The Making of the Soviet System: Essays in the Social History of Interwar Russia*. New York: Pantheon Books, 1985.

Manne, R. "The British Decision for Alliance with Russia." *Journal of Contemporary History*, 9, 3 (1974): 3-26.

_____. "The Foreign Office and the Failure of Anglo-Soviet Rapprochement." *Journal of Contemporary History*, 16, 4 (1981): 725-57.

Mastny, V. *Russia's Road to the Cold War*. New York: Columbia University Press, 1979.

McNeal, R. *Stalin: Man and Ruler*. New York: New York University Press, 1988.

Medlicott, W. *British Foreign Policy since Versailles 1919-1963*. London: Methuen, 1968.

Medvedev, R. *Let History Judge: The Origins and Consequences of Stalinism*. Edited by Colleen Taylor and translated by David Joravsky and Georges Haupt. New York: Vintage Books, 1973 (1967).

Meyer, A. "The War Scare of 1927." *Soviet Union/Union Soviétique*, 5, 1 (1978): 1-25.

Middlemas, K. *Britain and Russia: An Historical Essay*. New York: Kennikat Press, 1947.

Morrell, Gordon. "Sir Esmond Ovey: Britain's First Ambassador to Soviet Russia, 1929-1933." M.A. thesis, University of Waterloo, 1985.

————. "Britain Confronts the Stalin Revolution: The Metro-Vickers Trial and Anglo-Soviet Relations, 1933." Ph.D. dissertation, Michigan State University, 1990.

Naylor, J. *Labour's International Policy*. London: Weidenfeld & Nicolson, 1969.

Neilson, Keith. "My Beloved Russians: Sir Arthur Nicolson and Russia, 1906-1916." *The International History Review*, 9, 4 (1987), 517-688.

Northedge, F., and A. Wells. *Britain and Soviet Communism: The Impact of a Revolution*. London: Macmillan, 1982.

Owen, G. "The Metro-Vickers Crisis: Anglo-Soviet Relations between Trade Agreements, 1932-1934." *Slavonic and East European Review*, 44, 114 (1971): 92-112.

Pares, Bernard. *A History of Russia*. London: J. Cape, 1926.

Pearson, J. *The Life of Ian Fleming*. New York: McGraw Hill, 1966.

Peters, A. *Anthony Eden at the Foreign Office 1931-1938*. New York: St. Martin's Press, 1986.

Philips, H. *Between the Revolution and the West: A Political Biography of Maxim Litvinov*. Boulder: Westview Press, 1992.

Pope, A. *Maxim Litvinoff*. New York: L. Fischer Press, 1947.

Rassweiler, A. *The Generation of Power: The History of Dneprostroi*. New York: Oxford University Press, 1988.

Raymond, P. "Conflict and Consensus in Soviet Foreign Policy, 1933-1939." Ph.D thesis, Pennsylvania State University, 1979.

Reiman, M. *The Birth of Stalinism: The U.S.S.R. on the Eve of the "Second Revolution."* Translated from the German edition of 1979 by George Saunders. Bloomington: Indiana University Press, 1987.

Rigby, T. *Communist Party Membership in the U.S.S.R., 1917-1967*. Princeton, NJ: Princeton University Press, 1968.

Rittersporn, G. *Stalinist Simplifications and Soviet Complications: Social Tensions and Political Conflicts in the USSR, 1933-1953*. Philadelphia: Harwood Academic Publishers, 1991.

Roskill, S. *Hankey: Man of Secrets*, Vol. 2: *1919-1931*. London: Collins, 1972.

————. *Hankey: Man of Secrets*, Vol. 3: *1931-1963*. London: Collins, 1974.

Rothstein, Andrew, ed. *Wreckers on Trial: A Record of the Trial of the Industrial Party Held in Moscow, November-December 1930*. New York: Workers' Library Publishing, 1931.

Sakharov, V. "G.K. Ordzhonikidze vo Glave Bor'by za Tekhnicheskii Progress (1930-1935 gg.)." *Voprosy Istorii* (U.S.S.R.), 9 (1986): 81-91.

Schapiro, L. *The Communist Party of the Soviet Union*. New York: Random House, 1960.

Schinness, R. "An Early Pilgrimage to Soviet Russia: Four Conservative MP's Challenge Tory Party Policy." *Historical Journal*, 18, 3 (1975): 623-31.

Scott, J. *Vickers: A History*. London: Weidenfeld & Nicolson, 1962.

Sharlet, R. "Stalinism and Soviet Legal Culture." In *Stalinism: Essays in Historical Interpretation*, edited by R. Tucker. New York: W.W. Norton, 1977.

_____, and P. Beirne. "In Search of Vyshinsky: The Paradox of Law and Terror." *International Journal of the Sociology of Law*, 12 (1984): 153-77.

Sheinis, Z. *Maxim Litvinov*. Moscow: Progress Publishers, 1990.

Siegelbaum, L. *Soviet State and Society Between Revolutions, 1918-1929*. Cambridge: Cambridge University Press, 1992.

Slusser, R. "The Role of the Foreign Ministry." In *Russian Foreign Policy*, edited by Ivo Lederer. New Haven: Yale University Press, 1962.

Solomon, P. "Local Political Power and Soviet Criminal Justice, 1922-1941." *Soviet Studies*, 37, 3 (1983): 305-29.

_____. "Soviet Criminal Justice and the Great Terror." *Slavic Review*, 46, 3/4 (1987): 391-413.

Solzhenitsyn, A. *The Gulag Archipelago, 1918-1956: An Experiment in Literary Investigation*. New York: Harper & Row, 1974.

Sontag, J. "The Soviet War Scare of 1926-27." *The Russian Review*, 34, 1 (1975): 66-77.

Steiner, Z. *The Foreign Office and Foreign Policy, 1898-1914*. Cambridge: Cambridge University Press, 1969.

Stites, Richard. *Revolutionary Dreams: Utopian Vision and Experimental Life in the Russian Revolution*. Oxford: Oxford University Press, 1989.

Sutton, A. *Western Technology and Soviet Economic Development, 1917-1930*. Stanford: Hoover Institution Press, 1971.

Thompson, R. *Churchill and Morton*. London: Hodder and Stoughton, 1976.

Tucker, R., ed. *Stalinism: Essays in Historical Interpretation*. New York: W.W. Norton, 1977.

_____. "The Emergence of Stalin's Foreign Policy." *Slavic Review*, 36, 4 (1977): 563-89.

Ulam, A. *Expansion and Coexistence: Soviet Foreign Policy, 1917-1967*. New York: Frederick A. Praeger, 1968.

_____. *Stalin: The Man and His Era*. New York: The Viking Press, 1973.

Uldricks, T. "The Impact of the Great Purges on the People's Commissariat of Foreign Affairs." *Slavic Review*, 36, 2 (1977): 187-203.

_____. *Diplomacy and Ideology: The Origins of Soviet Foreign Relations*. Beverley Hills: Sage Publishers, 1979.

Vaksberg, A. *Stalin's Prosecutor: The Life of Andrei Vyshinsky*. New York: Grove and Weidenfeld, 1990.

Viola, L. *The Best Sons of the Fatherland: Workers in the Vanguard of Collectivization*. New York: Oxford University Press, 1987.

Volkogonov, D. *Triumf i Tragediia: Politicheskii Portret I.V. Stalina*, 2 vols. Moskva: Izdatel'stvo Agentstva Pechati Novosti, 1989.

Wark, W. *The Ultimate Enemy: British Intelligence and Nazi Germany, 1933-1939*. Ithaca: Cornell University Press, 1985.

Watt, D. *Personalities and Policies: Studies in the Formation of British Foreign Policy in the Twentieth Century*. South Bend: University of Notre Dame Press, 1965.

Weitz, B., ed. *Electrical Power Development in the USSR*. Moscow: INRA Publishing Society, 1936.

White, C. *British and American Commercial Relations with Soviet Russia, 1918-1924*. Chapel Hill: The University of North Carolina Press, 1992.

White, S. *Britain and the Bolshevik Revolution: A Study in the Politics of Diplomacy, 1920-1924*. New York: Holmes & Meier, 1980.

Wilson, Joan Hoff. *Ideology and Economics: U.S. Relations with the Soviet Union, 1918-1933*. Columbia: University of Missouri Press, 1974.

Wolin, S., and R. Slusser. *The Soviet Secret Police*. New York: Frederick A. Praeger, 1957.

Young, R. "Spokesmen for Economic Warfare: The Industrial Intelligence Centre in the 1930s." *European Studies Review*, 6 (1976): 473-89.

Zeiger, H. *Ian Fleming: The Spy Who Came in with the Gold*. New York: Duell, Sloan and Pearce, 1965.

Zile, Z., ed. *Ideas and Forces in Soviet Legal History: A Reader on the Soviet State and Law*. Oxford: Oxford University Press, 1992.

Index